ELITE
POLITICS IN
CONTEMPORARY
CHINA

ELITE
POLITICS IN
CONTEMPORARY
CHINA

JOSEPH FEWSMITH

An East Gate Book

M.E.Sharpe
Armonk, New York
London, England

An East Gate Book

Chapter 1 appeared in *Contemporary Chinese Politics in Historical Perspective*, Brantly
Womack, ed. New York: Cambridge University Press, 1991. Copyright © by Cambridge
University Press. Reprinted with permission of Cambridge University Press.

Chapter 2 appeared in *Informal Politics in East Asia*, Lowell Dittmer, Haruku Lee Fukui,
and N.S. Peter, eds. New York: Cambridge University Press, 2000.
Copyright © by Cambridge University Press. Reprinted with permission of
Cambridge University Press.

Chapter 3 appeared in *Democracy and Its Limits: Lessons from Asia, Latin America, and the
Middle East*, Howard Handelman and Mark Tessler, eds. © 1999 by University of Notre Dame
Press. Used with permission.

Chapter 4 is reprinted by permission of the publishers from *The Paradox of China's Post-Mao
Reforms*, Merle Goldman and Roderick McFarquhar, eds. Cambridge, Mass: Harvard University
Press, copyright © 1999 by the President and Fellows of Harvard College.

Chapter 5 appeared in *Asia Briefing 2000: The Continuing Transformation*, Tyrene White, ed.
Armonk, N.Y.: M.E. Sharpe, Inc., 2000. Reprinted with permission of the Asia Society.

Library of Congress Cataloging-in-Publication Data

Fewsmith, Joseph, 1949–
    Elite politics in contemporary China / Joseph Fewsmith.
        p. cm.
    "An East Gate book."
    Includes bibliographical references and index.
    ISBN 0-7656-0686-0 (cloth : alk. paper)—ISBN 0-7656-0687-9 (pbk. : alk paper)
        1. China—Politics and government—20th century. 2. Elite (Social sciences)—China. 3.
Political leadership—China. 4. Democratization—China. I. Title.

JQ1516 .F48 2000
306.2′0951—dc21   00-059589

Printed in the United States of America

The paper used in this publication meets the minimum requirements of
American National Standard for Information Sciences
Permanence of Paper for Printed Library Materials,
ANSI Z 39.48-1984.

BM (c)   10   9   8   7   6   5   4   3   2   1
BM (p)   10   9   8   7   6   5   4   3   2   1

In memory of Tang Tsou, 1919–1999:

He taught his students what it means to be a scholar,
a teacher, and, most of all, a person.
May those who come after see the "village" he so longed to see.

Contents

Acknowledgements

In writing these essays on contemporary Chinese politics, I incurred numerous intellectual debts. As will be evident from the dedication and introduction, my greatest debt continues to be to Tang Tsou, whose untimely death last year deprived the China field of perhaps its wisest voice. In addition, I have benefited from many conferences and conversations, including that convened at the John King Fairbank Center for East Asian Research by Merle Goldman and Roderick MacFarquhar that resulted in the chapter "The Impact of Reform on Elite Politics," the conference on democracy and its limits convened by Howard Handelman and Mark Tessler that resulted in the chapter "Institution Building and Democratization in China," and the panel at the Association of Asian Studies convened by Lowell Dittmer that resulted in the chapter "Formal Structures, Informal Politics, and Political Change in China." A sabbatical year of research, supported by Boston University and the Smith Richardson Foundation, provided the time to think about the issues discussed in the chapters below.

I am also grateful for the support shown by Doug Merwin of M.E. Sharpe, the production management by Angela Piliouras, and the proofreading of Nancy Hearst. All have made this a better volume, though I bear responsibility for the errors that remain.

Introduction

The study of elite politics has generally gone out of scholarly favor in recent years. This is largely because China has opened up considerably to research in other areas, which has led to the sort of in-depth studies of Chinese society that simply were not possible before.[1] There is a natural tendency to want to study materials that are available in depth rather than watch the "tea leaves" of a largely obscure process of elite politics. Moreover, disciplinary concerns have led the field to study such phenomena as "civil" society, property rights, and local elections, with the corresponding tendency to denigrate the study of elite politics as "China watching."[2] It is certainly true that the study of elite politics uninformed by questions derived from comparative or historical inquiry can degenerate into uninformed speculation about "who's up" and "who's down," but careful analysis of elite reactions to events is an important part of the study of contemporary China. Particularly in this day and age, when the press is filled with speculation about China's intentions, it is incumbent on the scholarly community to state as carefully as possible what we know, what we think, and what we do not know about elite politics.

There are many ways of trying to approach the study of elite politics. One approach is to try to understand the elite through their generational, educational, and social backgrounds. This is an approach that is deeply rooted in political science, even if that tradition is largely ignored these days.[3] For instance, in an important new book, Cheng Li has exhaustively studied the "fourth generation" of China's leadership, using both statistical and qualitative methods to describe the characteristics of this generation that is coming to power.[4] Li's book follows on Hong Yung Lee's earlier efforts to understand the changing composition of the Party elite over a longer period of time.[5] Another approach is to look at the institutions that make policy. Kenneth Lieberthal and Michel Oksenberg's pathbreaking study of energy policy, followed quickly by other studies of policy implementation, followed this approach.[6] Murray Scot Tanner's recent book on the National People's Congress also lies in this tradition.[7] Lucien Pye pioneered the use of political culture to study elite politics,[8] and Lowell Dittmer has extended such insights into the area of informal or personal politics.[9]

Somewhat in contrast, the essays in this book are largely informed by the approach that Tang Tsou took to the study of elite politics. It is useful, therefore, to elucidate Tsou's approach, or at least what I understand to be his approach.

Tsou's scholarly study of elite politics dates from the Cultural Revolution. Although his earlier study, entitled *America's Failure in China*, was informed by a deep understanding of Chinese politics, his topic was foreign policy.[10] The Cultural Revolution shredded scholarly assumptions about Chinese politics. The totalitarian model, then prevalent, was utterly unable to account for the Cultural Revolution. Franz Schurmann's superlative study, *Ideology and Organization in Communist China*, originally published on the eve of the Cultural Revolution, argued that ideology and organization coincided to produced an integrated polity, but that assumption was also rendered obsolete by the Cultural Revolution.[11]

It was under these circumstances that Tang Tsou and his colleague at the University of Chicago, Ho Ping-ti, convened one of the truly seminal conferences ever held on China.[12] In his own contribution to the conference proceedings, Tsou employed the then-popular notion of "integration" to examine both how the Chinese Communist movement had provided an integrating framework for contemporary China, and how it had come undone. In one of the most remarkable passages ever written in the China field, Tsou—in January 1967—wrote:

> A Maoist victory will establish a precedent under which the Chairman of the party may violate many, if not all, of its most important norms and prescribed features and ignore its regular structural arrangements, and under which personal legitimacy may be used to override structural legitimacy.... It will delay the process of routinization. . . . This precedent

can, however be nullified if Mao's successors repudiate implicitly or explicitly this particular aspect of the Cultural Revolution. This is a likely development in the long run.[13]

In retrospect one can see in this article and this assessment some of Tsou's assumptions about elite politics, and can also understand his preoccupation with finding better conceptualizations than were then available in American political science to aid in understanding Chinese politics. The effort to develop a better framework for analysis then became the primary focus of Tsou's intellectual inquiry for the remainder of his life.

I am not aware that Tsou ever employed the notion of "path dependence," but his understanding of elite politics was inseparable from his profound awareness that the Chinese Communist movement was rooted in the social, political, and intellectual problems of modern China. This was a world that Tsou understood in both intellectual and personal terms. Born into one of China's most prominent but conservative political families, Tsou, like many of his generation, became deeply involved in leftist politics. More or less by chance, he came to the United States in 1941 and soon migrated to the University of Chicago where, under the tutelage of Hans Morgenthau, he began to reflect on the history that he had lived. Always deeply conscious of the pull of politics (which he described as "like a drug"[14]), he remained apart from all political activities, devoting himself to intellectual understanding. It is impossible to read his essays, however, without a sense that they were informed by the intuitive understanding derived from his early participation in politics.

Perhaps what impressed him most about this period of history was the depth of intellectual crisis that China faced. As he expressed it later, the Chinese Communist movement rose as a totalistic response to a total crisis, and it was impossible to understand the later evolution of the Chinese Communist Party (CCP) without a grasp of the situation to which it was a response. One must say that Tsou was sympathetic to the rise of the CCP. Like other intellectuals of his generation, he was frustrated by China's international weakness and domestic chaos; he saw in the CCP an effective response—or at least a response more effective than any other political movement of the twentieth century—to the accumulated problems of imperialism, social decay, and political disarray. The Cultural Revolution forced him to confront the question of why this movement, which had previously appeared hopeful, had failed to construct a stable political order but rather had turned against itself and against the basic ways of organizing economic and political life in the twentieth century—markets and bureaucracy. Better than most at the time, Tsou understood the degree to which the Cultural Revolution undermined the basic prerequisites of modernity, which led him to believe, as quoted above, that eventually the CCP would reject the radical heritage of the Cultural Revolution and turn back to routinization.

When, a decade after this prediction, China finally turned its attention to reform, Tsou became more optimistic about the possibilities for the future. What caught his attention most about the early reform period was its combination of *restoration* of certain traditions within the Party, and the way that restoration opened the possibility for future change and innovation. In particular, Tsou saw Deng Xiaoping as restoring an earlier Maoist struggle *on two fronts* (against "bourgeois liberalization" on the one hand and "leftism" on the other), replacing the polarizing Cultural Revolution's emphasis on struggle *between two lines* ("proletarian" versus "capitalist"). In Tsou's estimation, this opened up a "middle course" that provided the possibility of political moderation, routinization, and institutionalization.[15]

If Tsou was hopeful, even optimistic, about the possibilities inherent in the Dengist reforms, he was constantly aware of the dangers. The danger that was uppermost in his mind was that of "winner-take-all" political conflict. It was unlike Tsou to write in a purely theoretical vein about Chinese politics; his preferred method was exposition via the case study approach. He would analyze a particular event or time period to see what lessons it revealed about the conduct of elite politics and where China was headed at a particular period of time. Rather than following the usual social science approach of explicitly stated hypotheses and testing against the evidence, Tsou pursued a more inductive approach, looking carefully at the evidence to derive broader generalizations. This was not because he was unaware of social science theory or methodology; to the contrary, he read widely in these areas, always gathering ideas that he would test against his understanding of Chinese politics. His usual modus operandi was, as he put it, to erect a theoretical scaffolding around which he would arrange the relevant data, creating a building in which the theoretical scaffolding was no longer clearly visible from the outside.[16]

Perhaps one reason he proceeded in this fashion was that he was not satisfied that the concepts developed in American political science could be applied directly to the study of China. Indeed, he fully expected that Chinese scholars, as political science eventually developed in that country, would build on the theoretical achievements of Western social science to create their own concepts and approaches, much as American political scientists had created new concepts based on concerns that differed from the earlier development of social science in Europe.[17] This is why one often finds Tsou introducing concepts from Western social science but then twisting their original meanings to better apply to the Chinese reality he observed. Indeed, Tsou himself spent a great deal of time trying to think of appropriate terminology and concepts for accurately describing Chinese politics, a project on which he felt he had made a good deal of progress by the end of his life.

Tsou departed from the case study approach in response to Andrew J. Nathan's well-known article on factional politics, which appeared in *China Quarterly* in 1973.[18] This was the only academic debate Tsou joined, and he did so only because he felt strongly about the issues involved. Tsou genuinely admired the theoretical sophistication of Nathan's article, but he could not agree with Nathan's conclusions. There were perhaps four core arguments Tsou could not accept. First, Nathan's description of Chinese politics as the product of factional alignments denied the importance of ideology in the political system. Tsou found ideology to be critical. Ideology certainly could be used cynically, but ideas were nevertheless important. Political actors might group together at one end or another of the political spectrum, but they did so for more than reasons of personal allegiance, however important personal ties may have been. Different groups (Tsou preferred the term "informal groups") contested for political power, but different policy orientations were always involved. Moreover, given the important role of ideology in the system, changes in policy had to be justified by changes in ideology. It was simply not true that ideology was unimportant.[19]

Second, the notion that Chinese politics revolved around factional struggles neglected the importance of the supreme leader, or what Deng Xiaoping would later call the "core" of the Party. Although warlord politics, the period for which Nathan originally developed his factional schema, could be described fairly accurately in those terms, the revolutionary movements of both the Guomindang (GMD) and the CCP self-consciously rejected factionalism (not always successfully). In the course of each of their struggles, one leader emerged above and beyond factional alignments, Chiang Kai-shek in the case of the GMD, and Mao

Zedong in the case of the CCP. Although the leader could manipulate factions (or groups) to enhance his own political power (something Chiang did more systematically than Mao), the leader could not be reduced to the head of the most important faction.

Third, by emphasizing personal relations to the exclusion of formal structure, Nathan's factional model suggested that formal institutions, including Party procedures, played no role. Tsou was hardly naïve about the often-dominant role that personal relations and informal politics have played in Chinese politics, but he argued that the role of formal structure could not be neglected entirely. Indeed, Tsou saw many of the problems in Chinese politics as arising from tensions between formal structures and informal politics. These needed to be brought into a stable relationship with each other before Chinese politics could stabilize.

Finally, and most importantly, Tsou rejected the factional model's assumption that a "code of civility" existed implicitly among political actors, limiting the depth of their conflict to restoring the *status quo ante*, a balance of power among factions. Whatever truth that assumption may have held for the warlord period, it was rejected by the GMD and particularly by the CCP. As Tsou put it, "[T]he basic assumption of CCP politics has been that a group or a coalition of groups can and does decisively defeat a major rival group or coalition, and eliminate it."[20]

As Tsou later developed this notion, political actors engaged in a contest in which one side would "win all" and the other side would "lose all." The precise standing of this proposition is not clear. It was, of course, derived from Tsou's observation of Chinese politics in the twentieth century, but was it rooted in culture, in ideology, or in the particular political conditions that prevailed at a given time? My own sense is that it was something of all three, that is, that Tsou saw this characteristic as rooted in Chinese culture (which is not to say either that it was culturally determined or that Chinese culture is incapable of supporting alternative political conceptions), but that it had been powerfully reinforced by the violent history of the twentieth century. Certainly Tsou developed a strong interest in game theory as a way of understanding the conditions under which such a "win all, lose all" political calculus might exist and how the game of politics might be played. In any event, Tsou argued strongly that Chinese political actors perceived political power as "monistic, unified, and indivisible,"[21] and that that view of political power was a powerful impediment to institutionalization and political stability.

There were several implications of this view of Chinese politics. One was that there was no legitimate division between state and society. Tsou continued to use the term "totalitarian" long after most in the China field gave it up for its Cold War associations, its inability to explain events such as the Cultural Revolution, and its static view of politics. But, as he did with many concepts he borrowed from social science theory, he distanced himself clearly from such classical formulations as that by Carl J. Friedrich and Zbigniew Brzezinski, preferring to view totalitarianism as one end of a continuum along which one could measure the degree of "stateness."[22] Tsou coined the term "totalism" (*quanneng zhuyi*) to try to capture the sense that even as the state withdrew from society over the course of reform (creating what Tsou called "zones of indifference"), it did not give up its right to intervene in society. Totalism was, in Tsou's words, a "political system that can violate the various aspects of any given legal, ideological, or moral (including religious) restrictions."[23] The state remained totalitarian in its claims if not its actions.

This totalistic political claim was related to the CCP's view of people as "masses" rather than as citizens. Masses are seen as a social stratum that is to be "mobilized and organized by political activists," rather than as individuals possessing legal and civic rights.[24] Because of the peculiarities of twentieth-century history, Tsou argued (or at least hoped) that China was reversing the Western pattern of first extending civil rights, followed by political and social rights (as laid out by T.H. Marshall in his classic work),[25] moving instead from social to political and eventually civic rights. Nevertheless, Tsou clearly recognized that a movement from "masses" to "citizenship" was necessary for political stability and the social well-being of the Chinese people. Moreover, parallel to this evolution from masses to citizens, there needs to be a corresponding change from cadres to functionaries.[26] Cadres mobilize masses; functionaries administer polities.

The fundamental difficulty with a "win all, lose all" approach to politics is that it is embedded in expectations of how the game of politics is played. If political actors play the game of politics in the expectation that sooner or later there will be a contest in which one side wins all and the other loses all, then either the "core" leader must garner sufficient political resources to prevent an effective challenge to his power, or rivals to political power must gear their actions toward an eventual showdown in which one will win all and the other will lose all. If this is the case, then, compromise can only be temporary and tactical. The expectation of eventual political showdown ultimately drives politics toward precisely such a showdown. It is a vicious cycle.

Much of Tsou's work in the latter years of his life was devoted to understanding the conditions under which this vicious cycle could be broken. Indeed, his article on the Dengist "middle course" was a tentative exploration of whether Deng had found a viable path for containing intra-Party conflict within certain bounds. The hope was that as political conflict was moderated or delayed, and as ideology was directed toward solving real-world problems ("refunctionalized"[27]), formal and informal power would increasingly complement each other, institutions would be strengthened, and the state-society relationship would be stabilized. Reform was clearly a transitional period, and incrementalism was essential to successful reform.

Unfortunately, ten years of reform and the undoubted achievements made in that period were insufficient either to "normalize" politics at the top or ameliorate state-society tensions. With the advent of student demonstrations in the spring of 1989, intra-elite tensions (already quite serious) were stretched to the breaking point, while the students, successful in their early demands, rejected the advice of moderate intellectuals, such as Dai Qing, and even sympathetic government officials, such as Yan Mingfu. When once again, political struggle was played out in terms of "win all, lose all," ending in bloodshed, Tsou was deeply discouraged. Indeed, he called himself an "all-out pessimist."[28] When he had published a collection of his essays in 1986, he had concluded the final one by quoting a then-popular poem:

> *Mountains multiply, streams double back—*
> *I doubt there's even a road;*
> *willows cluster darkly, blossoms shine—*
> *another village ahead!*

It was a verse that marvelously captured Tsou's sense of the difficulty and obscurity of China's incremental reforms but also the hope that there would indeed be "another village ahead." When he concluded his well-known essay on the Tiananmen tragedy, he quoted that verse again, and then added poignantly, "I no longer entertain the hope that I will see that 'village' with my own eyes."[29]

Although he was deeply discouraged by the events of Tiananmen, Tsou allowed himself to become cautiously optimistic by the course of Chinese politics in the 1990s. After a period of considerable uncertainty, Chinese politics began once again a process of incremental change that might, over time, lead to a deeper and more significant transformation, one that would provide for political stability and even political democracy. When Tsou read Li Zehou and Liu Zaifu's book *Farewell to Revolution*, he immediately wrote the authors a long letter, later published, in which he expressed complete agreement with their belief that Chinese politics must move away from the revolutionary impulse that has pulsated through the twentieth century.[30] As one who had lived through much of that history and studied the rest in great detail, Tsou concluded that China simply could not afford another round of violence. Sudden political change, he believed, was not likely to lead to democratic transition. China, he wrote, had been subjected to three major "operations" in the twentieth century (the 1911 Revolution, the Nationalist Revolution of 1926–1928, and the Communist Revolution of 1949) and could hardly stand a fourth: "China's political problems can only be resolved through incremental and evolutionary reform, problem by problem, drop by drop."[31] Violent upheaval or political collapse was likely to trigger a new round of "win all, lose all" political struggle, further embedding that pernicious tradition deeper in the Chinese body politic. Tsou was a political realist with a deep understanding of history; because of this, he had become a committed incrementalist, at least where late twentieth-century China was concerned.

The chapters that follow are deeply indebted to Tang Tsou's approach to the study of Chinese politics. Chapter 1, "The Dengist Reforms in Historical Perspective," was originally presented to a symposium convened by some of Tsou's students to mark his seventieth birthday and his retirement from teaching. Held in December 1988, it was already apparent that there were deep tensions in China's society and polity, tensions that were related to the very solutions China had adopted to resolve an earlier—and eerily similar—set of tensions. First the Nationalist and then the Communist revolutions were efforts to deal with the complex social, political, and international situations that existed following the fall of the Qing dynasty in 1911. Following a period of weak constitutionalism and warlordism, China turned to Leninist organization. In this essay, I prefer to follow Kenneth Jowitt's conceptionalization of "Leninist organization" rather than Tsou's usage of "totalitarianism" because is the various associations that cling to that term are difficult to expunge and because Jowitt's formulation is extremely useful in highlighting the tension that emerges when Leninist organization moves from "exclusion" to "inclusion." Stated succinctly, as Leninist organizations enter a period of reform and try to reduce the distance between themselves and the societies they govern, their particular organizational competence is undermined. That was very much the case with China in the 1980s; the tensions that brought down first Hu Yaobang and then Zhao Ziyang were very much those generated as the reform wing ("moderates") of the Party moved to reconcile with society while the more orthodox wing ("hardliners") resisted. Both the rapidity with which these tensions emerged and the fact that hardliners were dominated by first generation revolutionaries strongly biased the system toward suppression rather than transformation. Unfortunately, that suppression came quickly.

Chapter 2, "Formal Structures, Informal Politics, and Political Change in China," looks at the relationship between formal and informal politics in contemporary China, primarily in the 1980s. The history of the early reforms suggests that while formal structures were not without meaning, informal politics predominated. Ironically, it is unlikely that the Chinese political system would have displayed the flexibility that it did in the early 1980s without informal politics. Informal politics were important at both the local level, where personal relations could protect reform initiatives, and at the central level, where new ideas could be conveyed with surprising rapidity to the highest levels. A more formal system, such as grew up in the Soviet Union under Leonid Brezhnev, would likely have been far more resistant to the sort of reform initiatives China adopted in the late 1970s and early 1980s. But if the highly informal system displayed remarkable flexibility in the early reform period, it proved unable to contain the tensions that built up during the 1980s. Indeed, the very structures that emerged in that period tended to exacerbate tensions as reforms deepened. But while structures, both formal and informal, were important, the political meltdown in the spring of 1989 is incomprehensible without an appreciation of the "win all, lose all" approach to political contestation.

Chapter 3, "Institution Building and Democratization in China" tries to assess political developments in the 1990s and whether China is creating the sort of preconditions that are likely to make democratic transition and—more important—democratic consolidation likely. Much of the literature on democratic transition focuses on the dynamic of that transition, the role of elites and the possibilities of "pacted transitions," but relatively less attention has been paid in the recent literature to pre-conditions, not just in socioeconomic terms as an earlier generation of scholarship did, but in terms of institutions and political arrangements. Juan Linz and Alfred Stepan's *Problems of Democratic Transition and Consolidation* was a milestone in this regard. Comparing the democratic transitions of countries in southern Europe, eastern Europe, and Latin America, Linz and Stepan call attention to the importance of institutions, particularly the creation of a "usable bureaucracy" and law (a *Rechtsstaat*), as critical for successful transition.[32] With generational succession in China, as Jiang Zemin and the so-called third generation of leadership have replaced Deng Xiaoping and his generation, there have been palpable political pressures to move toward a more law-based form of governance. But the base from which such changes start is noticeably low, and there is clearly a long way to go. One hopes that the "village" Tang Tsou hoped to live to see will be viewed by another generation of Chinese, but the distance to travel still seems far.

Chapter 4, "The Impact of Reform on Elite Politics," approaches the same question from a different angle. It raises Tsou's question of political contestation as a matter of "win all, lose all" and asks whether there are trends afoot that will decisively change that debilitating rule of the game. It is worth noting that continuing to ask such a question marks me as something of an "outlier" in the China field. Most believe that Chinese politics has become institutionalized (the bureaucratic model has had a major impact in this view) and that Chinese political actors no longer "lose all" when they lose. Hu Yaobang was allowed to retain his seat on the Politburo after his ouster as general secretary, and even Zhao Ziyang has been treated well, though he is not free to leave his home without permission (and escort) or to see friends as he pleases. It should be noted that "losing all" has never necessarily implied losing one's life. Liu Shaoqi was persecuted to death during the Cultural Revolution, but generally losers in political struggles, since Kang Sheng's violent purge of the Party in the Yan'an period was curtailed, have been allowed to live. Indeed, it was this relatively benevolent tradition (compared with Stalin's purges) that preserved the lives of the veteran cadres who returned to power following the Cultural Revolution and oversaw the implementation of reform. "Losing all" simply means losing the ability to influence the political situation; losers do not generally die physically, just politically.[33] Moreover, especially under the conditions currently prevailing, losers in political contestation are frequently offered "sweeteners" to withdraw from active political life, as was apparently the case with former National People's Congress (NPC) head Qiao Shi.[34] Such "golden handshakes" may be the prelude to a more pluralistic conception of political power, but it should be noted that they are offered by winners to losers; instead of marking the end of win-all–lose-all struggles, they signal that no such struggle was ever triggered. One cannot yet assume that win-all–lose-all struggles are a thing of the past.

Given this, Chapter 4 is relatively optimistic about the possibility of leaving such struggles behind. Generational change is important, not only in that a new generation of technocrats has come to power, but also in that the current leadership lacks revolutionary legitimacy and therefore seems inclined to accept appeals to generalized norms and rules as a way of resolving differences rather than resorting to ideological combat. It may be, as Cheng Li argues, that technocrats are more prone by training to solve problems than their revolutionary predecessors, but it is also a matter of the type of problems confronting China today. A greater appreciation of the complexity of the tasks the leadership faces makes the leadership more interested in problems than ideology. If this continues to be the case, then China may defy the prediction inherent in Kenneth Jowitt's theorizing about the nature of Leninist organization.[35] His analysis leads to the conclusion that Leninist organizations are likely to collapse quickly and even violently; so far, the CCP has avoided that fate. If the discussion in these chapters is well grounded, one hopes the CCP can continue to avoid rapid collapse; institutionalization is not far advanced, and the possibility of a destructive new round of win-all–lose-all struggle cannot be discounted.

The final chapter, "Historical Echoes and Chinese Politics: Can China Leave the Twentieth Century Behind?" is perhaps a bit more somber about prospects for political change. Even after the trauma of Tiananmen, the process of incremental reform resumed, not only in terms of economics but also, though less substantially, in the political arena. (This process is laid out in chapters 4 and 5.) But by the mid-1990s, it was evident that new elements had appeared in the political equation. First, there was a clear change in the broad realm of "public opinion." On the one hand, many intellectuals had adopted a variety of postmodernist methodologies—referred to collectively as *houxue* (post-ist studies) in China—to examine their own society, modern Chinese history, and China's relationship to the rest of the world, though primarily the West. This was a major change in intellectual orientation in China. For most

of the twentieth century, intellectuals looked to the May Fourth enlightenment tradition for both intellectual and moral sustenance. This tradition had been reinvigorated by the reforms of the late 1970s and 1980s
as intellectuals sought both to explain how the Cultural Revolution could
have happened and to push ideological reforms that would make China
more democratic. The turn away from this enlightenment tradition in
the 1990s has come about as an increasing number of young intellectual
leaders have raised difficult questions about the meaning of modernity,
the impact of globalization, and the uniqueness of Chinese intellectual
and social history. This change has, to a certain extent, marginalized
liberal thought. On the other hand, at a more popular level, a forceful
wave of nationalism has emerged, contemptuous of the cosmopolitanism of the 1980s and intent on asserting China's interests (as its proponents see them).

Second, there has been rapid social change that will certainly continue and perhaps accelerate in the first decade of the new century. Although there has been impressive economic growth over the course of
reform, it is by no means certain that a "middle class," both in terms of
income distribution and independence from the political system, will
emerge. Perhaps the current tendency toward income polarization will
prove temporary as continued economic reform better clarifies property
rights and provides more protection for private property, but with a new
wave of unemployment expected as state-owned enterprises restructure,
disparities in income, accompanied by massive corruption, are certain
to cause social discontent.

Finally, despite the cautious optimism currently prevailing among
China scholars about the prospects for political stability, new questions
arose as the twentieth century gave way to the twenty-first. It was apparent that Jiang Zemin had not continued the path toward gradual political
relaxation that he had pursued following Deng Xiaoping's death. The
sudden emergence of Falun Gong (Buddhist Law Society), which was
only the best known (and best organized) of many similar religious sects,
was met with an unexpectedly harsh crackdown. Political and social
tensions were palpable in the months leading up to the fiftieth anniversary of the establishment of the PRC on October 1, 1999, and China's
relations with other countries seemed more uncertain after the tragic
bombing of the Chinese embassy in Belgrade in May 1999 and the
buildup of new tensions in the Taiwan Straits in the months prior to and
following Chen Shui-bian's election as president. Continued tensions

have been evident in early 2000 as Jiang Zemin has directed a new campaign against "rightist" tendencies.

Although not intended at the time of its writing, the final chapter revisits many of the themes developed in the first chapter. On the one hand, contemporary Chinese politics are very much a product of a century of political struggle, while, on the other hand, the evolution of politics inevitably raises historical cum political questions: What was the Chinese revolution about? Was it worth the millions of lives it cost? How can China define itself as a civilization vis-à-vis the rest of the world? Would the emergence of democratic politics set off a new round of settling scores and a struggle to "win all," thereby destroying the prospects of democratic politics? After a century of revolution and after two decades of largely successful reform, the answers to such questions are not clear.

Notes

The author would like to express appreciation to Marc Blecher, Cliff Edmonds, and Brantly Womack for their comments on an earlier version of this introduction.

1. Some of the works that have used this new access to good effect include Jean Oi, *Rural China Takes Off: Institutional Foundations of Economic Reform* (Berkeley: University of California Press, 1999); Jean Oi and Andrew Walder, eds., *Property Rights and Economic Reform in China* (Stanford: Stanford University Press, 1999); Dorothy Solinger, *Contesting Citizenship in Urban China: Peasant Migrants, the State, and the Logic of the Market* (Berkeley: University of California Press, 1999); and Edward S. Steinfeld, *Forging Reform in China* (New York: Cambridge University Press, 1998). Field work has also benefited efforts to understand the past, as in Elizabeth Perry, *Shanghai on Strike: The Politics of Chinese Labor* (Berkeley: University of California Press, 1993); Edward Friedman, Paul G. Pickowicz, and Mark Selden, *Chinese Village, Socialist State* (New Haven: Yale University Press, 1991); and Frederick Teiwes with Warren Sun, *China's Road to Disaster* (Armonk, NY: M.E. Sharpe, 1999).

2. David Bachman, "Emerging Patterns of Political Conflict in Post-Deng China," in Hung-mao Tien and Yun-han Chu, eds., *China Under Jiang Zemin* (Boulder, CO: Lynne Rienner, 2000), pp. 55–57.

3. The study of elite politics is rooted in the classic works of Vilfredo Pareto, *The Mind and Society* (New York: Harcourt, Brace, 1935); and Gaetano Mosca, *The Ruling Class* (New York: McGraw-Hill, 1939). For the United States, the classic work is C. Wright Mills, *The Power Elite* (Oxford: Oxford University Press, 1956).

4. Cheng Li, *China's Leaders: The New Generation* (Lanham, MD: Rowman and Littlefield, forthcoming).

5. Hong Yung Lee, *From Revolutionary Cadres to Party Technocrats in Socialist China* (Berkeley: University of California Press, 1991).

6. Kenneth Lieberthal and Michel Oksenberg, *Policy Making in China: Lead-*

ers, Structures, and Processes (Princeton: Princeton University Press, 1992); David M. Lampton, "Chinese Politics: The Bargaining Treadmill," *Issues and Studies*, 23, no. 3 (March 1987): 11–41; David M. Lampton, ed., *Policy Implementation in Post-Mao China* (Berkeley and Los Angeles: University of California Press, 1992); and Kenneth Lieberthal and David M. Lampton, eds., *Bureaucracy, Politics and Decision Making in Post-Mao China* (Berkeley and Los Angeles: University of California Press, 1992).

7. Murray Scot Tanner, *The Politics of Lawmaking in China: Institutions, Processes, and Democratic Prospects* (Oxford: Oxford University Press, 1999).

8. Lucien Pye, *The Spirit of Chinese Politics* (Cambridge, MA: Harvard University Press, 1992).

9. Lowell Dittmer, "Chinese Informal Politics," *The China Journal*, no. 34 (July 1995): 1–34.

10. Tang Tsou, *America's Failure in China*, 2 vols. (Chicago: University of Chicago Press, 1963).

11. Franz Schurmann, *Ideology and Organization in Communist China*, 2d ed. (Berkeley: University of California Press, 1971).

12. Ho Ping-ti and Tang Tsou, eds., *China in Crisis*, 2 vols. (Chicago: University of Chicago Press, 1968).

13. Tang Tsou, "Revolution, Reintegration, and Crisis in Communist China," in Tang Tsou, *The Cultural Revolution and Post-Mao Reforms: A Historical Perspective* (Chicago: University of Chicago Press, 1986), pp. 65–66.

14. Tang Tsou used this expression in conversation with me more than once. I always believed, though he never said, that it reflected his own early involvement in politics.

15. Tang Tsou, "Political Change and Reform: The Middle Course," in Tsou, *The Cultural Revolution and Post-Mao Reforms*, pp. 219–258.

16. Zhao Baoxu, "Zuihou yifeng nongsuo bisheng yanjiu jinghua de laixin—diaonian Zou Dang xuezhang" (A final letter reflecting the concentrated quintessence of a lifetime of study—mourning my elder classmate Zou Dang [Tang Tsou]), *Guoji zhengzhi yanjiu* (International politics research), special issue commemorating Tang Tsou, 1999, pp. 5–13.

17. See especially Tsou's essay, "Ruhe fazhan xin Zhongguo de zhengzhixue" (How to develop New China's political science), in Zou Dang, *Ershi shiji Zhongguo zhengzhi: Cong hongguan lishi yu weiguan xingdong jiaodu kan* (Twentieth century Chinese politics: Viewed from the perspective of macro history and micro action) (Hong Kong: Oxford University Press, 1994), pp. 22–40.

18. Andrew J. Nathan, "A Factional Model for CCP Politics," *The China Quarterly*, no. 53 (January/March 1973): 34–66.

19. Tang Tsou, "Prolegomenon to the Study of Informal Groups in CCP Politics," in Tsou, *The Cultural Revolution and Post-Mao Reforms*, pp. 95–111.

20. Ibid., p. 99.

21. Tsou, "Chinese Politics at the Top: Factionalism or Informal Politics? Balance of Power Politics or a Game to Win All?" *The China Journal*, no. 34 (July 1995): 95–156.

22. Tsou, "Introduction," in Tsou, *The Cultural Revolution and Post-Mao Reforms,* p. xxii. For the classic formulation of totalitarian theory, see Carl J. Friedrich and Zbigniew Bzrezinski, *Totalitarian Dictatorship and Autocracy,* rev. ed. (Cambridge, MA: Harvard University Press, 1965).

23. Zou Dang, "Houji: Cong chuantong quanwei zhengzhi xitong dao xiandai quanneng zhuyi zhengzhi xitong" (Afterword: From a traditional authoritarian political system to a modern totalitarian political system), in *Ershi shiji Zhongguo zhengzhi*, p. 223.

24. Tsou, "Reflections on the Formation and Foundations of the Chinese Communist Party-State," in Tsou, *The Cultural Revolution in Historical Perspective*, p. 272.

25. T.H. Marshall, *Class, Citizenship, and Social Development* (Chicago: University of Chicago Press, 1977).

26. Tsou, "Reflections on the Formation and Foundations of the Chinese Communist Party-State," p. 278.

27. Tsou borrowed this term from Peter C. Lutz, *The Changing Party Elite in East Germany* (Cambridge: MIT Press, 1972).

28. Personal conversation with Tang Tsou.

29. Tang Tsou, "The Tiananmen Tragedy: The State-Society Relationship, Choices, and Mechanisms in Historical Perspective," in Brantly Womack, ed., *Contemporary Chinese Politics in Historical Perspective* (Cambridge: Cambridge University Press, 1991), p. 322.

30. Zou Dang, "Du 'gaobie geming'—zhi Li Zehou, Liu Zaifu" (Reading *Farewell to revolution*—to Li Zehou and Liu Zaifu), in *Ershiyi shiji* no. 33 (February 1996): 62–67; and Li Zehou and Zaifu, *Gaobie geming* (Farewell to revolution) (Hong Kong: Cosmos Books Ltd., 1996).

31. Zou, "Houji: Cong chuantong quanwei zhengzhi xitong dao xiandai quanneng zhuyi zhengzhi xitong," p. 244.

32. Juan J. Linz and Alfred Stephan, *Problems of Democratic Transition and Consolidation: Southern Europe, South America, and Post-Communist Europe* (Baltimore: The Johns Hopkins University Press, 1996).

33. My understanding of Tsou's view on win-all–lose-all struggles was that the loser generally lost political influence (and perhaps more) for the rest of his or her career. A political leader might regain influence either if the supreme leader decided to restore that leader's posts (in which case, he or she would be serving at the sufferance of the supreme leader) or after the supreme leader died. Deng Xiaoping is, perhaps uniquely, an example of both. Mao brought Deng back in 1973 because he needed Deng's influence to steady the military after Lin Biao's death and because Zhou Enlai had been diagnosed with cancer. When Mao, apparently under the influence of the radical faction, became dissatisfied with Deng's performance, he purged him again. Deng was able to return to power following Mao's death because of the backing of such prominent leaders as Marshal Ye Jianying.

34. One area in which it would be useful to do additional research and conceptualization would be distinguishing between different levels of conflict. The reason Tsou focused on struggles to win all or lose all was that these were the points at which the developmental trajectory of the Party was changed decisively. Such struggles would certainly include Mao's victory at Zunyi, the purge of Liu Shaoqi in the Cultural Revolution, and Deng's emergence as "paramount leader" at the Third Plenum of the Eleventh Central Committee. Struggles in which a political leader loses power but which do not result in a major change of political direction might be conceived as something less than a struggle to "win all or lose all"—though they might well be part of the accumulating tensions that result in a struggle to "win all

or lose all." Thus, Hu Yaobang's ouster as general secretary in 1987 does not fit into the category of a struggle to "win all or lose all," though it certainly contributed to the tensions that led to the political meltdown of 1989. Qiao Shi's ouster resulted in no decisive change of political direction; indeed, I argue in this book that Qiao's ouster allowed Jiang Zemin to move more easily to espouse positions previously championed by Qiao—something quite different from what happened following the titanic conflicts of the past, when the winner would move decisively *away* from the direction espoused by the defeated rival. Indeed, if one accepts the interpretation that Wei Jianxing, who apparently has close ties with Qiao, was promoted to the Politiburo Standing Committee in "exchange" for Qiao's retirement, then it would suggest a level or type of conflict quite different than the old "win all, lose all" struggles of the past.

35. Kenneth Jowitt, *The New World Disorder* (Berkeley: University of California Press, 1992).

ELITE
POLITICS IN
CONTEMPORARY
CHINA

1

The Dengist Reforms in
Historical Perspective

The events of June 4, 1989, in a very real sense brought the Dengist period to a close. What defined the Dengist period more than anything else were three interrelated premises: The subordination of ideological struggle to economic development, the adoption of a "middle course," and the recognition of the "relative autonomy" of specific fields of knowledge. The crackdown on June 4 severely compromised each of those.

The Third Plenum of the Eleventh Central Committee, in December 1978—the meeting that marked the inauguration of the Dengist period—called for shifting the emphasis of work to economic development. The importance of that decision lay in its reversal of the relationship that had existed between ideology and economic policy in the preceding three decades of the People's Republic of China (PRC). Previously, ideology had been the linchpin around which economic policy revolved. At the Third Plenum, the effort to integrate the Party and nation around a common ideology, which had resulted in violent ideological struggle rather than unity, was abandoned in favor of an agreement on the primacy of economic development. The presumption was that with economic development both the urgency and the divisiveness of ideological questions would be reduced.

Ideology thus changed from an organizing principle to a boundary. As expressed by the "Four Cardinal Principles"—which affirmed the leading position of the Chinese Communist Party (CCP), the role of

Marxism-Leninism and Mao Zedong Thought, the people's democratic dictatorship, and the socialist road—ideology became a marker beyond which the expression of ideas was not to go, a barrier against "bourgeois liberalization." The Four Cardinal Principles were thus the counterpoint of the Third Plenum's emphasis on fighting "leftist" ideas, a thrust that found expression in such pragmatic slogans as "Emancipate the mind," "Seek truth from practice," and "Practice is the sole criterion of truth." The opposition to "leftist" ideas, on the one hand, and to bourgeois liberalization, on the other, thus defined, as Tang Tsou has pointed out, a "middle course" that struggled *against two fronts*. That middle course, then, attempted to build political consensus by rejecting the Cultural Revolution's emphasis on struggle *between two lines*.[1]

That focus on economic development and the demarcation of a middle course were accompanied by a recognition of the "relative autonomy" of specific fields of knowledge and the limits of state control. That recognition was based on an acceptance of what Tang Tsou calls the "sociological postulate," meaning that "every sphere of social life and its activities has its special characteristics (*tedian*) and is governed by special laws" and the corresponding injunction that the "political leadership can and should create the general conditions favorable to the operation of these laws to promote development, but it cannot violate these laws without suffering serious consequences.[2]

For most of the decade that followed 1978 those premises underlay a gradual, though not uninterrupted, depoliticization of the Chinese economy, polity, and culture. That trend was challenged at several points—most notably in the campaign to criticize the writer Bai Hua in 1981, the campaign against "spiritual pollution" in 1983, and the campaign against "bourgeois liberalization" in 1987—but, overall, the "center of gravity" of Chinese politics continued to shift toward greater depoliticization of society, greater use of market forces, and more recognition of societal diversity—until the use of force to suppress the democracy movement in 1989.

That shift was most apparent in the area of economic reform, with which the Dengist regime was so closely identified—the implementation of the rural responsibility system, the rapid development of rural enterprises, the adoption of various forms of the contract responsibility system, the experiments with shareholding, and the development of a significant individual and service economy. It also permitted greater decentralization of the economy and development of regional economics as local governments were given greater financial power and political latitude to guide their own developments.

Although the changes were most notable and most remarked upon in the area of economic reform and development, they were also apparent in the cultural and political realms. The "Resolution on Building Socialist Spiritual Civilization," which was adopted by the Sixth Plenum in 1986, for instance, was notable for its recognition of the diversity of Chinese society and the "immaturity" of the socialist system. It dropped the demand of the Twelfth Party Congress, held in 1982, that "spiritual civilization" be built "with Communist ideology as the core," calling instead for building spiritual civilization "with Marxism-Leninism as guidance." That less restrictive formulation allowed for greater stress on the development of a "common ideal" that could encompass "party members and nonparty people, Marxists and non-Marxists, atheists and believers, citizens at home and those living abroad."[3] The Thirteenth Party Congress in 1987 developed those ideas by expanding on the thesis that China was in the "primary stage of socialism" and by explicitly accepting limitations on the role of the Party, acknowledging the "diverse interests and contradictions" in society.[4]

As the Dengist regime pursued reforms in the economic, political, and cultural spheres, it adopted policies that built upon and reflected longstanding trends in Chinese history. That was most striking, of course, in the manner in which the rural reforms tapped China's long and vigorous commercial tradition. Those reforms were characterized by a retreat of state authority from the local level, allowing peasant households greater freedom in their choices of crop selection and marketing outlets. Rural markets were restored and expanded, and far greater levels of intraregional and interregional trade were permitted.

In allowing such markets to develop, the Dengist reforms yielded to the imperatives of China's economic geography. A large nation with poor transportation, China has traditionally been divided into economic macroregions, within each of which a hierarchical network of marketing structures has existed.[5] By permitting greater trade, the Dengist reforms revived those marketing structures and built on the natural economic structures of China. The rapid expansion of rural industry and the growth of small cities in recent years have similarly been built on those traditional structures. In a sense, then, the Dengist reforms revived the commercial structure and commercial orientations that had developed so vigorously throughout late imperial China, and particularly in the late nineteenth and early twentieth centuries.

At the same time, the Dengist reforms moved to correct the imbalance between "public" and "private" so manifest during the Cultural Revolution and the period of the PRC in general. As epitomized by the slogan *dagong wusi*—literally, "all public and no private" —the Cultural Revolution was the culmination of a fifty-year trend toward the politicization of increasingly greater areas of life. By depolitcizing large areas of social life, the Dengist reforms moved to rectify that imbalance, creating a "zone of indifference" in which "private" activities were permitted far greater scope.[6] In doing so, the Dengist reforms seemed much more in harmony with China's tradition of "totalistic" but noninvasive political power.

Along with the rectification of the balance between public and private, the acceptance of the sociological postulate that various areas of human endeavor are subject to their own laws implied an acknowledgment of the limits of ideology. That recognition contributed greatly to the relative depoliticization of wide areas of social and intellectual life and to a rapid expansion in the role of intellectuals in Chinese life. Though obvious restrictions remained on the expression of ideas, it was also true that intellectuals, prior to June 4, 1989, were generally given greater latitude to express themselves than at any time in the history of the PRC. The role of intellectuals in shaping public policy, particularly in the area of economic reform, was unprecedented in the history of the PRC.[7] Clearly, the denigration of intellectuals which reached an extreme in a Cultural Revolution slogan to the effect that the more one reads, the more stupid one becomes, was substantially altered. Although China's traditional society by no means guaranteed individual freedom of speech—as the literary inquisition of the eighteenth century showed— the status of intellectuals as a class was secure. Given the long and vibrant intellectual tradition of China, restoration of intellectuals to a higher status seems both inevitable and in keeping with China's past.

Finally, one might add, though with a lesser degree of certainty, the Dengist policy of "opening to the outside world" also corrected an imbalance toward national seclusion that reached an extreme during the Cultural Revolution. Though China has historically been an ethnocentric society, its modern history in particular has been marked by the rapid absorption of a wide variety of foreign influences—economic, political, and cultural. The seclusion of the Maoist era stood in contrast to the openness of the preceding period, and the decision of the Dengist regime to reopen China to a wide-ranging interaction with other countries seems more in keeping with the development of modern Chinese history.

This seemingly felicitous convergence between the Dengist reform strategy and the broad trends of China's historical development in the modern period might be taken as suggesting that the shift in the regime's goals from mobilization to development has brought about a reconciliation between the CCP and China's past.[8] The events of June 1989, however, suggest that such has not happened. On the contrary, the reforms generated a series of tensions that have made such a reconciliation neither easy nor certain. On another level, however, it is apparent that the reforms have brought about a number of unintended consequences (particularly the changing relationships between Beijing and the provinces and the tentative emergence or, better, reemergence of a "public sphere") that lead one to believe that China is facing a series of problems and tensions not altogether unlike those that confronted earlier generations. These developments will be seen as the lasting historical legacies of the Dengist period, and it is these developments that indeed suggest a convergence between the current period and the broad trends of the past. In turn, it is this convergence that is making the Maoist period look increasingly like an interregnum, rather than the historical solution to the dilemmas facing China that it was once thought to be.[9]

In looking at the relationship between the Dengist reforms and the Chinese past, it is apparent that the reforms stand in a Janus-faced relationship to the specific history of the CCP, on the one hand, and the broader trends of Chinese history, on the other. That is to say, although the Dengist reforms represent a reaction against the Cultural Revolution and the "leftist" traditions within the CCP, they also are forced to confront the very dilemmas that produced the communist movement and revolution in the first place. By opening up fundamental questions about the communist response to the dilemmas of modernization, the reformers themselves have been forced to confront the dilemmas that faced earlier generations of intellectuals, reformers, and revolutionaries of different stripes—questions about the relationships between state and society, the polity and the economy, and ideology and knowledge. Thus, there is a palpable feeling of déjà vu in reformers' efforts to come to grips with China's past.

Leninism and Tradition

In retracing the intellectual footsteps of preceding generations, contemporary reformers must work within the structure of a Leninist system that is itself a product of the historical, social, and intellectual pressures of an earlier period. Leninism, as Jowitt has persuasively argued, is a unique structure of authority that is able to combine the fundamentally conflicting orientations of "status" and "class" societies—the former based on the personalistic norms of corporate groups, the latter on the impersonal norms of economic relations. It unifies these conflicting orientations through the creation of a party that is an exclusive, "status" organization and also the enforcer of impersonal authority—a party characterized by "charismatic impersonalism."[10] The importance of this concept lies in its ability to capture the interrelatedness of the exclusive orientation of the Leninist party as a corporate group, the society to which it is a response, and the authority relationship that links party and society, namely, neotraditional authority.

The Leninist response, then, is a particular response to a particular set of historical circumstances. That set of circumstances includes the continued domination of status orientations over class orientations and a considerable overlap between the public sphere—that is, an independent realm of public life, including public opinion and public expression—and public authority, the legitimate exercise of state functions. Despite the extensive commercialization of China in the late imperial period, particularly in the "core" economic regions, there was never a "great transformation" comparable to that in early modern Western Europe.[11] Mercantile activities, despite their often close relationship with officialdom, continued to occupy an ambivalent status in China's Confucian order. Prescriptions granting trade a legitimate role in society— urging that the "people be made secure and trade facilitated" (*anmin tongshang*)—coexisted with a denigration of the profit-making sphere (*li*). As Susan Mann has recently put it, state policies protecting and fostering traders' activities were aimed not at improving the status of merchants, but at preserving the agrarian social order."[12]

As the traditional order crumbled and new commercial and industrial activities expanded in the late nineteenth and early twentieth centuries, a nascent bourgeoisie did develop, particularly in the coastal cities. Freed from the restrictions of the traditional order, by the 1920s, such businessmen had developed a sense of themselves as belonging to an independent class and as the purveyors of values essential to China's modernization. Merchants saw an emerging business ethic as containing both a dynamism that would break with the cultural conservatism of the past and a need for continuity and predictability that could provide the basis for both social stability and expansion of business. That newfound conviction that the values of the business community could and should become the basis for the nation underlay the oft-invoked phrase *yi shang jiu guo* (save the nation through business).[13]

That middle-class business ethic, however, remained too peripheral to Chinese society to provide the basis for a new political order. Having emerged in the context of both domestic political disarray and imperialism, such trends were soon overwhelmed by the nationalistic and nativistic impulses of first the Guomindang (GMD) and then the CCP. Both of those revolutionary movements, harking back to the status orientation of traditional society, imposed a form of "neotraditional" authority—a type of authority that, on the one hand, views economics as an extension of politics and, on the other hand, makes no legitimate distinction between public and private.

As the research of such scholars as Keith Schoppa, Mary Backus Rankin, William Rowe, and David Strand has shown, the great commercial expansion in late imperial China led to an important expansion of the public sphere that paralleled in interesting ways similar developments in early modern Europe. In particular, Rankin has used a tripartite division of *guan*, *gong*, and *si* (state, public, and private, respectively) to delineate the growth of "elite activism" that emerged in the gray area between state and society, particularly in the post-Taiping period. Following Rankin, David Strand has extended this concern with the public sphere into the 1920s in his recent study of Beijing society. Strand documents the important roles that legal groups *(fatuan)* played in the governance of local society and in the articulation of public interest.[14]

In a stimulating article, William Rowe has explored the comparability of these developments to Habermas's analysis of the emergence of the public sphere in Europe in the seventeenth and eighteenth centuries. In the European case, the emergence of bourgeois society led, in time, from the claim to a right to engage in free debate with the public authority to the right to regulate that authority, in short, to the right of the bourgeois reading public "to compel public authority to legitimate itself before public opinion."[15]

There are, as Rowe points out, ambiguities in the meaning of "public" in both the European and the Chinese cases. In both instances, the term "public" is used to refer to functions that are undertaken by the state on behalf of society (public education, public welfare, and public defense), as well as activities that are unique to society (public opinion and public charity). In the European case, however, there was, at least in an earlier period of time, a clear-cut distinction between state and society, a sense in which public opinion was directed *against* the state, and that indeed "compelled" public authority to legitimate itself (the apparent loss of a clear-cut distinction between state and society in the current age is a major concern of Habermas, but one that we need not take up). That opposition of the public sphere to the state rested on the emergence of bourgeois society, which in turn rested on notions of the legitimacy of private activities, particularly private property.[16]

In the Chinese case, the term *gong* shared the ambiguity of the European term "public" in that it could be applied to actions undertaken by either state or society, but it never developed the sense of independence and opposition to the state that typified the revolution described by Habermas. One might suggest that many of the public activities undertaken by the social elite were understood as being on behalf of the state, and that such public activities, as described by Rankin, Rowe, and Strand, were understood as being more of a bridge between society and state than an opposition between the two.[17]

The ambiguous relationship existing between the public sphere and the public authority (the state) was mirrored by the ambiguous relationship between the public sphere and private activities. The term *si* in China carries a variety of connotations. On the one hand, *si* is viewed in morally negative terms, as the equivalent of selfish, and hence is viewed as the opposite of *gong*. As Rowe points out, the *Shuowen* (the dictionary dating to the first century A.D.), analyzes *gong* etymologically as a compound of two simpler characters that together mean "turning one's back on the private."[18] Another tradition, which had its roots in the Confucian classic *The Great Learning*, saw the individual and society as existing on a continuum; thus, the way to bring tranquility to "all under heaven" was first to make one's thought sincere and to rectify one's heart. Rowe argues that by the time of late imperial China, the "traditional dichotomy between private and public came to be muted by a growing belief that private interest, if sufficiently enlightened, could simultaneously serve the interests of society." This view, which appears to have gone hand in hand with the growth of the public sphere in that period, did not imply, as Strand says, that "profits themselves are righteous or that private points of view or interests have a privileged claim on public discourse."[19] Both the relationship between private interests and the public sphere and that between the public sphere and public authority remained ambiguous.

The writings of Liang Qichao can be used to illustrate the complex interrelations between the concepts "public" and "private" and between the public sphere and public authority in late Qing China. Liang, who more than anyone else of his generation scathingly critiqued the old order, used the popular opposition of public and private to attack the legitimacy of the monarchy as an institution. Fundamentally challenging the traditional assumption that the monarch represented the public welfare, Liang argued that the monarch ruled the nation as his own private property. Rather than seeing the monarchy as the institutional expression of *gong*, Liang saw it as the institutionalized pursuit of *si*.[20]

This critique of the monarchy as not representing the public interest appears very much in line with Habermas's analysis of the emergence of a public sphere in Europe; in fact, it is a clear expression of an emerging public opinion engaging in debate with public authority. But that emerging debate never led in China, as it did in Europe, to the point that public opinion could "compel public authority to legitimate itself before public opinion." Nor did Liang Qichao try to push the argument along those lines. In part driven by the late-nineteenth-century desire to *strengthen* the state (unlike the development of European civil society, which emerged *against* the state), and in part drawing on deeply ingrained notions of how state and society should relate, Liang developed his notion of popular sovereignty in terms that were, ironically, very much compatible with the patterns of elite activism so well described by Rankin, Strand, and others.

In contrast to Western notions of popular sovereignty, which rest on the assumptions of individualism and the free interplay of competing—and private—interests, Liang viewed popular sovereignty as a coming together of like-minded (and public-minded) individuals. For Liang, each individual should develop within himself or herself the qualities necessary to create the nation. That is what Liang meant in drawing an analogy between the nation and a pile of salt—just as the quality of saltiness inheres in each grain of salt, the quality of "nationhood" must be present in each individual of the nation. Similarly, Liang liked to say that "a group of blind men cannot become a Li-hou [a man famous for his eyesight], a group of deaf persons cannot become a Shi-kuang [a man famous for his hearing], and a group of cowards cannot become a Wu-hu [a man famous for his courage]."[21] Thus, if the qualities needed for the nation were not present in the individuals of the society, then it would be impossible to construct a strong nation.

It was his belief that the qualities of nationhood inhered in individuals rather than in individualism that led Liang to be more concerned
with defining the content of citizenship (public virtue) than with design-
ing the structural arrangements of the state. Unwilling to trust the affairs
of the state to the subjective interests of individuals, Liang sought to
train a citizenry that would, collectively and individually, embody *gong.*
Thus, Liang's conception of popular sovereignty was double-edged. It
held the state responsible to an abstract notion of the public good, but at
the same time it held that society should live up to the same ideal; it was
not an assertion of the public interest against the state. When Liang tried
to redefine *gong* as inhering in society rather than in the monarchy, he
looked not to "the people," but to the "new people." Rather than asserting that private interests had a "privileged claim" on public discourse,
Liang continued to view state and society as existing along a continuum
in which the value of *gong* ran the entire length.

That concept of popular sovereignty is why Liang's concept of "grouping" (*qun*) bore no relationship to interest-group pluralism. *Grouping*
was a means by which the new people, infused with public virtue, could
be brought together in such organizations as study associations and cham-
bers of commerce to transmit their proposals and knowledge to the state.
Groups were to be the transmission belts by which the state could be
infused with the energy released by mobilizing the new people.

The congruence between this view of citizenship and grouping and the
patterns of elite activism described by Rankin, Strand, and others is apparent. Liang, who was very much a product of the culture that generated elite
activism, viewed groups neither as being based on private interests nor as
antagonistic to the state. He viewed groups as expressions of the public
interest, compatible with the interests of society as well as those of the state.

Thus, despite the emergence of a public sphere in late imperial and
early Republican China, there was no ideology that defined that sphere
as resting on the private interests of society or as being independent of
the state. One might argue that the sort of *fatuan* that Strand has studied
might have, over time, laid a foundation for the public sphere emerging
as independent of public authority, but such trends were cut short by a
rising tide of nationalism that viewed such nascent autonomy as hostile
to efforts to create a strong state. Organizationally, the Nationalists employed a combination of co-optation and coercion in the late 1920s and
the 1930s to extend the control of the state over society, and ideologically they promoted an image of organic unity that denied a legitimate

distinction between public authority and the public sphere.[22] The CCP's ideological hostility toward any sphere of private activity accompanied its organizational penetration of society, and the curtailment of societal autonomy begun under the Nationalists was radically extended.

The emergence of neotraditional authority, then, can be seen as a response to a situation in which there was an emergent public sphere, but it was not based on a highly developed economic foundation (a bourgeois class), nor did it have a coherent or persuasive ideology defining itself against the state. When nationalist demands found effective organizational expression, first with the GMD, and then to a much greater extent with the CCP, the nascent public sphere was crushed under demands for a strong state. The irony is that now the CCP must deal with the consequences of its own success. Reform not only engendered the implicit recognition of semiautonomous realms of knowledge but also fostered economic forces that have provided a basis for a tentative reemergence of a public sphere. These developments have revived many of the questions that faced Chinese intellectuals and politicians alike in the early twentieth century—such as the relationship between state and society, the tension between Chinese culture and modernization, and the relationship between China and the outside world—and at the same time they threaten the authority structure on which the CCP, as a Leninist party, has based its rule.

Leninism and Reform

If the unique characteristics of Leninist authority facilitate the quest for power and the initial mobilization of resources for modernization, they also present obstacles, and perhaps limits, to efforts to reform the system. For a party whose position in society is defined by its heroic orientation, the process of transformation from an all "exclusive" party that accentuated its differentiation from society to an "inclusive" party that attempts to incorporate societal elements is tenuous at best.[23] Although Leninist parties are willing to increase their responsiveness to societal demands in order to gain public support for regime goals, they find it difficult to suppress demands that they be "representative."

The difference between being "responsive" and being "representative" was dramatically highlighted by the debate between Fang Lizhi, then vice-president of the University of Science and Technology in Hefei, Anhui province, and Politburo member Wan Li, who traveled to Hefei in November 1986 to try to reduce the tensions that were soon to erupt in the largest student demonstration that China had seen up to that time. Wan Li apparently tried to persuade Fang that the views of people like himself could be reflected within the Party. Fang replied that "democracy is not something that can be given to lower levels from those above," but is something that must be "struggled for." Otherwise, said Fang, "what is given to you can be taken away."[24]

Moreover, as a party system based on neotraditional authority, the Leninist system is more compatible with planned economies than with market economies. Planned economies do not undermine the heroic ethos of the Leninist party. On the contrary, they often manifest that ethos, as in the heroic efforts required to build such projects as the Great Hall of the People, the bridge over the Yangzi River at Nanjing, and the Red Flag Canal in Henan (in addition to less successful undertakings such as the backyard furnaces of the Great Leap Forward). The tension inherent in this conflict between the heroic orientation of the Party and the requirements of economic modernization were vividly reflected in the fall of 1988—as the tensions that would result in the open division of the Party the following spring were becoming severe—when Party conservatives, in clear opposition to the reformist agenda, aired a highly nationalist television program chronicling the dedication and sacrifices of those who had developed China's nuclear weapons.[25] The results of such efforts are viewed not as the outcome of rational economic activity but as expressions of the Party's political wisdom and leadership.

In contrast, market economics are distinctly unheroic. It is precisely the day-to-day economic calculations of millions of independent individuals that underlie the constant flow of factor resources to the areas of greatest return. It is the essence of class-oriented societies that such decisions are made by individuals without regard to their positions in society. If there is a "hero" in a market economy, it is the successful entrepreneur, but the success of such people is distinctly individualistic; usually the attainment of such success comes not from relying on one's status but rather from acting in defiance of society's norms. Nothing could be more foreign to the notion of "comradeship"—a concept that implies a disciplined acceptance of a hierarchically based order harnessed to the party-state—than entrepreneurship.[26]

Socialist reform, which is initiated in large part because of the inefficiencies of centrally organized economics, inevitably involves all efforts to bring market forces to bear and a consequent deemphasis on planning. Socialist theoreticians have expended much effort trying to find formulas for integrating plan and market, but without success.[27] Chinese efforts to bridge the gap between plan and market culminated in the concept of a "planned commodity economy," which was given theoretical sanction in the 1984 Decision on Reform of the Economic Structure. Although that decision marked a theoretical breakthrough at the time, allowing reformers to pursue market-oriented reforms more vigorously, the notion of a "planned commodity economy" was more compromise than concept. As senior economist Liu Guoguang wrote, although everyone could agree with those words, some emphasized the "planned" part of the formula, whereas others stressed the "commodity" part.[28]

The debate on whether to give primary emphasis to the "planned" economy or to the "commodity" (market) economy reflected not simply an economic problem—though the difficulties in that regard were certainly formidable—but also a very real struggle between two conflicting principles of authority. As Jowitt has suggested, the incompatible orientations of class and status societies can coexist only under coercive auspices. A status society can have pockets containing modernized economics if they are "compartmented" and therefore do not threaten the larger society, or if they are so weak that they can be co-opted and thereby used to extend the power and scope of the stronger type.[29]

The relationship between guilds and the state in the status society of traditional China manifested that latter strategy. Guilds, as Susan Mann has pointed out, drew "strength from the government's sanction of their liturgical function, while at the same time depending on the state for their raison d'être."[30] In Dengist China, where the status orientation predominates, both strategies have been pursued. The creation of Special Economic Zones (SEZs) is a clear instance of compartmentalization (even if the intention behind their creation was to introduce new relations to the rest of society), and the rural reforms and the emergence of small-scale private entrepreneurship exemplify the latter approach. The state-owned economy remained so dominant, at least at first, that the more market-oriented sectors did not pose any real threat to the larger society.

This conflict between planning and market activities—and between status and class orientations—is reflected in the ambivalent attitude the Dengist regime has taken toward wealth. At various times, in order to promote economic reform and give ideological backing to the use of rnaterial incentives, the regime has urged people to "get rich." This theme, which became prominent in 1983, perhaps reached its apogee during the 1984 Spring Festival, when the Party newspaper *Renmin ribao* touted the virtues of "getting rich" in uncompromising terms. Later that year, Ren Zhongyi, then the reform-minded Party secretary of Guangdong province, declared that "the more revolution you make, the richer you should become."[31]

At other times—including the present—the Dengist regime has sought to dampen materialist urges. For instance, a 1981 *Renmin ribao* commentary said that, whereas material incentives are important, "it would be utterly wrong to think that in stressing material incentives we can ignore the importance of moral values to the extent of using the bourgeois attitude that 'money is all powerful' and egoism as a guide to all our actions." In 1985, in response to the assertion of materialist incentives the previous year, there was a campaign to oppose the idea that "money is above everything" *(yi qie wei qian kan)*. Similarly, in 1987, Guan Guangmei became famous for earning a sizable income from the state-owned retail stores she had leased, thereby becoming both a symbol for those who sought to tout the value of entrepreneurship and a target for those who thought that she, and China, were going down the "capitalist road."[32] Since the crackdown on June 4, 1989, the new general secretary, Jiang Zemin, has declared that admitting millionaires into the Party, which was proposed in 1988, is incompatible with the communist ethic that Party members are expected to uphold.

The same conflation of politics and economics posed a serious obstacle to reformist efforts to sort out relations of ownership and property rights. Reform-minded economists were aware of the need to redefine China's enterprises as independent (not "relatively independent") commodity producers restrained by market forces, but such hopes cut across four decades of socialist practice, during which, as Andrew Walder has observed, "employment [was] not primarily a market relationship, nor [was] the firm an economic enterprise in the capitalist sense."[33] The political obstacles to bringing about a fundamental change in that situation proved too great, and are likely to remain so for the indefinite future. As a result, economic reform could do little more than give enterprises greater autonomy, a change that was not sufficient to guide them toward economically rational behavior. Thus, China's economic reform followed the well-worn path of reform in Eastern Europe, where soft budget constraints led enterprises to "bear responsibility for profits but not for losses." Even in the countryside, where the results of reform were impressive in the first half of the 1980s, the failure to draw clear definitions of property relationships obviously has undermined the peasants' faith in reform and made them less willing to invest in agricultural production.[34]

Finally, as suggested earlier, the lack of differentiation between public and private finds expression in the relationship between ideology and knowledge. Despite the recognition of specialized areas of knowledge as separate from Party ideology, all areas of intellectual inquiry, including the natural sciences, remained subject to Party intervention when they seemed to violate important ideological tenets. Such intervention was most visible in areas where the distinction between professional norms and Party ideology was less clear. For instance, the demands of journalists to have greater editorial control over newspapers, though it was consistent with journalists' growing conception of themselves as an independent profession, led to periodic crackdowns on the press, including Hu Yaobang's well-known speech in 1986 in which he reiterated the Party's position that newspapers must be the "mouthpiece" of the Party, as well as the sharp curtailment of journalistic freedom that followed the June 1989 crackdown.

Openness, Leninism, and Nationalism

Although the policy of "opening to the outside world" has played a major role in China's reform program, it is clear that such openness has provoked opposition, thus raising questions about the degree and type of openness that China will be able to sustain over the long term. Such opposition has been apparent on three levels.

First, just as the inherent incompatibility between the status orientation of Leninist systems and the class orientation of market economies surfaces when market principles are introduced into the planned economies, there is a similar incompatibility between the basically autarkic economy traditionally practiced by socialist countries and the reforms intended to open them to the world economy. Becoming integrated into the world economy ultimately means establishing a convertible currency and accepting the inevitable disruptions of the domestic economy and the loss of Party control over the economy that such moves imply. It is precisely because of that threat that Leninist systems have traditionally "compartmentalized" their external economic activities through the use of nonconvertible currencies and state trading companies. Integration into the world economy implies acceptance of the market rules that prevail there, and, just as with the development of a domestic market economy, such acceptance undermines the "heroic" orientation of the Party.

Second, on an ideological level, openness undermines the antagonistic relationship presumed to exist between socialism and capitalism. To the extent that a policy of opening up is pursued, it is necessary to revise ideological tenets about both capitalism and socialism to show that whatever differences exist between the two systems, there are also underlying similarities. In China, that process started in the natural sciences, which were declared to have no class nature. Later, in order to extend market-oriented reforms, theoreticians argued that the concept of a "commodity capitalism" was not unique to capitalism, it was said that commodity exchange had existed long before the advent of capitalism and so could be adopted by socialist systems. In 1988, as reformers tried to press the gains they had made at the Thirteenth Party Congress, an effort was launched to "reunderstand" the natures of both socialism and capitalism. That endeavor sought to underline the commonalities between the two systems.

To the extent that capitalism and socialism are no longer seen as locked in a life-and-death struggle, but as being subject to common laws, there is an implicit convergence between the two systems. Just such a convergence was implicit in the use of the concept of the "new technological revolution." Thus, when Zhao Ziyang endorsed the concept of the new technological revolution, or the so-called third wave, in October 1983, he was not simply making an evaluation of the implications of new technology for China's modernization, but also was making an ideological statement about the relationship between superstructure and base: If socialism and capitalism are subject to the same laws of development, then the distinction between the two is attenuated at best.[35]

Precisely that implication was brought out in the summer of 1987 by an article in the Party's theoretical journal *Hongqi* that appeared to criticize Zhao's impending selection as Party general secretary. That article, written as a review of Alvin Toffler's *The Third Wave*, argued that Toffler's views "differ vastly from Marxist ones and we must not agree to them." Toffler's views were antagonistic to Marxism, the article said, because Toffler "preaches that scientific and technological progress can resolve various contradictions of the capitalist system and can even make the capitalist and socialist systems 'converge.'" As a result, "the question of 'which triumphs over the other' will disappear and give way to the unification of the two."[36] The subsequent meeting between Zhao Ziyang and Alvin Toffler in September 1988 marked a vivid—but ultimately unsuccessful—rejection of such views.[37]

On a third level, China's open policy is intertwined with deep visceral feelings about interaction with the outside world—feelings that historically helped bring about the downfall of the Qing dynasty and fueled the Nationalist and Communist revolutions. Inevitably, Chinese nationalism developed in the context of foreign imperialism. That was the case in 1874 when the authorities of the French Concession in Shanghai attempted to build roads through the cemetery of the local Ningbo Guild, touching off a protest now regarded as China's first political boycott against foreign imperialism. More virulent and more populist nationalist upsurges occurred in response to later events: the Sino-Japanese War of 1894–1895; the decision of the Versailles Conference in 1919 to grant Germany's concessions in China to Japan; the May 30, 1925, shooting of Chinese protestors, which led to the nationalist upsurge that culminated in the Northern Expedition and establishment of Nationalist rule; and the Sino-Japanese War of 1937–1945, which paved the way for the CCP's takeover in 1949.

Whereas that history of conflict with imperialism produced virulent nationalistic—and xenophobic—responses, such as the Boxer Rebellion of 1900 and the extreme antiforeignism of the Cultural Revolution, one can distinguish three other types of nationalistic responses that seem more likely to have a lasting impact on China's interaction with the world. Two of these traditions are suggested by the distinction that Paul Cohen makes between the "littoral" areas most exposed to Western influence and the "hinterland" most associated with both cultural conservatism and radical nativism.

The culture of the littoral areas was, in Cohen's words, "more commercialized than agricultural in its economic foundations, more modern than traditional in its administrative and social arrangements, more Western (Christian) than Chinese (Confucian) in its intellectual outlook, and more outward- than inward-looking in its general global orientation and involvement."[38] Although the distinction between hinterland and littoral is by no means absolute—there was much interaction between the two areas, and the hinterland was not always as agricultural or inward-looking as this dichotomy would suggest—it nevertheless provides a useful heuristic framework that highlights important differences in the ways in which Chinese reacted to the West.[39]

The littoral tradition of nationalism, associated with Chinese "liberalism," can be traced from such nineteenth-century reformers as Wang Tao, Ma Jianzhong, and Zheng Guanying, then to leaders of the 1898 reform movement such as Kang Youwei and Liang Qichao, and finally to Western-educated intellectuals such as Hu Shi and Ding Wenjiang in the 1920s and 1930s. In contrast, the hinterland tradition can be traced from such late-Qing cultural conservatives as Wo-ren; then to the later Liang Qichao (who turned away from his earlier infatuation with the Western model); and to promoters of the "national essence" such as Liu Shipei, neo-Confucian scholars such as Liang Shuming and Xiong Shili, and Sinocentric nationalists such as Tao Xisheng and Sa Mengwu.[40] In its radical nativist guise, the hinterland tradition found expression in the thought of Communist leaders such as Li Dazhao and Mao Zedong.

In between these two traditions, one can distinguish a third approach, that of "self-strengthening." Rooted in the Confucian tradition of "statecraft," the self-strengthening approach shares with the littoral tradition a concern for involvement in the world, yet remains, like the hinterland tradition, firmly embedded in China's cultural traditions. Finding its origins in late-Qing reformers such as Li Hongzhang and Zhang Zhidong, the self-strengthening approach tried to reinvigorate the Qing by blending Confucian traditions with the importation of Western technology. Summed up in Zhang Zhidong's famous aphorism, "Chinese learning as the essence, and Western learning for use" *(Zhongxue weiti, xixue weiyong)*, that tradition finds contemporary expression in the pragmatic approach of the Dengist regime, which is why the Dengist reforms bear such an uncanny resemblance to the self-strengthening efforts of a century ago.

The contrast between the hinterland and littoral traditions was reflected in a well-known debate—one that had clear echoes in the polemics of the late 1980s—involving Sa Mengwu, He Bingsong, Tao Xisheng, and other intellectuals on one side, with Hu Shi and others opposing them. In 1935, a group of ten professors, including Sa, He, and Tao, concerned that traditional Chinese values were being eroded by various modern influences, issued a manifesto declaring that Chinese cultural values must be preserved in the course of economic, political, and cultural modernization. They recommended that the Chinese should "adopt a critical attitude" and "absorb what should be absorbed" and reject the rest.[41]

In response, Hu Shi condemned the manifesto as a "fashionable reflection of the general reactionary atmosphere of the present." In contrast to the manifesto's expression of concern that "China's characteristics" were being lost, Hu said that "what is most worrying in China today is that the political form, social organization, and content and form of thought everywhere preserve all the sins that China has always had," and he recommended letting world culture "freely and fully come into contact with our old culture."[42] What China needed was not to preserve its traditional values but "complete Westernization."[43]

The different nationalistic responses reflected in that debate resonate with similar debates, both intellectual and policy-oriented, in contemporary China. One expression of this conflict has come in the course of building the SEZs, themselves an expression of a self-strengthening approach to modernization. During one period of heightened controversy over the SEZs, the conservative Party theoretician Hu Qiaomu gave voice to the hinterland tradition when he evoked the similarities between the SEZs and the foreign concessions in China's nineteenth-century treaty ports. Hu suggested that the Chinese government had given in to the "inordinate demands" of foreigners, and he charged that foreign businessmen "show no respect" for Chinese laws when they come to the SEZs.[44]

Precisely the same sort of conflict between different nationalistic traditions found echoes in the writings and speeches of the astrophysicist and human-rights activist Fang Lizhi and in the salvoes of the two campaigns (in 1987, and following June 4) against "bourgeois liberalization."

According to Fang Lizhi, China needs "complete Westernization," which he, like Hu Shi, defines as a "complete and total openness." Fang argues that China is backward not in one or two respects but "in all respects," so its opening cannot be preconditioned on the upholding of some aspects or the defining of some things as "the essence" (wei ti). It was on the basis of that belief that Fang went so far as to ridicule Deng Xiaoping's notion of "building socialism with Chinese characteristics." For Fang, the idea of "Chinese modernization" sets a prior limit on modernization, but what China needs is "complete" modernization.

Fang's fervent embrace of "complete Westernization" was sharply opposed by those whose intellectual and emotional roots lay in the hinterland tradition of nationalism. Shortly before the campaign against bourgeois liberalization that was launched at the end of 1986, the conservative party elders Bo Yibo, Wang Zhen, Hu Qiaomu, Deng Liqun, and Song Renqiong expressed their anger with the student movement then growing throughout the country, as well as with the liberalizing trends that had been developing in recent years, by meeting with a traditional storyteller known for his rendering of the Chinese classic *Ro-*

mance of the Three Kingdoms. Wang praised the storyteller for "raising our national dignity and sense of pride," contrasting his efforts favorably with "some people" who "advocate national nihilism, debase and negate China, and call for the complete Westernization of China." Similarly, Bo warned that the policy of opening to the outside world and studying the advanced science and technology of foreign nations should not cause Chinese to "belittle" themselves or to "consider all things foreign to be better than in China." "We must not think," he said, "that 'the moon in foreign countries is fuller than in China.'"[45]

There is, perhaps predictably, a close connection between these different nationalistic traditions and the ideological conflicts over the relationship between socialism and capitalism described earlier. The same *Hongqi* article that criticized Toffler's ideas went on to say that "we must never regard all foreign things as the correct standards to follow and blindly imitate them, and thus prostrate ourselves before Toffler's *The Third Wave.* Worshipping foreign things and inappropriately negating ourselves are like twins."[46] It was, after all, the hinterland tradition of nationalism that was the primary impulse underlying China's acceptance of Marxism and its understanding of socialism; it is not surprising that ideological conflict and different nationalistic impulses have become intertwined as China has struggled with redefining its ideology and opening to the outside world.

Chinese Culture and Modernization

Closely connected with these divergent strains of nationalism are contemporary reflections on Chinese culture, which similarly resonate with earlier periods of cultural introspection, such as the late Qing, the May Fourth period, and the 1930s. The continuity of such basic questions as the relationship between China and the West, and that between Chinese culture and Western culture, provides strong testimony to the continuing tension between China's cultural traditions and the task of modernization. Among other things, the evident and continuing force of this tension lays to rest Joseph Levenson's hypothesis that communist ideology had found a way out of the dilemmas that had entrapped earlier generations of intellectuals and had "museumified" Chinese history by rendering it irrelevant.[47]

What has resurrected these debates is the self-evident failure of the communist authorities, particularly during the Cultural Revolution, to modernize China economically, culturally, or politically. As China emerged from the Cultural Revolution, Chinese intellectuals of all sorts, whether they were in literature, history, philosophy, natural science, or social science, had to ask themselves certain questions: What went wrong? Was the Cultural Revolution an aberration that will not be repeated once the "good traditions" of the Party are reestablished? Or is there something in Chinese social structure and culture that supported the various manifestations of "leftism" throughout the history of Chinese communism and led, perhaps inexorably, to the Cultural Revolution?

Inevitably intellectuals find part of the answer lying in China's "feudal" history. They find that although the CCP has continually criticized both "feudalism" and "capitalism," the emphasis in practice has been on expunging every manifestation of capitalism, thus leaving feudal influences free to grow and develop. Thus, such intellectuals find the negative influences of feudalism strongly reflected in the practices of the CCP: overconcentration of power, rule by man rather than rule by law, one-man say, and the politicization of intellectual life.

Having found such feudal influences reflected in China's political life, intellectuals have naturally embarked on a search for the sources of those influences, and in doing so, they inevitably have found themselves retracing the steps of late-Qing intellectuals such as Liang Qichao and May Fourth intellectuals such as Hu Shi, Chen Duxiu, and Lu Xun.

Like their predecessors in earlier generations, Chinese intellectuals remain divided over the essential characteristics and value of Chinese tradition. One group of scholars, known as the "new Confucians," believe that it is necessary to find the seeds of modernization within Chinese tradition itself—though ironically they base this belief in no small measure on conclusions drawn from Western social science and philosophy. Building on the work of philosophers such as Liang Shuming, Xiong Shili, and Feng Youlan, this group has been strongly influenced by such non-PRC scholars as Mou Tsung-san and Tu Wei-ming. Such scholars emphasize that "modernization is not the same as Westernization" and argue that unless China finds the sources of modernization within its own tradition, it will become detached from its "roots" and continue to face a "crisis of identity." This approach, which has contributed greatly to a revival of interest in and understanding of traditional Chinese culture, after being criticized for so many years, finds powerful support in the developmental experiences of such Confucian-shaped societies as South Korea, Japan, Taiwan, Singapore, and Hong Kong.

For those who take this approach, Confucianism, like the Protestant ethic, can provide a basis for rapid economic development. Moreover, they argue, such "Confucian capitalism" can avoid the moral pitfalls of Western capitalist development. In this sense, a "third wave" of Confucian development not only can pave the way for economic development of China but also can provide a powerful corrective for Western nations.[48] Expressing this point of view, philosopher Tang Yijie concludes that "if a people lose the traditions of their national culture, then it is impossible for them to fully absorb foreign thought and culture much less to make their own thought and culture go to the forefront of other peoples."[49]

In response, philosophers such as Bao Zunxin have argued that even though modernization is not the same as Westernization, absorbing the experiences of Western nations is an inevitable part of modernization and nothing to worry about. In Bao's view, "using the excuse that 'modernization is not the same as Westernization' to refuse to absorb the fruits of other nations and to refuse to consult their modernization experiences is the same as erecting a stop sign on the way to modernization. The 'modernization is not the same as Westernization' that the new Confucians talk about is precisely such a sign."[50]

Those who, like Bao, espouse Westernization as a necessary component of modernization do so in large part because they see China's traditional culture as the problem rather than the solution. Like their predecessors in the May Fourth period, such intellectuals see the deep-rooted intellectual, social, and cultural habits of China's traditional culture as having been obstacles to China's modernization in the late nineteenth and early twentieth centuries and as continuing to retard modernization today. Although such intellectuals are willing to agree that there are many aspects of traditional culture worthy of praise and even cultivation, they see the "deep structure" of China's traditional culture as having formed an organic whole that is fundamentally antagonistic to the requisites of the modern world. For such intellectuals, the pressing intellectual task is to build on the tradition of the May Fourth movement by continuing, and deepening, the critique of China's traditional culture.

One attempt to view current political, economic, and cultural problems as stemming from weaknesses inherent in China's traditional culture is that by the literary critic Liu Zaifu and the historian Lin Gang. Not unlike many other critics, Liu and Lin see the relationship between traditional moral values and political power as corrupting of both and believe that contemporary China has been unable to escape the moral-political paradigm that shaped traditional China.[51]

Their critique is based on the belief that China's traditional culture was "pan-moralistic" *(fan daode zhuyi)*. Their contention is that Confucian morality, rather than remaining confined to a specific moral sphere, was infused throughout all spheres, particularly the political, thereby undermining both morality and the political system. Thus, they argue that "when good and evil are made the center of life and the foundation of the nation's organization, they are no longer a matter of conscience but attached to force." As a result, they become the haunting, dominating forces that Lu Xun described as "man-eating."

In the political realm, the fusion of morality and government brought about rule by man rather than rule by law. What counted in traditional rule was not an objective standard of legality but moral judgments of "right" and "wrong." On the other hand, that fusion of morality and political rule made the scope of government theoretically unlimited. Because the central concern of government was moral propriety, there was no area of life that could not become a legitimate subject of government interference. Thus, there was no sense of "privacy" in traditional culture.

Moreover, that fusion of morality and government, Liu and Lin argue, prevented improvement of the political system over time. When dynasties declined and fell, the influence of China's traditional moral system was such that people blamed political failings on the decline of morality, rather than looking to specific problems in the political system. That tendency only strengthened the grip of morality on politics, making it ever more difficult for China to work its way out of its dilemmas.

At the same time that the fusion of morality and government corrupted the method of rule and gave unlimited scope to the authority of the state, it undermined the very moral values it was designed to cultivate. Thus, Liu and Lin argue that because moral values were central to success in traditional society, that could only lead to hypocrisy and manipulation of moral values to achieve political success.

Finally, traditional moral concepts were always group-centered, stifling individualism. The individual who rebelled against the system not only would be rejected by family and friends but also could find the whole weight of the system thrown against him or her. Thus, pan-moralism led politically to totalism, on the one hand, and to a lack of privacy and individual vitality, on the other; morally it led to hypocrisy and selfishness, as well as withdrawal from society. Both public virtue and private virtue suffered accordingly. Such characteristics of China's traditional culture, then, stand in contrast to the "Faustian" spirit, the pluralist values, the emphasis on logic, and the action-oriented pragmatism said to characterize the West.

One of the most powerful intellectual frameworks for dealing with the cultural dilemmas described by such scholars as Liu and Lin has been developed by the philosopher Li Zehou.[52] Li has put forth the slogan "Western essence and Chinese use" *(xiti zhongyong)*—a deliberate play on Zhang Zhidong's famous aphorism—not only to be provocative but also to underscore his belief that China's difficulty in modernizing over the past century and a half has resulted from the age-old tendency of Chinese society to "Sinocize" foreign ideas, rendering them devoid of their original content. In sharp contrast to those, either in the past or in the present, who see Western ideas and culture as a threat to Chinese values, Li focuses on the way China has repeatedly taken foreign ideas, stripped them of their foreign essence *(xiti)*, and turned them into supports for China's essence *(zhongti)*—a critique that he applies widely (e.g., the importation of Buddhism from India, the adoption of Christianity by the leaders of the Taiping Rebellion, and the use of Marxism in modern China).

What gives the "Chinese essence" its strength, Li argues, is the combination of its economic structure, particularly its basis in "feudal," small-scale production, and an ideological consciousness that corresponds to that base. That essence can be changed, he believes, only with the development of a "commodity economy"; only then will "Western learning" be able to take root.[53] Despite his materialist conception of "essence," Li, like his forerunners in the May Fourth period, believes that changes in the economic base can be accelerated by appropriate changes in the "superstructure," particularly the spheres of culture and political organization. Hence his critique not only of traditional Chinese culture but also of the "new Confucians," who, he believes, are indirectly supporting the old economic base.

The tensions implicit in the different traditions of nationalism and the arguments over the compatibility between Chinese culture and the requirements for modernization dramatically entered the realm of elite politics with the broadcast of the television program *He shang* (River elegy) in the summer of 1988. Employing the contrasting metaphors of the Yellow River, the cradle of Chinese civilization, and the blue sea, connoting openness to the West, the program sharply criticized the conservatism of Chinese culture, viewing it as antithetical to modernization. The Party's general secretary, Zhao Ziyang, endorsed the film by presenting a copy to the Singapore prime minister, Lee Kuan Yew, during his visit to China. Meanwhile, conservatives, led by Vice President Wang Zhen, vehemently denounced the film. Since the student demonstrations of April–June 1989 and Zhao's ouster as Party head, the hard-line government in Beijing has repeatedly denounced *He shang*, and democratic activists abroad have appropriated its symbolism.[54]

The entire debate over the merits of Chinese culture and the way in which the debate became politicized marked a significant shift in the history of the Chinese Communist movement. The debate between proponents of the New Confucianism and those critical of traditional Chinese culture has been carried on almost entirely without reference to Marxist thought. That reflects not only the essential irrelevance of Marxist categories to contemporary intellectuals but also the reemergence of intellectuals as a partially autonomous interest group. That is to say, Chinese intellectuals, prior to June 4, were beginning to resume the position that they had held in Chinese society in the late Qing and early Republican periods as the articulators of a "public interest." This suggests that, however tentatively and problematically, a "public sphere" is beginning to reemerge in China. It seems premature, however, to talk in terms of an emergent "civil society," not simply because of the events of June 4 (which can only retard these trends, not stop them), but more importantly because of the continuing weakness of intellectuals as a group, because their relationship with government remains one of dependence, and because of the weight of tradition in which many (perhaps most) intellectuals continue to perceive their roles not as representatives of an independent civil society but as the articulators of a public interest within the scope of state authority.[55] The remarkable thing about the events of April–June 1989, was the degree to which intellectuals for a very brief time articulated the interests of an independent civil society. The possibility that this degree of articulation will become a long-term trend, however, seems remote.

The other thing that strikes one as remarkable about this debate is the posture of the Party. Fifteen years ago, when Michel Oksenberg and Steven Goldstein surveyed the political spectrum of the Party leadership, they could find no one supportive of traditional Chinese culture.[56] Rather, the Chinese Communist movement based its nationalism and nativism on the "little" tradition of the peasants and criticized the "big" tradition of Confucianism (the "four olds"). Today, however, no matter how uneasy some leaders may be about it, the Party has come to terms with Chinese tradition and Confucianism, and even views them as bastions of support against those who criticize Chinese culture from a perspective of "wholesale Westernization." The effort to transform society in the name of Marxism is over, and with it the "exclusive" orientation of the Party has been lost.

Conclusion

Placing the Dengist reforms in historical perspective not only highlights important continuities between pre-PRC China and the current period but also underscores the tensions involving China's historical tradition, Leninism as a unique form of authority, and the demands of reform. The dilemmas that Liang Qichao faced in trying to deal with relations between state and society and between public and private are very much the dilemmas of modern China. On the one hand, because Liang's critique of the traditional monarchy was rooted in nationalism, his denial that the monarchy represented *gong* (public interest) was not accompanied, as it was in Europe, by a concomitant assertion that an emergent public sphere could legitimately articulate a conception of *gong* against the state. On the other hand, as the bearer of a cultural tradition that viewed the scholarly class as upholding the general interest, his concept of *gong* was not rooted in notions of private interest or the interplay of private groups. Thus, his critique of the traditional monarchy was more savage than thorough. He argued neither against totalism per se nor against the absence of an autonomous public sphere in Chinese life, and his concept of the "new people" was not a concept of citizenship, but rather a delineation of the moral values Liang thought necessary for the creation of a modern, and stronger, state. Here, Liu Zaifu and Lin Gang's critique of China's traditional continuum between individual morality and political power rings true.

Liang's intellectual failure to adequately sort out the relationships between public and private and between state and society was "resolved" by the political imposition of neotraditional authority, first by the GMD, and then, more thoroughly and successfully, by the CCP. *Gong* was to be embodied in neither state nor society, but in the Party. In that view, a strong state could be created without statism, and society could be mobilized without the interplay of private interests. The seamless web between public authority and private interest would be maintained by the Party's supervision of both state and society. Thereby the basic assumptions of a status society could be harnessed to the goal of a modernizing state.

The Dengist reforms have called into question the basic assumptions of that "solution." Economic reform has challenged it by setting the class orientation of the market economy against the status orientation of the Party. Ideological reform has questioned it by setting autonomous realms of knowledge against Party claims of scientific truth. And the opening to the outside world has challenged it both ways—threatening both to integrate the Chinese economy into the world economy and to undermine ideological assumptions about the relationship between socialism and capitalism. At the same time, the opening revives old questions about the relationship between China and the outside world, thus provoking different strains of nationalist response.

The most significant long-term development brought about by the reforms, however, has been the reemergence of "society" as a meaningful participant in political life. This development, stimulated by the devolution of economic authority to local governments, makes the continuities between the pre-PRC period and the present all the more clear, while highlighting the very real sense in which the Maoist period has come to appear as an interregnum. This reemergence of society means that the questions that preoccupied earlier generations—defining the relationship between public and private and working out ways of relating local government to central government (possibly including some notions of a new federalist arrangement)—have once again appeared on the political agenda.

As the foregoing discussion suggests, however, one must be cautious about viewing this revival of society in terms of an emerging (or reemerging) "civil society." Going back to Habermas's description of the emergence of the public sphere in the West, it should be apparent that there exists little basis in China—culturally, sociologically, intellectually, or economically—for the emergence of civil society in the Western sense, that is, for an independent "public opinion" to establish the legitimate right to supervise the state. It seems more likely that a variety of intermediary entities (one cannot call them associations because they are neither voluntary nor, in most instances, nongovernmental) will emerge, but that they themselves will be of both state and society.

If such trends continue, it seems possible to conceive of a future in whisch greater authority might be delegated to officially recognized entities—

including local governments, interregional organizations, enterprises, and even intellectuals affiliated with research institutions—that would simultaneously articulate the interests of their constituents and enforce state policy. Such a development would certainly be in keeping with the many proposals made in recent years to establish a state asset management bureau, free from direct state intervention, that would manage state assets, as well as in keeping with the many discussions of "trade management."[57]

Such trends seem to point to the possibility of creating a type of state corporatist structure that could draw on China's guild tradition as well as its traditional preference for a limited, but not delimited, state. Such a structure would balance centralism and decentralism, providing for local autonomy as well as state control. It would suppress and limit the scope of interest representation, yet allow the expression of interests within a certain scope. Such a decentralized system would necessarily be less ideologically rigid, permitting the expression of a wide, but not unlimited, range of ideas. It would be open to the outside world, and perhaps integrated in part into the world economy, but it would retain a degree of central control over foreign-trade activities. Such a development might provide a means of reconciling China's past with its present, its diversity with its need for unity, its ideology with the expression of divergent views, and its nationalism with a continuing opening to the outside world.

Such an outcome seems conceivable whether or not China remains a Marxist system. The revival of regional economics, the failure of Marxism as all-integrating ideology, the increasing scope of the state's "zone of indifference," and the tentative reemergence of a public sphere over the past decade all suggest that trends strengthening society vis-à-vis the state are likely to continue. At the same time, however, the absence of a tradition legitimating the role of an independent public sphere suggests that the relations between public and private and between state and society will continue to be focuses of intellectual and political contention. It seems that China's century-long effort to reconcile its past with its postrevolutionary present will remain problematic.

Notes

I would like to thank A. Doak Barnett, Paul Cohen, and Brantly Womack for their comments on an earlier draft of this chapter.

1. Tang Tsou, "Political Change and Reform: The Middle Course," in *The Cultural Revolution and Post-Mao Reforms: A Historical Perspective* (Chicago: University of Chicago Press, 1986), pp. 219–258.

2. Tang Tsou, "Political Change and Reform," p. 220.

3. "Communiqué of the Sixth Plenary Session of the Twelfth Central Committee of the Communist Party of China," Xinhua, September 28, 1986, trans. Foreign Broadcast Information Service (FBIS), September 29, 1986, pp. K1–K15.

4. "Continue Along the Road of Socialism with Chinese Characteristics," Beijing Domestic Service, October 25, 1987, trans. FBIS, October 25, 1987, pp. 10–34.

5. G. William Skinner, "Marketing and Social Structure in Rural China" (parts 1–2), *Journal of Asian Studies*, 24, no. 1–2 (1964–1965); G. William Skinner, "Cities and the Hierarchy of Local Systems," in G. William Skinner, ed., *The City in Late Imperial China* (Stanford: Stanford University Press, 1977), pp. 275–351.

6. Tsou, "Introduction," in *Cultural Revolution*, p. xxiv.

7. See, for instance, Nina Halperin, "Information Flows and Policy Coordination in the Chinese Bureaucracy," paper presented at a conference entitled The Structure of Authority and Bureaucratic Behavior in China, Tucson, AZ, June 19–23, 1989.

8. The classic statement of that shift in regime goals is by Richard Lowenthal: "Development vs. Utopia in Communist Policy," in Chalmers Johnson, ed., *Change in Communist Systems* (Stanford: Stanford University Press, 1970), pp. 33–116.

9. Suggestive in this regard is Arthur Waldron's article, "Warlordism Versus Federalism: The Revival of a Debate?" *The China Quarterly*, no. 121 (March 1990): 116–128.

10. Kenneth Jowitt, *The Leninist Response to National Dependency* (Berkeley: Institute of International Studies, University of California, 1978), p. 36.

11. The term "great transformation" is borrowed from the title of Karl Polanyi's book *The Great Transformation: The Political and Economic Conditions of Our Time* (Boston: Beacon, 1944).

12. Susan Mann, *Local Merchants and the Chinese Bureaucracy, 1750–1950* (Stanford: Stanford University Press, 1987).

13. See, for instance, "Shang xiguan yu shangye" (Business customs and business) and "Shangye yu zhengfu" (Business and government), in *Shanghai zongshanghui yuebao* (Journal of the general chamber of commerce of Shanghai), 3, no. 12 (December 1923), and 6, no. 5 (May 1926).

14. See Keith R. Schoppa, *Chinese Elites and Political Change: Zhejiang Province in the Early Twentieth Century* (Cambridge, MA: Harvard University Press, 1982); William T. Rowe, *Hankow: Conflict and Community in a Chinese City, 1796–1895* (Stanford: Stanford University Press, 1989); Mary Backus Rankin, *Elite Activism and Political Transformation in China: Zhejiang Province, 1865–1911* (Stanford: Stanford University Press, 1986); and David Strand, *Rickshaw Beijing: City, People and Politics in 1920s China* (Berkeley: University of California Press, 1989).

15. William T. Rowe, "The Public Sphere in Modern China," *Modern China,* 16, no. 3 (July 1990): 309–329; Jürgen Habermas, *The Structural Transformation of the Public Sphere*, trans. Thomas Burger, with the assistance of Frederick Lawrence (Cambridge: MIT Press, 1989).

16. Habermas, *Structural Transformation*, pp. 79–85; Rowe, "The Public Sphere in Modern China," pp. 311–312.

17. The parallel with conceptions of regionalism are suggestive in this regard. Diana Lary argues that regional leaders in the early twentieth century envisioned

regionalism as a "bridging phenomenon" that would give way as the center reasserted itself. See her *Region and Nation: The Kwangsi Clique in Chinese Politics, 1925–1927* (New York: Cambridge University Press, 1974), pp. 8–9.

18. Rowe, "The Public Sphere in Modern China," p. 316.

19. David Strand, "Protest in Beijing: Civil Society and Public Sphere in China," *Problems of Communism* (May–June 1990): 5.

20. Hao Chang, *Liang Ch'i-ch'ao and The Intellectual Transition in China, 1890–1907* (Cambridge: Harvard University Press, 1971), p. 103.

21. Liang Qichao, "Xinmin shuo" (On the new people), in *Yinbingshi quanji* (Essays from the ice-drinker's studio) (Taipei: Wenhua tushu gongsi, 1967), pp. 2–3.

22. On the imposition of Nationalist control over society, see Joseph Fewsmith, *Party, State, and Local Elites in Republican China* (Honolulu: University of Hawaii Press, 1985).

23. Kenneth Jowitt makes the distinction between inclusion and exclusion in his article "Inclusion and Mobilization in European Leninist Regimes," *World Politics*, 28, no. 1 (October 1975): 69–96.

24. Fang Lizhi, "Minzhu bushi ciyude" (Democracy is not something given), in *Women zhengzai xie lishi* (We are writing history) (Taipei: Commonwealth Publishing, 1987), pp. 132–133.

25. A seminar lauding the television program "The Motherland Cannot Be Forgotten" was reported in *Guangming ribao*, November 1, 1988, p. 1. Synopses of the four-part program appeared in the same newspaper on November 3, 6, 8, and 9. That show clearly was intended as a rejoinder to *He shang* (River elegy), the controversial program highly critical of China's traditional culture that had been broadcast the previous summer, as discussed later.

26. The classic discussion of comradeship is by Ezra Vogel in "From Friendship to Comradeship: The Change in Personal Relations in Communist China," *The China Quarterly*, no. 21 (January–March 1965): 46–60.

27. In his most recent book, Janos Kornai states baldly that "the basic idea of market socialism simply fizzled out. Yugoslavia, Hungary, China, the Soviet Union, and Poland bear witness to its fiasco." See *The Road to a Free Economy* (New York: Norton, 1990), p. 58.

28. Liu Guoguang, "Guanyu woguo jingji tizhi gaige de mubiao moshi ji moshi zhuanhuan de ruogan wenti" (The target model of China's economic structural reform and some problems in changing the model), in Liu Guoguang, ed., *Zhongguo jingji tizhi gaige de moshi yanjiu* (Studies on the model of China's economic structural reform) (Beijing: Zhongguo shehui kexue chubanshe, 1988), p. 3.

29. Jowitt, *The Leninist Response to National Dependency*, p. 15.

30. Mann, *Local Merchants and the Chinese Bureaucracy*, p. 24.

31. Guangdong provincial radio, September 23, 1984.

32. See the fascinating description of contention over Guan Guangmei's activities in Li Honglin's "Yi jiu ba qi, Zhongguo di wu hao xinwen renwu—Guan Guangmei jishi" (1987, China's number 5 newsmaker—an account of Guan Guangmei), *Dangdai*, no. 2 (February 1988). See also the recent controversy over whether a millionaire should be permitted to join the CCP: Xinhua, September 6, 1988, trans. FBIS, September 7, 1988, p. 27.

33. Andrew G. Walder, *Communist Neo-Traditionalism: Work and Authority in Chinese Industry* (Berkeley: University of California Press, 1986), p. 11.

34. Joseph Fewsmith, "Agricultural Crisis in the PRC," *Problems of Communism,* 37 (November–December 1988): 78–93.

35. As Carol Hamrin brings out, Zhao's endorsement of the concept of a new technological revolution was also very much a part of the ideological struggle then taking place among the leadership. See *China and the Challenge of the Future* (Boulder, CO: Westview Press, 1990), pp. 75–78.

36. Tian Sen, "Jottings Written After Reading 'The Third Wave'—Also Commenting on Comments on 'The Third Wave' and 'A Big Lever,'" *Hongqi,* no. 12 (June 16, 1987): 30–34, trans. Joint Publications Research Service, JPRS-CRF-87–006 (August 20, 1987): 49–55. Tian was the general editor of the *Contemporary Sociology (Dangdai shehuixue)* book series. His article was based on remarks made at a December 1986 meeting that was called for the purpose of discussing Toffler's book. See Gao Fang, ed., *Ping "Di san ci chaolang"* (Evaluating 'The Third Wave') (Beijing: Guangming ribao chubanshe, 1988), pp. 207–212.

37. On Zhao's meeting, see Xinhua, September 13, 1988, trans. FBIS, September 21, 1988, p. 5.

38. Paul Cohen, *Between Tradition and Modernity: Wang T'ao and Reform in Late Ch'ing China* (Cambridge: Harvard University Press, 1974), pp. 241–242.

39. The distinction between hinterland and littoral is not meant to imply geographical determinism, although it is true, as Paul Cohen points out, that many Western ideas took root first in the coastal areas and that a majority of pioneering reformers grew up in or had extensive exposure to the culture of the coastal areas. Particularly as time went on, the geographical dimension of this distinction became less pronounced. Inland areas such as Changsha were notable for their cosmopolitanism, and coastal cities such as Shanghai also bred rejection of Western values. In borrowing this concept to describe different nationalistic traditions, my intention is to focus not on geographical differences (though they are not negligible) but on the relative openness of different people to foreign ideas. In the preface to the paperback edition of his book *Between Tradition and Modernity*, Paul Cohen has suggested the continued usefulness of the distinction between hinterland and littoral.

40. The thoughts of many of these conservative intellectuals have been explored: Charlotte Furth, ed., *The Limits of Change: Essays on Conservative Alternatives in Republican China* (Cambridge: Harvard University Press, 1976).

41. "Zhongguo benwei de wenhua jianshe xuanyan" (Manifesto on the construction of a China-based culture), *Wenhua jianshe* (Shanghai), October 1, 1935.

42. Hu Shi, "Shiping suowei 'Zhongguo benwei de wenhua jianshe'" (Critique of the so-called 'construction of a China-based culture), in *Hu Shi wencun* (Collected essays of Hu Shi) (Taipei: Yuandong tushu gongsi, 1953), vol. 4: 535–540.

43. Hu did not actually use the term "complete Westernization" in his critique of the ten-professor manifesto, but he did use it in his essay on cultural conflict in contemporary China, which appeared in the 1929 *Christian Year-Book.* He later expressed a preference for the term "fully cosmopolitan" rather than "complete Westernization." See his essay "Chongfen shijiehua yu quanpan xihua" (Fully cosmopolitan and complete Westernization), in *Hu's Hu Shi wencun,* 4: 541–544.

44. "Hu Qiaomu Warns in Xiamen That Foreign Investment Enterprises Are Not Concessions; Their Inordinate Demands Cannot Be Given Tacit Consent," *Ming pao,* June 22, 1985, trans. FBIS, June 24, 1885, p. W8; "Special Economic Zones

Are Not Special Political Zones; China's Laws Must Be Upheld, Says Hu Qiaomu," *Zhongguo fazhi bao*, June 28, 1985, trans. FBIS, July 8, 1985, pp. K19–K20.

45. Xinhua, December 28, 1986, trans. FBIS, December 30, 1986, pp. K6–K8.

46. Tian, "Jottings Written After Reading 'The Third Wave,'" p. 55.

47. Joseph R. Levenson, "The Problem of Historical Significance," in *Confucian China and Its Modern Fate: A Trilogy* (Berkeley: University of California Press, 1972).

48. See, for instance, the interview with Tu Wei-ming in *Dushu*, October 1985, pp. 118–128.

49. Tang Yijie, "Zhongguo xin wenhua de chuangjian" (Creating a new Chinese culture), *Dushu*, July 1988, pp. 6–10.

50. Bao Zunxin, "Xiandaihua he xihua" (Modernization and westernization), *Wenhui bao*, September 23, 1986, p. 2.

51. The description of the views of Liu Zaifu and Lin Gang that follows is based on their two-part essay "Chuantong daode de kunjing" (The dilemma of traditional morality), *Shehui kexue zhanxian*, nos. 2–3, 1988. For a more complete statement of their argument, see Liu Zaifu and Lin Gang, *Chuantong yu Zhongguoren* (Tradition and the Chinese people) (Hong Kong: Sanlian shudian, 1988).

52. See Li Zehou, *Zhongguo jindai sixiangshi lun* (History of modern Chinese thought) (Beijing: Renmin chubanshe, 1979); Li Zehou, *Zhongguo xiandai sixiangshi lun* (History of contemporary Chinese thought) (Beijing: Dongfang chubanshe, 1987).

53. See Li Zehou, "Man shuo 'xiti zhongyong'" (Discussing "Western learning as essence, Chinese learning for use"), in Li, *Zhongguo xiandai sixiangshi lun*, especially pp. 331–333.

54. Su Xiaokang and Wang Luxiang, *He shang* (River elegy) (Hong Kong: China Books, 1988). The literature for and against *He shang* has become voluminous. An early description of the political battle over it is provided by Liu Yen-ying, "Dianshi zhenglun zhu 'He shang' zhenjing Zhongnanhai" (The controversial television drama "River elegy" shakes Zhongnanhai), *Ching pao*, August 1988, pp. 40–42.

55. This discussion has benefited from conversations with Corinna-Barbara Francis.

56. Michel Oksenberg and Steven Goldstein, "The Chinese Political Spectrum," *Problems of Communism*, 23 (March–April 1974): 1–13.

57. Senior economist Xue Muqiao is one of those who have advocated reviving the federations of trade and commerce as guild-type organizations to provide indirect management over various trades. See his article "Establish and Develop Non-Governmental Self-Management Organizations in Various Trades," *Renmin ribao*, October 10, 1988, p. 5, trans. FBIS, October 18, 1988, pp. 33–35.

2

Formal Structures, Informal Politics, and Political Change in China[1]

Western studies of China have offered sometimes dramatically different images of the way the political system works and how policy decisions are made.[2] In recent years, studies of China's political system have drawn on Western understandings of bureaucratic processes to develop a picture of a highly institutionalized, albeit fragmented, administrative system. In particular, Kenneth Lieberthal and Michel Oksenberg's monumental study of the energy bureaucracy depicts a system in which there is an elaborate division of labor and institutionalized operating procedures that direct the paper flow and greatly influence the decision-making process.[3] Their work, as well as that of others, has highlighted the fragmentation of power and consequent bargaining that takes place in the system.[4] The richness of this work suggests the intellectual mileage that can be gained by looking carefully at the formal, institutional structure of the system. Yet as Lieberthal and Oksenberg clearly recognize, China's political system is far less institutionalized at the highest levels of the Party, and there are policy arenas in which bargaining models are far less useful. As Jonathan Pollack remarked in a recent article on the People's Liberation Army, "The closer to the acme of the system, the less command derives from specified rules and norms. . . ."[5] Lieberthal has similarly noted that the "fragmented authoritarianism" model was largely constructed around studies of investment projects and does not necessarily have the same utility in other areas.[6]

In contrast, other studies that draw explicitly or implicitly on notions of Chinese political culture stress the informal nature of the Chinese political process and the importance of "relation networks" (*guanxi wang*).[7] Viewed from this perspective, laws, regulations, and institutions count for little; what matters is who knows whom. The present chapter systematically explores this dimension, stressing the importance of informal politics for "who gets, what, when, and how." As Lowell Dittmer and others emphasize, however, informal politics are given shape in large part by the "trellis" of formal politics. It is, in other words, the interaction between formal and informal politics that should be the focus of our attention. Western studies of organizational behavior have long recognized the importance of this interaction, but studies of the Chinese political system have generally neglected this interaction. Yet even a cursory glance at the Chinese political system suggests the importance of both factors. This chapter thus makes a modest effort to address this interaction by looking at the way formal and informal politics interacted in the 1980s.

It seems evident that certain interests in Chinese society do find institutional expression in China's bureaucracy, and thus efforts to reform China's bureaucracy are often successfully resisted. For instance, in 1988, the State Council abolished the State Economic Commission, but beginning in 1993 it was gradually resuscitated until it had reappeared, in a more powerful form, as the State Economic and Trade Commission. On the other hand, many important policy decisions apparently receive only cursory review, at best, by China's bureaucracy. For instance, personal relations and political interests were critical in the promotion of the rural reforms in the late 1970s and early 1980s. The interaction between formal and informal structures of power is also apparent in the difficult-to-measure, but nonetheless real, ebbs and flows of power over the course of time. Viewing the policy-making process over time, it seems apparent that power shifts from one individual or institution to another according to the issue involved, and according to the overall political atmosphere. To take but one dramatic example, between 1983 and 1984 neither the composition of the Politburo nor that of the Central Committee of the Chinese Communist Party (CCP) changed significantly, yet the politics of the two years differed dramatically. In 1983, the Party launched a campaign against "spiritual pollution," whereas in 1984 it adopted a landmark decision on economic structural reform. Such rapid shifts along the political spectrum from "left" to "right" are not explicable by reference to bureaucratic or bargaining models. Bureaucratic models would lead one to expect slow, incremental shifts in policy, but in fact the policy behavior observed is rapid and nonincremental.

One could argue that the reason the campaign against spiritual pollution, like the campaigns against bourgeois liberalization in 1987 and 1989–1990, did not last was that bureaucratic interests reasserted themselves. But such a line of reasoning only underscores the question of why bureaucratic interests were overruled in the first place. It seems apparent that there is a large element of nonbureaucratic politics that needs to be examined and explained. Bargaining models are not of much help in explaining such campaigns as that against spiritual pollution, precisely because such campaigns have an ideological component that does not lend itself to the sort of bargaining that goes on in other areas such as capital construction.

A factional model seems potentially more helpful, but there is no known explanation for the shifts in factional alignments in this period.[8] Moreover, the factional model is not compatible with the ideological components of either the campaign against spiritual pollution or the subsequent Decision on the Reform of the Economic Structure. It is important to recognize that reform decisions, like the movements that have interrupted the reform process, have an important ideological dimension. Such ideological components are not compatible with the "culture of civility" said to typify factionalism.

Moreover, whether one is looking at such policy shifts as that from 1983 to 1984 or at other periods of political change, such as the emergence of reform in the late 1970s, it seems that there are factors other than bureaucratic or factional politics involved. In particular, it seems that one cannot explain such shifts without an understanding of how broad issues affect the decision-making process, yet discussions of Chinese politics have rarely discussed how such issues get into the political system.

In his wonderful study of the American political system, Hedrick Smith uses the term "power float" to suggest the way in which power flows among the individuals and institutions in Washington.[9] It seems that power "floats" in Beijing as well as Washington, albeit in quite different ways. This chapter cannot offer a complete explanation of the ways in which power floats in Beijing, but can simply suggest that any explanation of the Chinese political system and policy-making process must take account of informal politics, formal structure, and political issues. Moreover, as Smith's study of American politics suggests, one wants to try to understand how these elements change over time. Looking at how these elements interact may help us understand not only past transformations of the political system but also the post–Deng Xiaoping transition.

Informal Politics and Formal Structure in the Inauguration of Reform

Chinese politics in the period following the death of Mao and the subsequent arrest of the Gang of Four can be seen as a period in which formal structures, battered but not destroyed by the Cultural Revolution, overlapped and interacted with informal politics, Party norms (which continued to exist as an ideal), uncertain ideology, and burgeoning social issues. When one looks back at the political transition that took place in China fifteen years ago—the only political transition to have taken place between the establishment of the PRC and the death of Deng—one sees that reform emerged from a complex process in which Deng Xiaoping used a set of issues that could mobilize a constituency, distinguish him from Hua Guofeng, and thereby legitimate his own displacement of Hua as the paramount leader of China. It is important to emphasize, as Frederick Teiwes does, the revolutionary legitimacy Deng possessed by virtue of his long participation in and major contributions to the victory of the CCP and the administration of the PRC prior to the Cultural Revolution.[10] Nevertheless, despite such revolutionary legitimacy, Deng did not challenge Hua Guofeng in an intra-Party meeting and then articulate an agenda but rather the other way around, underscoring the importance of issues in legitimating leadership.

Thinking counterfactually for a moment about alternative scenarios can perhaps shed some light on the implicit "rules of the game" by which Chinese politics are played, at least in this period. Given Hua Guofeng's rather junior standing in the Party, his weak personal network, and his apparently modest work capabilities, it might seem logical to suppose that a group of veteran leaders would get together, either formally or informally, and decide to oust Hua and replace him with someone more acceptable. This could have been done in an extra-legal fashion, as with the ouster of the Gang of Four, or legally through the convening of a Party plenum. Having disposed of Hua, Deng and the new leadership could then consider the direction of policy. Indeed, given the strength of Deng's leadership credentials—his Party experience, his extensive personal connections, and his links to the military—this seems a logical scenario. That the political situation evolved along rather different lines tells us a great deal about Chinese politics.

The first point that this counterfactual scenario brings out is the degree of legitimacy that Hua Guofeng possessed, both because of Mao's endorsement of his leadership ("with you in charge, I am at ease") and because of Hua's holding of formal office. The Gang of Four had been seen as so dangerous that they had to be removed by extra-legal means; even then, without the legitimation provided by Hua Guofeng's approval as the *formal* head of the Party, the plotters might have desisted. Hua Guofeng was hardly regarded in the same category as the Gang of Four and removing him needed to be legitimated. Whatever the Party constitution said about the members of the Central Committee electing the head of the Party, it was clear that Hua had to be delegitimated before he could be removed.[11]

The need to first delegitimate Hua highlights a second point in this counterfactual scenario, namely the link between personal leadership and political line. If Chinese politics were either more formalized or more informal, line would not be so important. Political line is what connects individual leaders to policy direction and to a broader ideological framework. As is well known, Hua attempted to secure his leadership by vowing to continue the policies of Mao Zedong (even if he modified them in practice). The Dazhai model, which emphasized collective labor, was confirmed in agriculture, as was the Daqing model, which similarly emphasized ideological incentives in industry. Most of all, Hua vowed to uphold the results of the Cultural Revolution and the "all-round dictatorship of the proletariat." These policies, summarized as the "two whatevers" ("whatever decision Chairman Mao made, we resolutely support; whatever instructions Chairman Mao made, we will steadfastly abide by"),[12] were intended to legitimize Hua's position as Chairman Mao's revolutionary successor and to limit the return and influence of those veteran cadres purged during the Cultural Revolution, particularly Deng Xiaoping (after all, Mao had "instructed" that Deng be purged). Without challenging this line, it would have been difficult if not impossible to remove Hua Guofeng, much less to inaugurate a new line of reform and opening up.

The process of delegitimizing Hua Guofeng and legitimizing Deng Xiaoping illuminates the interconnections between formal position, informal politics, political issues, and ideology. Frequently we think of Chinese politics as dominated by informal politics, but clearly there are limits to informal politics (just as Hua Guofeng could not be removed through informal means). A closer look shows the ways in which the formal structure, informal processes, and broader ideological framework interact. At least three issues were vital to Deng in this quest: rural policy, enterprise policy, and ideology.

Rural Reform

The inauguration of rural reform is too complex to discuss in detail here, but some aspects that underscore the interaction between the formal and informal processes in Chinese politics can be mentioned. Although many people played an important role in rural reform, perhaps no one was more critical than Deng's close associate Wan Li. Wan was appointed as Anhui Party secretary in June 1977, a month before Deng's rehabilitation, though there is every reason to believe that Deng and his colleagues were behind Wan's appointment. Almost as soon as Wan arrived in the province, he began challenging the then prevailing Dazhai model; Wan was openly contemptuous of the commune system, dismissing communes as "labor camps." Wan completely ignored the provincial "learn from Dazhai" office and sought help from people like Zhou Yueli, who was then holding a sinecure position as head of the provincial policy research office. Zhou had previously been the personal secretary to Zeng Xisheng, the former provincial CCP secretary of Anhui who had first enthusiastically endorsed the policies of the Great Leap Forward, bringing famine and death to millions, but then with equal enthusiasm endorsed the household responsibility system. By the end of 1961, shortly before Zeng Xisheng was criticized and transferred out of Anhui, some 80 percent of the province was practicing the household production responsibility system.[13]

Wan's actions in Anhui were "aided" and spurred on by the severe drought that hit the province in 1978. A Xinhua film crew reportedly went to Anhui and caught graphic pictures of horrific suffering. Shown to a meeting of the Politburo, the film allegedly brought tears to the eyes of the viewers. The film had brought into stark relief the contradiction between the youthful ideals of those former revolutionaries and the present reality of continued privation, thus contributing to the salience of rural poverty as a political issue.[14] Of course, the political leadership was not moved just by pictures of wretched suffering in the countryside. Leaders were concerned as well about the possibility of widespread social disorder. Thus, Chen Yun warned the Central Work Conference that immediately preceded the 1978 Third Plenum that if the livelihood of the peasants were not bettered, rural Party secretaries would lead peasants into the cities to demand food.[15] As Luo Xiaopeng has observed, "The astonishing reality of the rural poverty not only proved to be an effective weapon for Deng and Chen in their political fight with Hua Guofeng, it also created a sense of crisis within the new leadership."[16]

Wan Li's protection of early reform efforts in Anhui and the film produced by Xinhua were actions that took place within the structure of formal politics,[17] but informal politics were also critical in gaining central support for rural reform. One story that exemplifies the important role of personal relationships and the salience of poverty as a political issue in the early rural reform is that of Guo Chongyi. Guo, a member of the Anhui Provincial People's Congress, came to Beijing in the summer of 1979 with a report on the success of the early implementation of the household responsibility system in parts of that province. Because that system was still contrary to Party policy, several high-level officials refused to meet Guo or to read his report. Finally, he was introduced to Chen Yizi, then a researcher in the Agricultural Institute of the Chinese Academy of Social Sciences (CASS). Chen was excited by the report and took it that evening to both Hu Yaobang and Deng Liqun. Hu immediately wrote a note supporting continued implementation of the household responsibility system on an experimental basis.[18] Guo's report would never have made it through bureaucratic channels to rise to the top of the system, especially if the bureaucracy had been charged with overseeing the implementation of Cultural Revolution–era agricultural policies, as any institution prior to the inauguration of reform would have been.

Informal politics were also in great evidence in the role that young reformers played in the promotion of rural reform. Whether one looks at the role of the so-called four gentlemen[19] or at that of the Rural Development Group, it is apparent that informal politics were central to their activities. On the one hand, the members of these groups came together on the basis of personal relationships, either because they had known each other during the Cultural Revolution or because someone had introduced them as they and others were returning to Beijing following the end of the Cultural Revolution. Personal relationships formed quickly, and these became the basis for promoting various reform policies. On the other hand, such groups would have been impotent had they not quickly formed relationships with senior political leaders. The presence of Wang Qishan, the son-in-law of Yao Yilin, and the patronage of Ma Hong guaranteed the "four gentlemen" access to very high levels of the Party leadership. Similarly, the relationship between Chen Yizi and Party leaders Hu Yaobang and Deng Liqun; the participation of Deng Yingtao, son of Deng Liqun; and the close relationship between various group members and He Weiling, a close friend of Deng Xiaoping's son, Deng Pufang, all gave the nascent Rural Development Group access to high-level leaders within the Party.

Throughout the early reform period, the Rural Development Group played a critical role as a source of new information and policy innovation, yet it existed on the fringes of China's bureaucratic system. The Rural Development Group was initially formed by a group of young intellectuals and had no formal standing within China's bureaucratic system (which made it unique within China's policy-making structure). It was not until late 1981 that the CCP Secretariat formally affirmed the work of the group and gave it bureaucratic standing by attaching it to the Agricultural Institute of CASS. Even then, the group members maintained separate identity, separate funding, and regarded themselves—as they were regarded by others—as outside the regular bureaucratic structure.

This brief description of the origins of rural reform is not meant to suggest that either Deng or Wan had a blueprint for reform that Wan took with him to Anhui. The reality was a complex mixture of high-level support for innovation and a bottom-up push by peasants and lower-level cadres to break free of the confines of collectivization. But Wan did focus quickly on rural issues and made no effort to support the then-prevailing policy of the center, which suggests his desire to undermine policies associated with Hua Guofeng.

Enterprise Reform

The inauguration of enterprise reform inevitably involved a more bureaucratic process than rural reform. Whereas rural affairs had been overseen primarily by the Rural Work Department of the CCP Central Committee, industrial affairs were supervised by the various commissions and ministries of the State Council that oversaw the administration of the planned economy. Despite the disruption and decentralization that had taken place during the Cultural Revolution, this was still an extensive bureaucratic apparatus. Moreover, the industrial economy—particularly that which involved the large- and medium-sized state-owned enterprises that made up the core of the planned economy—was interrelated and interdependent in ways that the rural economy was not. It was possible to experiment with rural reform in one area (particularly poor and backward areas) without it affecting directly rural production in other areas. The same was not true of the industrial economy. With the economy already faring poorly and central government finances severely strained, the risk of enterprise reform was simply greater—one part of the industrial economy could not be easily isolated from other parts, so disruption in one area might have major repercussions for the overall economy. The combination of a more bureaucratic structure and the potential risk of enterprise reform generally produced a more centralized decision-making process.

Nevertheless, the inauguration of enterprise reform involved formal structure, informal politics, and ideology just as rural reform did. At the same time that Wan Li was undermining the Dazhai model in Anhui, Hu Qiaomu and others were working on a theoretical critique of the theories behind the economic policies of the Gang of Four, but that had implications for Hua Guofeng's economic policies as well. This effort resulted in Hu's July 1978 report to the State Council, "Act in Accordance with Economic Laws, Step Up the Four Modernizations." This report was drafted by Hu and others in the Political Research Office (*Zhengzhi yanjiu shi*) of the State Council. This office, established by Deng in 1975 when he was fighting the Gang of Four, was responsible for the drafting of the policy documents that were later denounced as the "three poisonous weeds."[20] The office was never formally closed after Deng was purged in 1976. As the political climate shifted following the arrest of the Gang of Four, the staffers—including Hu Qiaomu, Deng Liqun, and Yu Guangyuan—could go back to the office. Even before Deng's own rehabilitation, the people in this office apparently provided Deng with up-to-the-minute reports on the political atmosphere at the highest levels of the Party.

In the event, it was this office that drafted Hu Qiaomu's report. The purpose of Hu Qiaomu's report was to justify in Marxist ideological terms the reform of the Chinese economy. Drawing on the economic thought of Sun Yefang and others, Hu refuted such Cultural Revolution charges as that paying attention to material incentives would lead to "economism." Hu's report also laid out the case for emphasizing the "law of value" and for "proportionate development in a planned way." In short, Hu Qiaomu's report laid out the basic ideological premises of reform and thereby undermined Hua Guofeng's policy line.[21]

The irony is that despite the ideological issues involved in enterprise reform being joined (successfully from Deng's point of view) earlier and at a higher level than was the case with rural reform, enterprise reform proceeded more slowly than rural reform. It got under way in Sichuan province in the fall of 1978 and was extended the following spring (following Deng's victory at the Third Plenum), but the reforms undertaken were modest and had little impact initially. The pace of reform, such as it was, slowed even further following the December 1980 Central Work Conference, which called for the implementation of retrenchment policies. Undoubtedly, the reason enterprise reform proceeded more slowly was the interdependence and greater bureaucratization of the industrial economy mentioned above. This process confirms the ability of formal structures—China's bureaucratic apparatus—to resist changes that they do not like, just as the work of Lieberthal, Oksenberg, Lampton, and others suggests.

Ideological Reform

As many have noted, the cornerstone in the effort to delegitimize Hua Guofeng was the discussion on practice as the sole criterion of truth. Promoted by members of Hu Yaobang's intellectual network in the Central Party School, at the *People's Daily*, and elsewhere,[22] the discussion on practice as the sole criterion of truth reflected the relationship between power, political line, and policy. The issue of practice was raised in opposition to Hua Guofeng's "two whatevers," which were, in turn, rooted in an effort to prevent Deng Xiaoping from challenging Hua for power.

At the National Propaganda Symposium on November 18, 1976, Wang Dongxing sharply attacked Deng, saying, "This person Deng Xiaoping is wrong, and his errors are very serious. He did not listen to Mao Zedong, and continued to do those things that he had done before."[23] Shortly thereafter, Wu Lengxi told a meeting of the National People's Congress (NPC), "Whatever Chairman Mao instructed or Chairman Mao affirmed, we must strive to do and strive to do well." He also tried to link criticism of Deng Xiaoping to criticism of the Gang of Four on the grounds that both were opposed to Mao. Shortly thereafter, Wang Dongxing ordered Li Xin and his Central Theoretical Study Group to write the February 7 editorial, publishing it prior to the March Central Work Meeting in an effort to parry demands for Deng to return to work. Apparently it was Li Xin who penned the famous sentence about the two whatevers and inserted it into the draft of the editorial.[24] In a joint report to the 1979 Theory Conference, *Renmin ribao* (People's daily) editor-in-chief Hu Jiwei and his colleagues argued, "The roots of the divisions over line, orientation, and policies the past two years lie in division over the theoretical line."[25] Without challenging Hua Guofeng's theoretical line, it was impossible to justify Deng Xiaoping's return to power or the adoption of reform.

The discussion on practice as the sole criterion of truth, launched in May 1978, was thus the linchpin linking the reform agenda that was implicit in Wan Li's permissive attitude toward rural reform in Anhui, and also implicit in Hu Qiaomu's report to the State Council, to a broader ideological framework that could delegitimate Hua Guofeng and justify Deng Xiaoping's return to power. Had this campaign been defeated, the Dengist reforms would likely have been stillborn, and Hua Guofeng would have remained in power. The connection between policy and political line was very close.

This very brief overview of the inauguration of reform brings out several analytical points. First, although the competition between Hua Guofeng and Deng Xiaoping can be called a power struggle, it was not simply a power struggle. The policies and ideology articulated by each side were not just used cynically but rather marked distinctly different political lines. The struggle for power was a struggle to implement very different policy visions. Second, despite the fluidity of the political situation following Mao's death, the formal political structure still had meaning. This was evident in the need for Hua to authorize the arrest of the Gang of Four, in the bureaucratic processes involved in early enterprise reform, and in the use that reformers made of their formal political positions to push their agenda. Thus, Wan Li was Anhui Party secretary, Hu Qiaomu and others were assigned to the Political Study Office of the State Council, and Hu Yaobang was vice-president of the Central Party School. Just as clearly, however, the formal political structure was not determinative. Wan Li's actions in Anhui violated the policies of his formal superiors and supported Deng Xiaoping's rise to power. Similarly, the activities of Hu Qiaomu and his colleagues in the Political Study Office were undertaken on behalf of Deng Xiaoping rather than the head of the State Council, Hua Guofeng. Likewise, the actions of Hu Yaobang and his intellectual network were based on the informal ties that existed among individuals and were intended to subvert rather than reinforce the formal structure by campaigning for Deng Xiaoping to replace Hua Guofeng. Moreover, political issues, such as rural poverty, could enter the system and be promoted through informal ties such as those that linked the Rural Development Group to high-level Party leaders. Thus, in the political transition from Hua Guofeng to Deng Xiaoping one can see that informal politics were critical, even predominant, but that nevertheless Party norms (including the importance of ideology), Party traditions (which linked power to policy), and formal structure still played important roles.

China's Political System in the 1980s

As the Dengist coalition replaced Hua Guofeng and his colleagues at the center of China's political system, it moved to reinforce long-held (and long-ignored) Party norms and to strengthen the formal structures of the system. There was a greater emphasis on collective leadership (at least rhetorically and to some extent in reality), on not wielding "big sticks" in criticizing opponents (which did not stop such campaigns as those against spiritual pollution and bourgeois liberalization but may have limited them), on intra-Party supervision and control (through a reestablished Central Discipline Inspection Commission), on routinizing cadre promotion, and on establishing a retirement system. The National People's Congress (NPC) and the Chinese People's Political Consultative Conference (CPPCC) were restored and began to take on a greater role, particularly as the NPC became more active in formulating economic legislation. The policy-making process, while ultimately still tightly controlled, became more open and consultative than it had ever been under Mao or Hua.

Although there seemed to be clear movement toward the strengthening of formal institutions and the routinization of politics, the process was far from complete. In particular, the notions of a political "core" with a corresponding political line remained deeply embedded. These notions, which are inherently incompatible with procedural rationality, skewed the political process by perpetuating the perception that political conflict necessarily involves the struggle for power, that the struggle for power is ultimately a "game to win all,"[26] and hence the belief that compromise should be tactical rather than an integral part of the political process.

As Deng emerged as the core of the political system, a role that combines both formal position and informal networks, his power was constrained by other Party elders, most notably Chen Yun. There were many areas of agreement between the two Party elders, including the need to turn away from class struggle to emphasize economic construction, to rejuvenate Party ranks, and to strengthen Party norms. But there were also many areas of disagreement. As one policy researcher described their relationship, Deng and Chen were "opponents within cooperation" (*hezuo zhong de duishou*).[27]

Although Chen initially sought to give greater emphasis to market forces, by the winter of 1980 he was reemphasizing planning. This gave rise to a debate over the relationship between planning and markets. Conservative economists apparently allied to Chen emphasized the primacy of planning; they called for integrating the *planned economy* with *market regulation*. Market-oriented reformers derided this form of integration as *bankuai jiehe* ("board and plank integration"), suggesting the effort of conservatives to maintain a separation between the central, planned core of the economy and the limited role that market forces that would be allowed to operate around the periphery. In contrast, market-oriented reformers such as Liu Guoguang, called for an "organic" integration (*youji jiehe*) between the *planned economy* and the *market economy*, suggesting both that planning and markets should have equal status and that they should be encouraged to permeate each other so that planning would take the market economy into account and vice versa. By 1981 market-oriented reformers had raised internally the concept of a "planned commodity economy." The notion of a commodity economy, by suggesting that exchange of equal value should predominate, flew in the face of Marxist orthodoxy and the belief that the planned economy was the sine qua non of socialism. Conservatives won this first round. Liu Guoguang made a self-criticism, and the resolution of the Twelfth Party Congress enshrined Chen Yun's formulation regarding the integration of the *planned economy* and *market regulation* (which was also written into the Party and state constitutions).[28]

The reason for going into this otherwise obscure debate is that it makes very clear that, in endorsing the commodity economy as the central concept of the 1984 Decision on Economic Structural Reform, Deng was clearly rejecting Chen's counsel and adopting a different development strategy. It is true that Chen did not openly oppose this decision (in this and much else that Chen did vis-à-vis both Mao and Deng, Chen would make known his views internally but then maintain silence if the decision went against him), but Chen gave only qualified support. Chen has been quoted as stating, "I agree with Zhao's letter outlining the reform decision] but I would like to point out our practice in the past is not simply copying the Soviet model. We have our own development and very good experience. Now, the only thing we should do is change it, improve it, and develop it to comply with the new situation."[29] Thus, Chen apparently rejected the reformers' charge that China's economic system had been copied from the Soviet Union and suggested that incremental improvement on China's own developmental experience would be better than rejecting that experience in favor of new models of development (which is apparently what Chen believed the 1984 decision was doing). As China's economy encountered problems of one sort or another in the coming years, Chen and conservative economists allied with him did not hesitate to criticize the failings of reform. Following the Tiananmen tragedy, when Deng again endorsed the integration of the planned economy and the market economy, conservatives edited his remarks to call for the integration of the *planned economy* and *market integration*.[30] The return to the pre-1984 formulation was hardly accidental.

Chen's disagreement with Deng was most apparent in the economic area, but it extended to the ideological and organizational spheres as well. Chen, it seems, not only feared that the emphasis on markets would destroy the socialist economy but also that markets and opening up to the outside world would undermine the ideological legitimacy of the system and the organizational integrity of the Party. In short, Chen Yun did not simply disagree with this or that policy or with the pace and scope of reform. He and his supporters disagreed with the direction of reform and presented a systematic alternative to Deng's vision. To Chen's credit, he always chose to abide by the norms of the Party and seems genuinely never to have wanted to challenge Deng's role as core of the Party. Nevertheless, when the opportunity arose following Tiananmen, Chen and other conservatives did take the initiative to implement a policy line quite distinct from that of Deng. It took Deng three years of sometimes rather strenuous infighting before he could once again dominate China's policy agenda.[31]

The relationship between Deng and Chen had a major impact on the distribution of power below the apex of the system and on the decision-making process. It is important to note that Deng's subordinates, Hu Yaobang and Zhao Ziyang, who were charged with carrying out the reforms, existed on a distinctly different political level from that of Deng, Chen, and the other elders. According to associates of both men, neither was in a position to go to see Deng and chat about the economic or political situation on a more or less equal basis. Some old cadres such as Wang Zhen could do that, but Hu and Zhao could only make reports and ask for instructions (*huibao, qingshi*); there was a very real difference in status, and Deng apparently took pains to maintain that status differential.

At least in part because of the status differential between Deng (and the other elders, particularly Chen Yun) and second-echelon leaders such as Hu Yaobang and Zhao Ziyang, the most important personnel decisions were not in the hands of those charged with implementing policy, namely Hu and Zhao. For instance, as head of the Party organization, Hu Yaobang had ultimate responsibility for ideological affairs. Yet throughout the period, Hu had to contend with Deng Liqun, who headed the Propaganda Department until 1985 and who obviously thought himself more qualified than Hu Yaobang to be general secretary.[32] The fact that the Party head, charged with overseeing ideology, could neither appoint nor remove the head of the Propaganda Department may have violated the principle of democratic centralism, but it certainly reflected the informal structure of power.

Hu was not the only one who suffered from this inability to oversee the apparatus he was charged with running. From September 1980 until the Thirteenth Party Congress in October 1987, Zhao Ziyang was premier of the State Council, but the evidence suggests that Zhao never dominated this apparatus. In part, Zhao's problem was that his career had been in the provinces and he had never developed the extensive ties throughout the bureaucracy that were needed to manage it. But the bigger part of Zhao's difficulties stemmed from the same source as Hu Yaobang's. Because Zhao was a second-echelon leader and senior appointments were controlled at a level higher than his own, he could never control the most important bureaucratic elements of the State Council, particularly the State Planning Commission. The State Planning Commission, headed at various times by Yao Yilin and Song Ping, remained loyal to Chen Yun; Zhao could pressure, cajole, and compromise with the State Planning Commission, but he could not command it and he could not have its leaders changed.

At the risk of considerably oversimplifying political relations in China, one can heuristically sketch the power structure of Chinese politics in the mid- to late-1980s as shown in Figure 2.1. As schematic as this diagram is, it nonetheless suggests two important aspects of politics in the Dengist period. First, it highlights, as discussed above, Chen Yun's role as the proponent of a policy line, or perhaps one should say a latent policy line, that differed significantly from that espoused by Deng. Second, the diagram suggests the very carefully constructed balances that

Figure 2.1 **Schematic Diagram of Informal Power Relations**

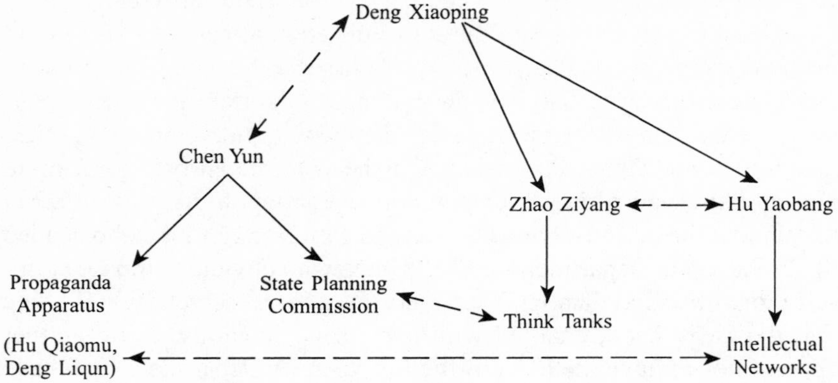

Deng Xiaoping

Chen Yun

Zhao Ziyang ← — → Hu Yaobang

Propaganda
Apparatus

State Planning
Commission

Think Tanks

(Hu Qiaomu,
Deng Liqun)

Intellectual
Networks

Note: Unbroken lines indicate subordinate relationship; dotted lines indicate a conflictual relationship.

Deng established in order to maintain the stability of the Party while still biasing the structure toward his own policy agenda. From the diagram, one can see how Deng both balanced reformers off against conservatives and maintained rivalries between reform leaders, including Zhao Ziyang and Hu Yaobang. To say that Deng maintained a balance among different forces within the Party suggests neither that those forces were fixed and unchanging (as a factional model implies) nor that Deng acted simply as one of many forces within the Party. On the contrary, the balances constructed or maintained by Deng were intended to reinforce Deng's role as the core of the Party and therefore to support his policy line (even as the existence of different forces suggested the difficulty of maintaining and implementing a consistent line). As suggested above, no one leader or group was able to control all the instruments of policy that "rightfully" belonged to him. As the diagram illustrates, this system of checks and balances was crafted out of an intermingling of informal politics and bureaucratic institutions; indeed, it frequently juxtaposed informal politics and bureaucratic institutions.

This system was viable in the mid-1980s because it reflected a certain balance of power within the Party, but it was not sustainable over the long run for two reasons. First, the very structure of power meant that policy decisions could not be optimal. Indeed, policy decisions are rarely, if ever, optimal. The point is that policy decisions that are suboptimal because they are designed to parry opponents, rather than to reach compromise, are almost certain to lead to counterattacks when their flaws become evident in the implementation process. In thinking about economic reform, Zhao Ziyang had to constantly keep in mind the power and opposition of the State Planning Commission and other conservative organs. This meant that thoughts about price and ownership reform had to be trimmed back to what was politically viable—which meant that their chances of working smoothly was correspondingly diminished.

Second, and more important, is the basic assumption of Chinese politics that power is monistic and indivisible, and hence that compromise is tactical rather than fundamental. As Tang Tsou put it in his eloquent and insightful article on the Tiananmen tragedy:[33]

> It is true that at times there were compromises, concessions, admissions of defeat, negotiations, and even cooperation with such opposing forces, but those were tactical measures that did not lead to permanent institutions and fundamental processes according to which all political forces would have to conduct their contestations, promote their interests, and accept the results. In other words, Chinese political culture has not yet accepted the politics of compromise that are so vital to democratic governance.

This suggests that informal politics play a role in Chinese politics that is significantly different from their role in, say, American politics. In the American context, informal politics are frequently seen as ameliorating political conflict. Backroom deals, logrolling, and the venerable Washington institution known as "let's do lunch" are all seen as ways of working things out among divergent interests and opinions—sometimes at the expense of the American public. They are, for better or worse, ways in which political conflict can be contained. Chinese politicians certainly cut deals just as their American counterparts do, but sooner or later political conflict in China seems to result in political rupture.

To refer back to the schematic diagram of the Chinese power structure shown above, it is apparent why, given the opposition of the State Planning Commission to market-oriented reform and given the relationship of that organization to Chen Yun (an instance of a bureaucratic organization being tied to a political patron through informal means), Zhao Ziyang was forced to rely increasingly on his think tanks and to adopt policy measures that went around the limits of control of that organization. In other words, Zhao had to rely on a series of informal relationships in order to maintain the momentum of reform and his own position within the system.

Although the use of think tanks enlivened policy debate and led to policy innovation, it also led to political competition with such bureaucratic organs as the State Planning Commission. This competition was, in the final analysis, a struggle for dominance. If Zhaoist reform were successful, the State Planning Commission and Chen Yun would inevitably lose politically, just as problems in reform would diminish Zhao Ziyang and Deng Xiaoping while enhancing the influence of Chen Yun. Thus, conservative planners never failed to lose an opportunity to criticize a variety of sins, including inflationary pressures, loss of revenue to the central government, and so forth. The debacle of the 1988 price reform effort gave them a ready-made issue, and Zhao Ziyang paid the price. Thus, it was not so much informal politics per se that were so debilitating for Chinese politics as the combination of informal politics and ingrained assumptions about the role of "line" and political core, and the corresponding rejection of the politics of compromise, which led to the escalating tensions within the Party that finally exploded during the protest movement of 1989.

Chinese Politics in the 1990s

Tiananmen left China's political system badly shaken. Recriminations ricocheted through the Party as people tried to lay the blame for what had happened at the feet of their political opponents. The fall of socialism in Eastern Europe in the fall of 1989 exacerbated intra-Party tensions in China, even as international tensions fed domestic doubts about China's policy of opening up. Restoring intra-Party stability was the most difficult domestic political task Deng Xiaoping had undertaken since 1978.

There were several factors that facilitated stabilization. The simple fact that the collapse of socialism in Eastern Europe and subsequently in the Soviet Union did not cause any major domestic upheaval in China perhaps gave Party leaders a confidence that they could in fact survive. Indeed, it can be argued that the collapse of the Soviet Union facilitated the restoration of political stability in China by making it evident to many, most notably to Deng, that the CCP's only chance of political survival lay in further reform—a conclusion that Deng pushed by way of his dramatic trip to Shenzhen in early 1992.

Domestically, the most important factor was the complete inability of the conservatives, under the leadership of Li Peng, to implement a successful economic program. After years of carping about the various failings of reform, conservatives at last had a relatively free hand to implement their preferred policies. The failure of the so-called double-guarantee system (which restored greater central control and planning over 200 major industries), the escalation of interenterprise debts, and the dramatic decline in the profits of state-owned enterprises punctured conservatives' illusions about the viability of a restoration (even partial restoration) of the old planning system.[34] At the same time, the continued vitality of the township and village enterprise sector (under a less than ideal policy environment) underscored the successes of market-oriented reform. Although new debates over the role of the large- and medium-sized state-owned enterprises would soon emerge, the debate over planning and markets as it had been cast in the 1980s was basically over; for all intents and purposes the planned economy was dead.

These international and domestic factors were accompanied by generational change. Deng Xiaoping gave up his last major position, that of head of the Party Central Military Commission (CMC), in November 1989. Although Deng was still the paramount leader (and indeed his continued presence in the early 1990s was critical to the restoration of political stability and the vigorous reassertion of reform), his retirement as head of the CMC marked the beginning of the shift in power from the generation that had fought and won the revolution to the first postrevolutionary generation. This generational shift was given a push by the deaths of several major conservative leaders: CPPCC deputy secretary Wang Renzhong in March 1992, former president and CPPCC chairman Li Xiannian in June 1992, former Mao secretary Hu Qiaomu in September 1992, and Chen Yun in April 1995. By 1996, Deng Xiaoping appeared incapable of further intervention in the political system, and in February 1997 he finally passed from the scene. Some eight years after Tiananmen, the shift to the so-called third generation of leaders (with Mao Zedong and Deng Xiaoping representing the first and second generations, respectively) was complete.

The question that hangs over the Chinese political system is whether the trends just sketched foreshadow a more stable, institutionalized system in the future or whether China's political traditions (such as viewing power in monistic terms) and the Party's history of ideological cum power conflict will lead to renewed instability and, perhaps, the collapse of the system. Put in the terms that we have been using in this article, the question is whether the formal aspects of the system are becoming more institutionalized so that conflict within the Party can be resolved through procedural means.

This is obviously a very complex question, and opinions within the field vary tremendously.[35] No doubt the trends that seem so ambiguous now will appear self-evident a few years hence. Instead of trying to foretell the future, perhaps one can outline the contingencies on which the future will hang by making a few comparisons with the trends of the reform period that have been sketched in the previous pages.

Perhaps the most consistent, and indeed ominous, feature of Chinese politics in the reform era has been the continuation of the interrelated notions that power is monistic, that one person must emerge as the "core" of the political system, and that policy is linked to power through political "line." Such a political system inherently rejects a politics of compromise, resists institutionalization, and is antagonistic to procedural rationality. These features were very evident in the political transition from the death of Mao to the emergence of Deng as the new core. Moreover, these features continued to characterize Chinese politics through the first decade and more of reform. They affected the structure of the political system (that is, the real distribution of power), distorted the reform process, and exacerbated tensions within the elite (not just between conservatives and reformers but also among reformers). They certainly contributed to the tragedy of Tiananmen.

It must also be noted, however, that the existence of these features did not lead to the breakdown of the system during the reform era as it did during the Cultural Revolution. Conflict was real and had a major impact on the second echelon, but it did not trigger a struggle to "win all" at the highest level. This was no doubt due in part to Chen Yun's personality. Perhaps more than any other high-level political leader, Chen took Party norms concerning the expression of political differences seriously. This reticence did not go so far as to cause him actually to refrain from interfering in reform measures that he disagreed with. But it did stop him from openly criticizing Deng or challenging Deng for the core position. For his part, Deng tolerated Chen's criticisms of the problems of reform and the interference of the State Planning Commission in the implementation of reform. There was perhaps a mutual recognition that the Party could not survive another struggle to "win all."

If the scope of conflict between Deng and Chen was bounded, consciously or unconsciously, by such a recognition, there was also a more positive element that restrained conflict, namely an emphasis on Party norms. Perhaps the most important of these norms was that Party meetings would be held on a regular basis. Thus, since 1977, Party congresses have met every five years, as required by the Party Constitution, and plenary sesssions of the Central Committee have met at least once a year, also as required by statute. Given the history of the CCP, this is a remarkable record. The convention of regular Party conclaves does not mean the complete routinization of Party affairs. After all, both Hu Yaobang and Zhao Ziyang were dismissed without benefit of a Party plenum (in Zhao's case one was called within a month of his effective dismissal), and three weeks prior to the convening of the Fourth Plenum of the Thirteenth Central Committee, Deng Xiaoping called in Premier Li Peng and Politburo Standing Committee member Yao Yilin to inform them that Jiang Zemin would be the next general secretary (following Zhao's ouster). Deng said that he had checked with Chen Yun and Li Xiannian—giving a fairly accurate account of the range of consultation needed to make the most critical decisions in the Party. Nevertheless, the regular convening of Party meetings suggests a broader range of consultation on a wider range of issues (but not including top leadership issues!) than ever before in Party history.

Another factor that has affected the conduct of elite politics (even if tracing its impact is difficult) is simply the growing complexity of managing a nation with a large and rapidly growing economy, diverse and frequently conflicting interests, and a wide range of international interests and commitments. Efforts to manage an increasingly complex social and economic system have led to the growing importance of the NPC, to a growing emphasis on law (though there is still a very long way to go), to a far more consultative policy-making process, and perhaps, though it is difficult to tell, to a greater emphasis on institutions to manage society. When most problems are complex and technical in nature, ideological formulas are not very helpful. Moreover, *if* (and it is a big "if") there is greater consensus at the elite level on the general direction of reform (which is to say, if disagreements really are over the pace and scope of reform measures rather than over fundamental issues of orientation), then the salience of "line" issues seems likely to decline. If power is no longer so closely linked to policy, political competition is more likely to be "normal" (more about competence than ideology, as Michael Dukakis once put it).

If these trends suggest that the formal political structure and norms limiting political conflict have gained ground over the past two decades, it must still be recognized that they exist on shaky ground. China is not simply an authoritarian system undergoing democratization, but is a

Leninist system undergoing both political change (one dare not call it democratization) and economic reform.[36] This is a formidable challenge that no Leninist system has yet successfully negotiated. If China has managed the process of economic reform without political collapse better than the Soviet Union or other socialist states did, it nevertheless remains true that marketization undermines the legitimacy of the CCP. This may not be a problem as long as economic development remains strong and social conflicts remain under control, but it is easy to envision scenarios in which economic or social problems prompt questions of legitimacy and/or generate intense intra-elite conflict. In such an event, the lack of institutionalization at the highest level could yet prove to be a fatal flaw. Even in the absence of such system-threatening conflict, there are a variety of issues that could trigger elite conflict. The perilous state of state-owned enterprises, the influx of peasants into the cities, growing income inequalities, corruption, and rising nationalism have already generated a growing neoconservative movement.[37]

Conclusion

This overview of the interaction of formal structure and informal politics in the reform era suggests some of the ways these and other factors have interacted to produce political outcomes. Although informal politics have always been important, even dominant, formal structure has nevertheless played an important role. Thus, as noted above, Hua Guofeng's endorsement of the arrest of the Gang of Four was important more because of Hua's formal status as head of the Party than because of any informal influence he wielded. Perhaps conversely, Deng Xiaoping's position as the core of the Party has depended first and foremost on his extensive personal connections throughout the Party, but Deng has never neglected the formal bases of power. Even though Deng declined the positions of chairman and general secretary, he accepted a position on the Politburo Standing Committee and headed the Party's powerful Central Military Commission. When Deng gave up his position on the Politburo Standing Committee, as we know from Zhao Ziyang's revelation to Gorbachev, the Thirteenth Party Congress passed a secret resolution to refer major issues to him as the "helmsman" of the Party.[38] This action suggests that Party norms were sufficiently institutionalized that Deng needed such a formal resolution in order to justify his continued access to important documents and his continued involvement in the political system.[39]

Just as Deng combined formal position and informal influence, so did Chen Yun. Indeed, Chen was such a formidable rival to Deng largely because of Chen's own extensive personal relations throughout the bureaucracy, particularly the planning system. But Chen's power was not based solely on personal politics and influence; until his death, he was either on the Politburo Standing Committee, head of the Central Discipline Inspection Commission, or head of the Central Advisory Commission.

Informal politics, of course, are not wholly negative. Indeed, they have provided Chinese politics with a degree of flexibility, even vitality, that the formal political structures alone could not provide. The great virtue of informal politics is that low- or mid-level officials can cut through or go around bureaucratic organizations, taking new information or policy proposals quickly to the highest levels and sometimes getting immediate decisions.

Informal politics have been vital to reform because reform is necessarily characterized by rapid change and the transformation of institutions. It is a process that almost by definition cannot be carried out through bureaucratic channels; indeed, one of the critical differences between the reforms in the former Soviet Union and in China is the far higher level of institutionalization in the former, something that turned out to be a disadvantage. Throughout China's reform, informal politics have been critical for identifying and raising issues, for bringing new information to bear on the analysis of problems, and for proposing new policy recommendations. The emergence of reforms in the late 1970s certainly cannot be understood as the outcome of bureaucratic politics, and the current political transformation will necessarily involve more than bureaucratic politics as well. The difference is that if the current political transformation is to be successful, the role of formal politics vis-à-vis informal politics will have to increase.

Indeed, the role of informal politics in the People's Republic of China (PRC) appears to be diminishing—though by no means disappearing—over the course of the reforms. Party conclaves are held regularly, the bureaucracy is larger but better led, and economic and other legislation has acquired an unprecedented importance. Moreover, the role of the Central Committee seems to be gaining in political importance, as Susan Shirk has argued.[40] At the same time, however, informal politics remain important. As Dittmer and Xiaobo Lu point out, formal structure and informal politics can expand at the same time.[41] Frederick Teiwes has argued persuasively that the reduction of Party demands on society and the open-ended nature of the reform process have resulted in a corresponding reduction of demands on Party members, thus allowing them to maintain, and express, differences of opinion.[42] Similarly, Andrew G. Walder has argued that reform has changed the incentive structure for cadres, so that those at the lower reaches of the state have more interests in common with the local society than with the central state, thus reducing their willingness to comply with orders from above.[43] Whether such trends will undermine the growing importance of formal politics or complement their functioning is one of the major questions as China heads into the twenty-first century.

Notes

1. The ideas in this article were first presented at the Shorenstein symposium entitled East Asian Development Strategies and International Conflict: Issues for the Twenty-First Century, in Berkeley, CA, in 1995; and at the Forty-seventh annual meeting of the Association for Asian Studies, in Washington, DC, 1995. The same ideas were published in "Institutions, Informal Politics, and Political Transition in China," *Asian Survey*, 36, no. 3 (March 1996): 230–245. The present version has been extensively revised from these earlier versions. I have greatly benefited from the comments of Lowell Dittmer, Brantly Womack, Dorothy Solinger, and others.

2. Harry Harding, "Competing Models of the Chinese Communist Policy Process: Toward a Sorting and Evaluation," *Issues and Studies*, 20, no. 2 (February 1984): 13–36.

3. Kenneth Lieberthal and Michel Oksenberg, *Policy Making in China: Leaders, Structures, and Processes* (Princeton: Princeton University Press, 1988).

4. David M. Lampton, "Chinese Politics: The Bargaining Treadmill," *Issues and Studies*, 23, no. 3 (March 1987): 11–41; David M. Lampton, ed., *Policy Implementation in Post-Mao China* (Berkeley: University of California Press, 1992); and Kenneth Lieberthal and David M. Lampton, eds., *Bureaucracy, Politics and Decision Making in Post-Mao China* (Berkeley: University of California Press, 1992).

5. Jonathan Pollack, "Structure and Process in the Chinese Military System," in Lieberthal and Lampton, eds., *Bureaucracy, Politics, and Decision Making in Post-Mao China*, p. 169.

6. Kenneth G. Lieberthal, "The 'Fragmented Authoritarianism' Model and Its Limitations," in Lieberthal and Lampton, eds., *Bureaucracy, Politics and Decision Making in Post-Mao China*, p. 14.

7. Lucien W. Pye, *The Spirit of Chinese Politics* (Cambridge: Harvard University Press, 1992).

8. Andrew J. Nathan, "A Factionalism Model for CCP Politics," *The China Quarterly*, no. 53 (January–March 1973): 34–66.

9. Hedrick Smith, *The Power Game: How Washington Works* (New York: Ballantine, 1988).

10. See Frederick C. Teiwes, "The Paradoxical Post-Mao Transition: From Obeying the Leader to 'Normal Politics,'" *The China Journal*, no. 34 (July 1995): 55–94.

11. See Tang Tsou, "Chinese Politics at the Top: Factionalism or Informal Politics? Balance-of-Power Politics or a Game to Win All?" *The China Journal*, no. 34 (July 1995): 115.

12. "Study Well the Documents and Grasp the Key Link," *Renmin ribao*, February 7, 1977, trans. Foreign Broadcast Information Service, *Daily Report–China* (hereafter, FBIS-Chi), February 7, 1977, pp. E1–E3.

13. Joseph Fewsmith, *Dilemmas of Reform in China: Political Conflict and Economic Debate* (Armonk, NY: M.E. Sharpe, 1994), chapter 1. See also Dali Yang, *Calamity and Reform in China* (Stanford: Stanford University Press, 1996).

14. Wang Lixin, "Life After Mao Zedong: A Report on Implementation of and Major Consequences of Major Chinese Agricultural Policies in CCP Politics," *Kunlun*, no. 5 (December 1988), trans. Joint Publication Research Service, JPRS-CAR-89–079 (July 28, 1989).

15. See Chen Yun, "Jianchi an bili yuanze tiaozheng guomin jingji" (Readjust the national economy in accordance with the principle of proportionality), in *Chen Yun wenxuan, 1956–1985* (Selected works of Chen Yun, 1956–1985), (Beijing: Renmin chubanshe, 1995), p. 226.

16. Luo Xiaopeng, "Rural Reform and the Rise of Localism," in Jia Hao and Lin Zhimin, eds., *Changing Central-Local Relations in China: Reform and State Capacity* (Boulder, CO: Westview, 1994), p. 115.

17. Wan's formal position as Party secretary was no doubt important, but clearly his loyalties were to Deng Xiaoping rather than to Hua Guofeng or Ji Dengkui, then in charge of rural policy. Thus, Wan's position was formal, but his alliances and policy positions reflected informal structures.

18. Fewsmith, *Dilemmas of Reform in China*, pp. 32–33.

19. *Sida junzi* (the four gentlemen) was the name given to Huang Jiangnan, Wang Qishan, Weng Yongxi, and Zhu Jiaming, four young reformers who contributed both to the early rural and the enterprise reforms.

20. On the Political Study Office, see Tan Zongji and Zheng Qian, eds., *Shinianhou de pingshuo* (An evaluation ten years later) (Beijing: Zhonggong dangshi ziliao chubanshe, 1987); and Su Shaozhi, *Shinian fengyu: Wenge hou de dalu lilunjie* (Ten years of storms: Mainland theoretical circles after the Cultural Revolution) (Taipei: Shibao wenhua, 1996), pp. 20–21.

21. Hu Qiaomu, "Act in Accordance with Economic Laws, Step Up the Four Modernizations," Xinhua, October 5, 1978, trans. FBIS-Chi, October 11, 1978, pp. E1–E22.

22. Merle Goldman, "Hu Yaobang's Intellectual Network," *The China Quarterly*, no. 126 (June 1991): 219–242; and Michael Schoenhals, "The Discussion on Practice as the Sole Criterion of Truth," *The China Quarterly*, no. 126 (June 1991): 243–268.

23. Su, *Shinian fengyu*, p. 65.

24. Ibid., pp. 44, 65.

25. Ibid., p. 64.

26. Tsou, "Chinese Politics at the Top."

27. Author's interview.

28. Fewsmith, *Dilemmas of Reform in China*, chapter 3, esp. pp. 109–116.

29. Author's interview.

30. Richard Baum, *Burying Mao: Chinese Politics in the Age of Deng Xiaoping* (Princeton: Princeton University Press, 1994), p. 294.

31. Joseph Fewsmith, "Reaction, Resurgence, and Succession: Chinese Politics Since Tiananmen," in Roderick MacFarquhar, ed., *The Politics of China* (2d ed): *The Eras of Mao and Deng* (New York: Cambridge University Press, 1997).

32. On the rivalry between Hu Yaobang and Deng Liqun, see Baum, *Burying Mao.*

33. Tang Tsou, "The Tiananmen Tragedy," in Brantly Womack, ed., *Contemporary Chinese Politics in Historical Perspective* (Cambridge: Cambridge University Press, 1991), p. 319.

34. Barry Naughton, *Growing Out of the Plan: Chinese Economic Reform, 1978–1993* (Cambridge: Cambridge University Press, 1995), p. 286.

35. The range of opinion stretches from William H. Overholt's optimistic scenario in his *The Rise of China* (New York: W.W. Norton, 1993) to James Miles's pessimistic portrait in his *The Legacy of Tiananmen: China in Disarray* (Ann Arbor: University of Michigan Press, 1996).

36. Minxin Pei has emphasized the importance of dual transition (economic and political) in Leninist systems as opposed to authoritarian systems. See his *From Reform to Revolution: The Demise of Communism in China and the Soviet Union* (Cambridge, MA: Harvard University Press, 1994).

37. Joseph Fewsmith, "Neoconservatism and the End of the Dengist Era," *Asian Survey*, 35, no. 7 (July 1995): 635–651.

38. Beijing television, May 16, 1989, trans. FBIS-Chi, May 16, 1989, p. 28; and *Renmin ribao*, May 17, 1989, trans. FBIS-Chi, May 17, 1989, p. 16.

39. Precisely what powers were conferred by such a resolution was obviously ambiguous, as the contention over publicizing Deng's views during his 1992 trip to Shenzhen revealed.

40. Susan Shirk, *The Political Logic of Economic Reform* (Berkeley: University of California Press, 1993).

41. Lowell Dittmer and Lu Xiaobo, "Personal Politics in the Chinese *Danwei* under Reform," *Asian Survey*, 36, no. 3 (March 1996): 246–267.

42. Teiwes, "The Paradoxical Post-Mao Transition."

43. Andrew G. Walder, "The Quiet Revolution from Within: Economic Reform as a Source of Political Decline," in Andrew G. Walder, ed., *The Waning of the Communist State: Economic Origins of Political Decline in China and Hungary* (Berkeley: University of California Press, 1995).

3

Institution Building and Democratization in China

In recent years, some of the bloom has faded from the euphoria generated by the "third wave" of democratization, particularly the collapse of socialism in Eastern Europe and the Soviet Union. It has been seen that democratic transition does not lead automatically to sustainable democratic governance ("consolidation") and that the outcomes of democratic transition depend on both the legacies, cultural and institutional, of the preceding regimes as well as the modalities of the transition itself.[1] The gap in democratic governance between those countries of the former socialist world that are geographically (and culturally) closer to Europe and those farther east has been noted. Yet hopes remain high for a "fourth wave" of democratic transition, and China looms large in these projections. As Larry Diamond puts it, somewhat breathily, "half of these 2.2 billion people [who continue to live under authoritarian rule] live in one country: mainland China." For Diamond, the prospects for the future of world democratization—both the absence of a reversal of the recent wave of democratizations and the development of a new wave of democratization—hinge primarily on events in one country: China.[2]

This is a heavy burden to place on any given country, and perhaps gives too much weight to the potential influence of any "Chinese model." Yet the attention that Diamond and others have focused on China make it important to assess realistically where China is politically at the present time; whether liberalization and perhaps democratization are realistic

61

options; and, most important, under what conditions China is most likely to democratize successfully. A "democratic transition" that leads not to sustainable democratic governance but to the collapse of political authority, with all the potential for civil violence, famine, and exodus of refugees that that would entail, would hardly advance the cause of either human rights or global democratization. Yet the "downside risk" of political change in China is rarely considered. This is no doubt in part because worries about "chaos" can and have been used by the political authorities in Beijing to justify repressive measures. Nevertheless, such a liberal observer of contemporary China as Ding Xueliang worries openly about the impact of political implosion. "If an anarchic situation appears in China," he warns, "the violence that Chinese will inflict on each other will far exceed the barbarism inflicted by the Japanese army when it invaded in the 1930s."[3]

The question that must be addressed, therefore, is whether China has developed or is developing the political, institutional, and social conditions that would allow not only for democratic transition but, more important, for democratic consolidation. Knowledgeable observers of China can and do assess these factors quite differently. Optimists point to the vast improvements in China over the past decade and more, and assume that the future will see similar improvements. They also generally assume that the more China develops economically and the more it enters the international arena, the more it will develop a middle class and the more likely it will be to democratize. The "East Asia development model" plays an important role in many people's thinking—both inside and outside China—even if specifying precisely what such a model is or the dynamic development of any such model is not as easy or straightforward as sometimes assumed.[4] In contrast, pessimists view China's human rights record, the government's penchant for rejecting even modest moments in the direction of democratization, efforts to modernize the military, and the growth of nationalism as indications that China will develop into a strong, menacing presence in the Asia-Pacific region. In addition, there have been suggestions from time to time that China may break up, which could be an optimistic or a pessimistic prediction, depending on the person making it.[5]

In recent years, Juan Linz, Alfred Stepan, and others have called attention to the importance of institutions (a "usable bureaucracy"), a state effectively subjected to a rule of law (a *Reichstaat*), institutionalized economic society, a "free and lively" civil society, and a "relatively autonomous" political society for successful transition to democratic governance.[6] Even to list such factors suggests the gap between China's current reality and effective democratic governance. The question then is whether China is moving in a direction that will at least narrow this gap.

Much has been said about China's economic reforms, which have propelled China to a nearly 10 percent per annum growth rate over the last decade, an unprecedented achievement for such a large country. The impact of economic reform on China's political system, however, has achieved considerably less attention. While it is widely noted that the economic reforms have shredded faith in Marxism-Leninism, thus undermining the legitimacy of the regime, fewer questions have been asked about the degree to which China's economic reforms have supported the creation of new political institutions that might sustain the polity in the course of democratic transition.

The purposes of this chapter are to sort through a number of different pressures facing Chinese society and government, to look at some of the ways China is dealing with them, and to try to assess whether China is institutionalizing or deinstitutionalizing. The basic conclusion of this chapter is that the pressures on the contemporary polity are forcing institution-building changes that are necessary and healthy over the long run. This conclusion is advanced cautiously because it is also apparent that there is a long way to go and that there are still important obstacles to the building of sound economic and political institutions, much less to the construction of a democratic polity.

Where do institutions come from? In his monumental comparative study of the development of bureaucracy in four polities, Bernard Silberman argues that bureaucracies (as well as important characteristics of their relations with the political system) emerge and are shaped as solutions to political problems.[7] Under certain circumstances, there is a perceived political need to shift contentious issues from the political arena to the "neutral" zone of administration. Viewed from this perspective, there is much reason for pessimism in the Chinese case. Relations between the Chinese Communist Party (CCP) and the state bureaucracy have always been an issue of contention, and each time there has been some movement toward establishing a separate and institutionally autonomous state bureaucracy, the Party has, for one reason or another, reintervened to curtail the process.[8] Yet the past need not be prologue. There is reason to believe that the process of economic reform has set in motion forces that may lead to the separation of Party and state, between the state and the economy, and thereby to a substantial reordering of state-society relations. The basic argument of this chapter is that economic reform, diminished ideological legitimacy, generational succession, and even political conflict are generating pressures for the separation of politics and the economy, for institutionalization of the state (creating a "usable bureaucracy"), and for the application of rule-based solutions to the resolution of political conflict. This process has been uneven at best, but it has been present and it may provide a window of opportunity through which China may emerge successfully from its difficult transition.

The Dynamics of Reform

Beginning in 1978, the Chinese government undertook a program of economic reform largely because it had no other choice. Politically, the Cultural Revolution had undermined Maoist ideology by driving it to extremes; economically, the country was on the "the brink of collapse." A massive oil-exploration program in 1978–1979, which might have supported a program of economic development without significant marketization, turned up little but dry holes.[9] Political stability in the face of economic stagnation could not be taken for granted. In an important report to the State Council in July 1978, Hu Qiaomu, Mao's former secretary and the Party's foremost ideological authority, declared, "The basic purpose of all communists is to work for the interests of the majority of people. If communists fail to work for the interest of the majority of people, then why do the masses need the Communist Party and why should they support it?"[10] Senior Party leader and economic specialist Chen Yun was even blunter, warning the Central Work Conference that met in the fall of 1978 that if the livelihood of the peasants did not improve, Party secretaries would lead the peasants into the cities to demand food.[11] This recognition that political stability and the Party's continued rule required improving the livelihood of the people found concrete expression in the decision to raise the procurement price of grain by 50 percent and to increase the wages of urban workers by 20 percent in 1979. In short, it was the decline of regime legitimacy that prompted the Party to switch from ideological legitimacy to performance legitimacy.

This shift set off a logic that remains in place today, one that demands that living standards increase continuously and hence that economic reform continue apace. Once reform was inaugurated, it became impossible to set the clock back. The closest the Party came to attempting to do so, prior to Tiananmen, was in the 1980–1981 period when inflation and other imbalances emerged from an initial round of reform. Planners inaugurated a period of economic retrenchment, but reductions in procurements through the plan created new and important incentives for enterprises to seek new outlets for their products. Once the window of markets was opened, efforts to tighten control through the plan could only create incentives to increase marketization.[12] Indeed, the increased marketization in this period helped keep the economy going in a period of retrenchment and laid a foundation for the next wave of economic reform, which began in 1984.

The economic growth that has occurred since then and the structural changes that have been brought about have been largely, though not exclusively, due to the emergence of township and village enterprises (TVEs). Although the enterprises existing at what were then the commune and brigade levels predate the inauguration of reform, such enterprises were extremely backward and, surprisingly, capital intensive. With the inauguration of reform and the subsequent transformation of agricultural organization (that is, the implementation of household farming, the dissolution of communes and brigades in favor of townships and villages, and the emergence of rural markets), labor flowed into newly created TVEs. Such industries, taking advantage of the shortage of consumer products in the economy and the high prices such products garnered under China's distorted price structure, grew quickly and under conditions of market competition. Not controlled by China's planned economy, TVEs purchased their raw materials and sold their produce at market prices.

The emergence of the township and village enterprises, which played to China's comparative advantage of a nearly inexhaustible supply of inexpensive labor, not only imparted a new dynamism to China's economy (in 1996 the TVE sector accounted for about 60 percent of China's industrial output) but also eroded the plan and spearheaded the emergence of a market economy. By the mid-1990s, less than 10 percent of consumer goods and only about 15 percent of capital goods were still being sold at state-determined prices under the old plan.[13] Reforms of state-owned enterprises, the bulwark of the planned economy, took place slowly and under pressure from the competition provided by the TVEs and then from foreign products entering the market.

Reform not only set in train a series of economic pressures that have led to tremendous economic growth, it also generated pressures to reform in important ways China's political and administrative systems. The increasing marketization of the economy has done much to force the government to develop the tools to begin to manage the economy through economic means. It has diminished and transformed the role of the State Planning Commission, the nerve center of the old planned economy; has strengthened new economic organs, especially the State Economic and Trade Commission; and has increased the still incomplete role of the central bank, the People's Bank of China.

Perhaps more important, the demand for economic development and the politics of reform put a premium on economic expertise. As Hu Qiaomu put it in the report cited above, "Economics is a science for studying economic laws. To be able to act according to economic laws, we must step up the popularization of the study of economics and raise its level. . . . This calls for vastly expanding our country's economics-study contingent, because we must study many economic problems, many of which require meticulous and quantitative study."[14] Economic reform has produced vast growth in the number of professional economists and a growing acceptance of their role in the polity. Just as the implementation of reform in late-nineteenth- and early-twentieth-century Europe created a demand for the services of the growing numbers of social scientists, so reform in China created a new demand for expertise.[15] The expansion of expertise and the growth of economic organs have meant that information acquisition is better, and it is better utilized in the decision-making process.

Reform also created an unprecedented demand for regularizing retirement. The need to develop a retirement system was in part a by-product of one of the peculiarities of reform, namely, that reform was inaugurated by a group of aging revolutionaries who had been purged during the Cultural Revolution and returned to power late in life. Many were quite old—Deng Xiaoping was seventy-three in 1978—and most had lived difficult lives. Moreover, political conflict deepened the need to develop a retirement system. Many of those who came back into power at the end of the Cultural Revolution, however much they had opposed it, had neither the desire nor the ability to lead reform. They were generally reluctant to implement even modest change, much less the rapid marketizing reforms Deng had in mind. Thus, both the age structure of China's political leadership and the political need to "ease out" those opposed to reform converged to form a new norm in favor of retirement. Such a shift was incremental; it was eased at the highest level by providing a variety of perks, including membership in the newly created

Central Advisory Commission, which would allow retired officials to continue to participate in China's political affairs (sometimes with very detrimental results). Initially, many exceptions to the retirement age were allowed. Nevertheless, the Central Advisory Commission was abolished in 1992, a decade after it had been established, and over time fewer exceptions to the age of retirement were allowed.[16] Although it is difficult to say that a firm commitment has been made to complete retirement at all levels, the results of the Fifteenth Party Congress in 1997 and the National People's Congress in March 1998 suggest considerable movement in this direction.

At the same time, economic reform and the implementation of retirement policies required the recruitment of a new generation of bureaucrats. This need was all the more imperative because so many careers had been sidetracked during the Cultural Revolution. In the course of the Party Rectification of 1983–1986 and in successive Party conclaves in 1985, 1987, 1992, and 1997, those too old or unqualified for high office were weeded out or passed over, while those better qualified were promoted. Although the official slogan for the recruitment and promotion of younger officials was to promote "more revolutionary, better educated, more professionally competent, and younger," in practice the term "more revolutionary" was difficult to define and highly contentious. The result has been to rely on more objective criteria, particularly education and age, for selecting the Party elite and state cadres. Because the social sciences were highly suspect in the early part of the PRC, and even remain so today, there has been a very strong tendency to recruit those who have had technical training, particularly engineering, thus giving China's political elite a very technocratic cast. An issue that is highly contentious—whom to recruit—has been delimited if not resolved by falling back on "objective" indicators such as age and education.[17]

Obviously these new criteria have not resolved all problems of recruitment and bureaucratic building. Often there are several individuals who satisfy the "objective" criteria, leaving promotion decisions up to political and other considerations. China has been slow to develop a civil service system, although there has been movement in that direction in recent years.[18] But even in the absence of an effective civil service system, there are some indications that more objective criteria are being applied to promotion. Prior to an official being promoted, the views of subordinates, peers, and superiors are solicited in an effort to weed out objectionable people. Such a process hardly eliminates personalism, but perhaps it limits its worst abuses.

Although reform generated a variety of positive pressures, as suggested above, it also produced negative effects and conflict, both within the state and between state and society. One of the central consequences of reform was to undermine the legitimacy of the socialist system. The divergence between ideological understandings of socialism and the reality of what was happening stretched credulity and generated cynicism. The problems of partial reform were everywhere, straining the relations between those who insisted that problems could be resolved only through more reform and those who insisted the problems were caused by reform itself. "Hardliners" wanted to reemphasize socialist ideology in order to rein in the consequences of reform, while "moderates" wanted to push ahead. It did not help that moderates ("reformers") were themselves badly divided, as followers of Hu Yaobang (the general secretary ousted in January 1987 for his supposed "laxness" in the face of "bourgeois liberalization") often engaged in acrimonious disputes with those who looked to Premier (then General Secretary) Zhao Ziyang for leadership. (This was particularly visible in the debate over the so-called new authoritarianism.)[19] But such disputes reflected the real problems involved in deciding how to move forward in the face of both economic difficulties and political opposition.

At the same time, there was an ever-widening gulf developing between state and society, particularly with the younger generation that had grown up not knowing the Maoist period and were thus frustrated with the distance that remained between the reality they did know and their expectations for the future. Anger was increasingly focused on corruption and bureaucratic privilege. The example of the West, both presumed and real, helped fuel expectations, while Gorbachev in the Soviet Union and popular efforts to bring about democracy in the Philippines and South Korea suggested what might be done to realize those expectations.

Tensions at the highest political level and the growing estrangement between state and society created a tinderbox that exploded in the spring of 1989. The tragedy that ensued dashed hopes for an easy and rapid transition. For a while, it seemed that the possibility of resuming market-oriented economic reform, much less political reform, was small, but the evolution of events has confounded the expectations of domestic and foreign observers alike and opened up possibilities not only of continued economic reform but also, eventually, of political change.

The Impact of Tiananmen

This is not the place to analyze the dynamics of Tiananmen; that has been done elsewhere.[20] It is important to point out, however, that the suddenness with which the demonstrations arose and the ferocity with which they were then suppressed ensured that China would not follow the path of the "classic" four-actor model said to characterize the most successful transitions to democracy.[21] Within the regime, there was a division between hardliners and moderates, but the unique role of Deng Xiaoping as the supreme leader meant that this division could never really develop as two separate, roughly evenly balanced wings of the Party. Deng hesitated a long while during the Tiananmen crisis, as various political forces played themselves out, but then threw his full weight behind the hardliners. Similarly, within the student movement there was a similar tendency for the leadership to divide between "moderates" and "radicals," but the dynamic of the movement continuously pushed it in a more radical direction. Moderate student leaders never had a chance to emerge as a separate and viable political force. In the event, the whole movement was over in seven weeks. There was a chance, but only a brief chance, for moderates within the leadership to work with moderates within the student movement. It was a chance that was not seized, and the possibility of a "pacted" transition of some sort passed quickly from the scene.

The crushing of the student movement appeared to end any chance that China could embark on a period of gradual transition. It seemed that hardliners were in total control and there were fears, not altogether unfounded, that they would use their power to roll back the reforms. However, there were a number of factors, both particular and structural, that prevented this from happening. One, of course, was the role that Deng Xiaoping played. Deng threw his support behind the hardliners and ordered the military to end the demonstrations, but he also denied the fruits of victory to the hardliners. Talking to hardliners Li Peng and Yao Yilin, who no doubt expected to gain from the demise of Zhao Ziyang, Deng explained the choice of Jiang Zemin as the new general secretary. Almost contemptuously he said, "The people see reality. If we put up a front so that people feel that it is an ossified leadership, a conservative leadership, or if the people believe that it is a mediocre leadership that cannot reflect the future of China, then there will be constant trouble and there will never be a peaceful day."[22] At the same time, Deng insisted that economic reform and opening up be continued. Deng's position was much weakened in the aftermath of Tiananmen and his policy preferences hardly prevailed. But his power was sufficient to prevent hardliners from consolidating their position and finally, in 1992, Deng struck back; by the end of the year he was once again able to dominate China's policy agenda.[23]

Deng's role in the immediate post-Tiananmen period was thus primarily as a stabilizer, preventing the Chinese political system from lurching completely out of control, and then as the promoter of a new round of reform. In this sense, Deng's role was unique and critical. But there were also other forces at work that contributed not only to the revival of reform but more important to greater, albeit still nascent, institutionalization.

The first factor was the further disintegration of the role of ideology. The role of ideology was one of the most contentious issues in the post-Tiananmen period, with conservative ideologues arguing that it had been precisely the implementation of marketizing reforms that had eroded the legitimacy of ideology and thus weakened the Party. This argument intensified when socialism collapsed in Eastern Europe as the Soviet Union disintegrated. Deng opposed the arguments of hardliners by turning their logic upside down. He argued that economic reform was not the cause of the Tiananmen crisis but had, on the contrary, provided the Chinese system with the resiliency to survive that upheaval. By way of contrast, Eastern Europe and the Soviet Union had not carried out economic reform successfully and were therefore more vulnerable. In making this argument, however, Deng was pushing performance legitimacy to a new level. In effect, Deng was arguing that Marxism-Leninism had lost all effectiveness in ensuring the regime's legitimacy; the only way the regime could "buy" the acquiescence of the people was to improve their livelihood through developing the economy. In his critical tour of Shenzhen in early 1992, Deng defined "socialism" in terms of the so-called three advantages. Reforms were to be judged by three criteria: Whether they were advantageous to the development of socialist productive forces, whether they increased the comprehensive strength of a socialist nation, and whether they raised the people's standard of living.[24] Clearly, Tiananmen had shattered whatever legitimacy remained in Marxism-Leninism, forcing the regime to base its continued existence ever more firmly on its ability to "deliver the goods."

A second critical factor has been that of leadership succession, both personal and generational. Jiang Zemin, born in 1926, was seventy-one years old when the Fifteenth Party Congress convened in September 1997. Whatever his abilities, Jiang clearly does not carry the political authority of a Mao Zedong or a Deng Xiaoping (and Deng's authority was certainly less than Mao's). There was considerable doubt whether senior political leaders, including his own age cohorts who might regard themselves as being as well qualified as Jiang to hold the top position, would be willing to accept his authority. No doubt Party norms give a considerable advantage to incumbency; to be seen as "splitting" the Party is a serious offense, making challenges to the top leadership difficult and hazardous. Still, there are ways of challenging the scope of the leader's authority without directly challenging his position, and it was widely expected that a number of top leaders might undermine Jiang's authority directly or indirectly.

To an important extent such challenges are extra-institutional in that there is no defined forum in which conflicts are mediated or to which decisions can be referred. In other words, politics at the top remain uninstitutionalized, and their outcome is based on who has more power. In the Mao period, there was little doubt about who had the most power. In the Dengist period, Deng remained preeminent and was willing to exercise the prerogatives that came with that position from time to time, but he was also more willing to accede to, and even encourage, the emergence of norms that curtailed the arbitrary exercise of power—at least to some extent.[25] With less personal authority and unable to appeal to historical contributions in the revolution (Jiang was only a student organizer in Shanghai in the late 1940s), Jiang Zemin has tried to respond to challenges to his position and authority by invoking rules. One can take the invocation of rules as a shallow exercise in formalism, and it may turn out that way, but it is also possible that the invocation of rules will prove binding, setting the political system on a course of institutionalization.

In personal terms, there have been three major challenges to Jiang's authority so far.[26] The first came in 1992 when in response to Deng Xiaoping's trip to the south and his implicit criticism of Jiang's tolerance of the "left," Yang Shangkun, then permanent vice chairman of the Central Military Commission, and Qiao Shi, then head of the National People's Congress, apparently joined forces in an effort to oust Jiang. What precisely happened is in doubt, and many different versions have swirled through the rumor mill, but it appears that there was a significant challenge to Jiang's authority. This was the sort of challenge that Jiang could hardly meet on his own, given Yang's seniority in the political system and position in the military. Whatever the details, Jiang eventually was able to win Deng Xiaoping's support, and in the presumed interest of maintaining long-term stability in the political system, Deng turned against his longtime friend, removing Yang's younger half-brother, Yang Baibing, from his critical position in the Central Military Commission and effectively depriving Yang Shangkun of much of his influence. This move allowed Jiang to shake up the military structure and to begin to promote officers who at least appeared to be loyal to him.

In important ways, this shake-up was an old-fashioned political struggle. Conflict revolved around generational differences, personalities, and professionalization. In getting rid of the Yang brothers and their supporters, Jiang was able to promote a number of younger military officers, many of whom had been promoted on the basis of their military professionalism. In order to develop a younger and more professional officer corps, Jiang invoked longstanding rules about factionalism in the military as well as rules regarding the military's obedience to the Party. None of this ensures the loyalty of the military to Jiang or to the civilian Party leadership in general, but it *could* pave the way for greater professionalization and regularization of civilian-military relations, trends that have been under way for some time in any event.[27]

The second challenge to Jiang's authority came from Beijing Party secretary and Politburo member Chen Xitong. It is not clear the extent to which Chen posed a threat to Jiang or merely resisted his authority, but it seems clear that Chen felt his own connections to top-level leaders, including Deng Xiaoping, would protect him and permit him to defy the Party general secretary. As later events demonstrated, there was also enormous corruption involved—Chen apparently had amassed a fortune of some 18 billion yuan (over $2 billion). This conflict also came at a time when Jiang was concerned with being able to assert his authority over China's provincial leaders, some of whom were increasingly resisting Beijing's demands. Thus, Chen Xitong's case cut across a number of issues, and Jiang no doubt considered the impact of ousting Chen for increasing Jiang's authority in a number of these areas.

It appears that Jiang waited until Deng was seriously ill before acting to oust Chen, and apparently he did so only after cutting a number of deals with other members of the Politburo Standing Committee. As in the Yang Baibing–Yang Shangkun case, Jiang's conflict with Chen Xitong contained significant elements of a power struggle. But Jiang handled it by referring the case to the Party's Central Discipline Inspection Commission (which, in turn, eventually referred it to the court system, which three years later finally sentenced Chen to sixteen years in prison), and used Chen's dismissal to raise the profile of Jiang's struggle against corruption. That strategy raised Jiang's profile both as protector of the common interest and as advocate of a law-based society. Apparently, Chen's corruption was of a degree that, when Jiang made an issue of it, Chen could hardly rally support to his cause.[28]

Chen's dismissal on corruption charges, as Melanie Manion notes, was part of a broader *campaign* against corruption rather than part of an institutionalized enforcement of anticorruption laws.[29] Yet the seriousness of corruption in contemporary China, and Jiang's apparent desire to avoid being tagged with charges of pursuing personal power struggle, could lay the foundation for a more routinized effort to deal with that issue. The problem is so large and complex, involving so many vested interests, however, that it will be some time before it becomes clear whether China can deal with corruption on more than an episodic basis. In any case, Jiang's ouster of Chen for specific cause—rather than on the grounds of loosely defined ideological criteria such as being lax against "bourgeois liberalization"—and especially the decision to refer Chen's case to the legal authorities (rather than define it simply as a matter of Party discipline) lays a foundation for bureaucratization of anticorruption efforts, if such efforts can continue to be followed up regularly.

Perhaps the most intriguing case has been that of Qiao Shi, the third-ranking member of the Politburo Standing Committee and head of the National People's Congress, who was not reelected to the Central Committee, much less the Politburo, at the Fifteenth Party Congress in September 1997. Qiao's dismissal occasioned a great deal of public comment because Qiao represented the "liberal" wing of the Party, calling more explicitly and continuously than any other Party leader for institutionalizing the rule of law and strengthening the role of the National People's Congress. Qiao's public statements certainly did champion the rule of law, but it had become increasingly apparent that, whatever might be his feelings about law per se, he was using the issue to distinguish himself publicly from Jiang Zemin, who continuously emphasized democratic centralism and obedience to the "core" (himself).[30] In short, there was a personal power struggle going on as well as a difference in political emphasis.

According to the various rumors circulating since the Fifteenth Party Congress, Jiang apparently invoked the age criterion to force Qiao's

ouster.[31] As noted above, retirement norms have been increasingly institutionalized over the past two decades, but they had remained loose at
best at the highest level. This time, Jiang apparently invoked age as a
reason to retire both the eighty-three-year-old Liu Huaqing (the military's
representative on the Politburo Standing Committee) and the seventy-
two-year-old Qiao Shi. Qiao is only one year older than Jiang, and both
men were slightly above the officially mandated retirement age of sev-
enty that was invoked to force Qiao out. So it appears a bit disingenuous
to say that Qiao was ousted on grounds of age. Nevertheless, Jiang's
invocation of an "objective" criterion now makes it more difficult for
others to stay on the Politburo Standing Committee past the age of sev-
enty; accordingly, it is widely expected that Jiang will retire after serving his current five-year term in office.[32] If he does indeed retire, it could
pave the way for a more orderly succession process than China has been
blessed with in the past.

While Jiang has tended to invoke "objective" rules and standards (factionalism, corruption, age) in order to thwart personal challenges to his
power, the more interesting trend has been the invocation of such decision-making rules to ensure large-scale change in the Central Committee. The transition from Deng's generation of aging revolutionaries to
Jiang's generation of Party bureaucrats has evoked the most discussion,
but it is the rejuvenation and promotion of better-educated cadres to the
Central Committee that is more important in institutional terms. This is
a change that has been taking place for some time. A special "Party
representatives" meeting in 1985 saw a large-scale turnover in the membership of the Central Committee, as many younger and better-educated
cadres were promoted. This trend continued in the Party congresses of
1987 and 1992. At the Fifteenth Party Congress in September 1997,
almost 60 percent of the Central Committee was replaced, ensuring the
promotion of younger and better-educated cadres, particularly in the
provinces. Such trends are important in terms of both formal and informal authority. In terms of the formal structure, norms concerning retirement and educational criteria are increasingly institutionalized—only 3
of the 193 members of the newly elected Central Committee came to
prominence as "model workers." Moreover, all three have long since
demonstrated administrative competence in a variety of important positions, showing that they have qualifications beyond just being "model
workers." In terms of the informal power structure, it is simply much
more likely that Jiang will be able to gain compliance from those who

are clearly his juniors and, moreover, owe their promotion at least in part to him.[33]

The third major pressure for rationalization (in a Weberian sense) comes from the economic realm. As noted above, the growth of the TVE sector spurred economic growth, marketization, and important structural changes in industry (including the rapid growth of a consumer goods sector and the development of horizontal linkages among industries). It also brought competitive pressures to bear on the state-owned sector, which had previously enjoyed large economic rents. Over time, the profits of state-owned enterprises (SOEs) eroded and subsidies to those enterprises increased. The pressures facing SOEs provoked one of the most critical political debates in the late 1980s. When conservatives had a free hand to try to revive aspects of the planned economy in the wake of Tiananmen, they attempted to shore up the role of SOEs. These efforts, however, were mishandled, not to mention misconceived, and profitability declined sharply and interenterprise debt (so-called triangular debt) exploded.

By the mid-1990s, the problems of SOEs were threatening state solvency and the entire fiscal system. Whereas approximately 20 percent of China's SOEs perennially ran deficits in the 1980s, the figure rose to more than 30 percent by the early 1990s. By 1995 it was close to 40 percent, and it reached 43.7 percent the following year.[34] Meanwhile the volume of losses surged almost 30 percent to 61.6 billion yuan ($7.4 billion). These losses were particularly disturbing because they were beginning to exceed the surplus generated by the SOEs that were profitable. In the first four months of 1996, China's SOEs ran a net loss. Although the situation improved somewhat in later months, it remained very serious: In the first nine months of the year, net profits were only 20.2 billion yuan ($2.43 billion), a decline of 62.1 percent from the previous year. Even in the prosperous coastal areas of Shanghai and Guangdong, losses were up and profits were down.[35]

Because taxes from SOEs continue to account for more than 60 percent of central government revenues, such figures mean that the fiscal situation facing the government, already tight for many years, will remain precarious. It also means that so-called triangular debts (the money enterprises owe each other) are increasing. Such debts rose from 300 billion yuan ($36.1 billion) in the early 1990s to 700 billion yuan ($84.3 billion) in 1994 and 800 billion yuan ($84.3 billion) in 1995.[36] These developments cannot be good news for China's banking system where at least one-third of outstanding loans are said to be nonperforming.[37]

Such figures suggest the economic and fiscal pressures behind continued economic reform in the 1990s and the endorsement by the Fifteenth Party Congress of restructuring, reorganizing, and selling off SOEs.
A major feature of these reforms is the effort to clarify property rights.
Although there remain sharp debates within China over how to clarify
those rights,[38] the very effort to do so reflects an important turning point
in China's economic reform. It can be argued that economic reform progressed as rapidly as it did in the 1980s because China sidestepped the
complicated and contentious issue of property rights. The deepening of
reform, the plight of state-owned industries, and the emergence of financial markets, however, are creating new and intense pressures to
clarify them. This is a difficult and politically contentious issue that will
not be solved quickly. Nevertheless, a large number of smaller SOEs are
likely to be privatized, while a smaller number of large SOEs will implement some form of a shareholding system—a step that requires the evaluation of assets and the assignment of ownership. To the extent that
property rights are clarified, there will be a greater separation between
the political sphere and the economic, again with the caveat that there is
a long way to go.

One sees the same pressures in the fiscal area. The structure of China's
planned economy and SOEs were established in large measure to direct
fiscal resources to the state,[39] and even in the reform era, as the role of
SOEs has diminished, the central state has relied disproportionately on
those enterprises for its fiscal revenues. The role and financial health of
SOEs have declined in part because of the rapid growth of TVEs. These
township and village enterprises have grown rapidly not only because
they supplied consumer goods, which had been neglected under the
planned economy, but also because they have been supported by local
governments, which have benefited from the increased tax revenues TVEs
provide.[40] At the same time, as TVEs have grown, they have cut into the
monopoly rents once enjoyed by the SOEs, causing the revenues available to the central government to decline (relatively) as those taken in
by local governments have grown rapidly. Central government revenues
as a share of gross domestic product (GDP) have declined from 35 percent in 1978 to only 12 percent in 1994. This rapid decline in fiscal
resources to a point that is considered quite low in comparative terms—
a point which leading Chinese and U.S.-based scholars such as Hu
Angang and Wang Shaoguang fear could lead to the physical breakup of
China—prompted a major reform of the tax system in 1994.[41] That re-

form constituted an important effort to diversify the sources of central government revenue so as to reflect the changing composition of the economy and, most importantly, to establish a genuinely independent, central tax system. Previously, taxes had been collected at the local level and remitted to the center, an arrangement that exists in no other modern state. Fears that continued fiscal decentralization would undermine the ability of the state to carry out its functions—from welfare to national defense—and to exercise macroeconomic control prompted rationalizing reforms. Although such reforms are far from complete, they mark an important step toward institution building.

This pressure to separate the political realm from the economic and to rationalize the administrative system took a major step forward in the spring of 1998 when the first session of the Ninth National People's Congress announced a major reorganization of the government to reduce the number of ministries and commissions under the State Council from forty to twenty-nine and to cut government personnel by 50 percent. Perhaps the most important feature of this government reorganization, assuming it proceeds more or less as intended, is to separate the ministries from direct control of enterprises. This change strikes at the very heart of the old planned economy, and appears to be a serious effort to address the institutional basis of much corruption, namely the control that government bureaucrats exercise over scarce resources.[42]

If one of the distinctions between authoritarian and Leninist political systems is the general separation of the political and economic spheres and the recognition of property rights in the former and the conflation of politics and economics and the nonexistence of property rights in the latter, then China has moved quite far in the authoritarian direction over the past two decades. Authoritarianism does not necessarily lead to a successful transition to democracy, but if space is provided for the growth of institutions, the prospect for democratization appears better than for a more Leninist regime.

Problems of Partial Reform

This chapter has argued that important political and economic pressures are pushing China toward the creation of more effective institutions. These are noteworthy trends because the nation's tumultuous history over the past century has not allowed state building to take place, and as Linz and Stepan have argued, one cannot have a democratic state unless one has a *state*.[43] Although a variety of caveats have been registered above, it is nevertheless necessary to emphasize that the trends outlined above remain nascent and are offset to a considerable degree by countervailing developments that could overwhelm the progress made.

One such tendency is that the conflation of public and private continues to grow, even as there are simultaneous pulls in the opposite direction. This conflation takes place on two levels, one at the local level and the other at higher levels. At the local (county) level, reform and the development of TVEs have strengthened the role of government, while Party secretaries act more like chief executive officers (CEOs) of holding companies than government officials. Local Party and government officials are deeply involved in the economy, often deciding how to allocate resources among competing demands and deciding on local development strategies.[44] Although the government has encouraged and fostered private entrepreneurship in some areas, the more prevalent pattern is for the government itself to be entrepreneurial. To the extent that such patterns become entrenched, and that appears to be considerable, there is a lack of separation between economic and political society and a corresponding conflation of state and society.[45]

At other levels, there is similarly a widespread tendency for the political and economic arenas to overlap. Government officials can frequently collect "rents" on their control over everything from scarce resources to permits. Similarly, leaders in large SOEs are frequently able to siphon off state-owned resources to set up enterprises controlled by their families or friends. An important part of enterprise reform allows SOEs to buy and sell capital goods as their businesses requires, but opening up such capital goods markets, where state-owned assets are often not valued fairly, creates enormous opportunities for corruption. Although such "stripping" (*liushi*) of state assets is difficult to define or quantify, one recent estimate states that in the decade between 1982 and 1992, some 500 billion yuan (approximately $60 billion)—nearly a fifth of all state-owned assets— was drained legally or illegally into private accounts.[46] Another estimate claims that in the 1980s, some 50 billion yuan ($5.8 billion) worth of state assets was being stripped per year, and that that figure has almost doubled to 80–100 billion yuan ($9.5–11.8 billion) in the 1990s.[47] Although such trends could lead to de facto privatization of a significant portion of the Chinese economy (a process referred to ironically as "primitive socialist accumulation"), in the short run there is a very substantial overlap between the public and private economies.

In part as a result of this asset stripping or direct corruption, income inequality has increased rapidly in recent years. Between 1981 and 1996, urban residents with the lowest 20 percent of income increased their incomes only by 1.6 times, whereas the highest 20 percent increased their incomes by 12.7 times.[48] According to one report, income inequality in China now parallels that in the United States and is worse than in Japan.[49] Another report states that the wealthiest 7 percent of China's urban residents possess over 30 percent of urban wealth.[50]

If there has been a concentration of wealth at the top of the system, there has also been suffering at the lower end of the spectrum. Increasingly Chinese workers are "furloughed" (*xiagang*) from state-owned enterprises that are trying to cut losses. In 1996, it was authoritatively estimated that over 8 percent of urban workers had had their wages reduced or stopped, and that some fifteen million urban residents had been affected by the loss and reduction of wages.[51] As a result, labor discontent has grown. According to Vice Premier Wu Bangguo, between January and August 1996, there were a total of 4,032 strike actions, over half of which were caused by disputes over delayed payment of wages. Some were reported to have signs of organization and planning.[52]

Thus, the conflation of economic and political societies is directly related to volatile social issues such as income inequality and corruption. In its survey of fifty-four countries, Transparency International reported that China is the fifth most corrupt country, trailing only Bangladesh, Kenya, Pakistan, and Nigeria. Moreover, as Melanie Manion has recently observed, repeated efforts to tighten controls against corruption have yet to reveal visible results. Corruption was one of the focal points of the 1989 Tiananmen demonstrations, and it remains one of the most volatile issues in China's public life. A survey of urban workers in 1996 found that corruption was at or near the top of most workers' concerns.[53]

Another particularly difficult issue is the continued conflation of Party and state. In the 1980s, reformers pressed concerns about separation of Party and state. After the Thirteenth Party Congress in 1987, Party groups (*dangzu*) were removed from most ministries of the State Council and efforts were made to create a professional civil service. Following the upheaval of 1989, these trends were reversed and Party groups were reestablished. In 1992, the Fourteenth Party Congress increased the overlap between Party and state by making the top four members of the Politburo Standing Committee simultaneously the heads of the major state organs (Jiang Zemin as president, Li Peng as premier, Qiao Shi as head of the NPC, and Li Ruihuan as head of the Chinese People's Political Consultative Conference), a trend that was continued at the Fifteenth Party Congress in 1997 (although Zhu Rongji replaced Li Peng as premier, and Li Peng replaced Qiao Shi as head of the NPC). The same trend of strengthening the Party at the expense of the state has been apparent in recent years as Jiang Zemin has tried to consolidate his power. Although there have been trends toward rationalizing and regularizing politics at the highest level, as pointed out above, the rallying cry Jiang used to reinforce his own power was strengthening democratic centralism, a Leninist norm rather than a statist norm. Nevertheless, at the Fifteenth Party Congress in September 1997, Jiang made a strong pitch for rule by law.[54] How the tension between the different norms of democratic centralism and law will be worked out remains one of the critical issues of the coming years.

To the extent that the economic and public spheres and the realms of Party and state are conflated, it is difficult at best either for a vital civil society to emerge or for law to become more than an adjunct to administration. These are important weaknesses when we look at China today. The state has retreated significantly from society, giving individuals greater freedom than ever before in Chinese history, but studies of "civil society" point to a high degree of intermingling of public and private and of dependence on the state.[55] Similarly, law has become increasingly important in the course of economic reform, but it has yet to emerge as really independent from the state. Rule by law remains far stronger than rule of law.[56] The possibility of a Chinese *Reichstaat* remains a distant hope.

Conclusion

Discussions on democratic prospects in China have generally revolved around whether or not there is widespread public support for democracy, the activity of political dissidents, whether or not there is an emergent civil society or pressures for democracy from below, and the presence or absence of democratic traditions in Chinese history.[57] Generally speaking, these discussions have focused on the possibility of democratic transition in China. The experience of other countries and the burgeoning literature on the difficulties many countries have had following democratic transitions, however, have focused greater attention to the social, economic, and political requisites of successful transitions as well as the modalities of the transitions themselves.[58] Such literature should force those who study China as well as those who are concerned about the country's democratization to rethink the categories and modes of analysis they use. Accordingly, this chapter has been an attempt to look realistically at the "state of the state" in China and at the political and economic dynamics of the post-Tiananmen period, so as to assess not just the possibility of democratic transition in China but, more importantly, the probability of sustainable democratic governance in the future.

Accordingly, the emphasis in this chapter has been on the development of institutions. Institutions can be both formal, as in the development of a "usable bureaucracy," and informal, as in regular behavior patterns. Formal institutions and informal patterns of behavior can be mutually reinforcing, but it is difficult to develop formal institutions if informal behavior is destructive of stable expectations. In general, twentieth-century Chinese politics have witnessed a continual clash between informal patterns of behavior and emergent institutions, to the detriment of political stability and state building.[59]

China has now been undergoing a reform process for nearly two decades. With the notable exceptions of the 1979 border war with Vietnam and the violent suppression of demonstrators in 1989, these two decades have been the longest period of sustained domestic and international peace and economic development since the Opium War. Given the violence of China's political history over the past century and a half, it is not surprising that China has not been able to develop formal institutions and informal patterns of behavior that are mutually supportive. The question that China's reform process raises is whether such a mutually supportive pattern is taking shape. This chapter has offered a cautiously optimistic assessment of this possibility. It has been noted that there were both positive and negative trends in the 1980s, followed by the perhaps unexpected reemergence of positive trends in the 1990s. The dynamics of economic reform, political conflict, and generational succession have generated pressures to separate political and economic society, to build more competent and "rational" bureaucratic structures, to regularize political promotion and change through the use of more objective criteria for promotion and by enforcing norms for retirement.

It has also been noted that this process remains tentative, ambiguous, and fragile. China faces a number of enormous challenges, including reform of the SOEs, the pressures from those to be thrown out of work and those coming into the job market (at a rate of about eight million per year), the building of a viable system of social security, the need to address growing regional and income inequalities, the reform of the health

82 ELITE POLITICS IN CONTEMPORARY CHINA

care system, addressing deteriorating environmental conditions, and so forth. These or other issues could provoke large-scale protests of various sorts that could once again cause political upheavals that would set back the progress made in recent years.

If such challenges are to be addressed adequately and tensions between state and society and within the political system ameliorated, China will have to develop more effective institutions, particularly at the central state level. Building a stronger, more bureaucratic state is not necessarily incompatible with greater democratization. In a narrow, limited sense, bureaucratization means professionalization, which, in turn, implies a widening of the consultative process as professional competence spreads through the policy community, encompassing both state bureaucrats and the broader intellectual community. In a broader sense, it seems likely that the central state will have to grant greater political participation to local governments if it wants to convince the latter to yield control over revenue sources.[60] Neither the development of broad policy communities nor the participation of local levels of government in decision making necessarily implies voting and democratization. But it does imply the development of institutions and the sort of "soft authoritarianism" that prefaced the successful transition to democracy in Taiwan and elsewhere. Perhaps China can follow in this path.

Notes

The author would like to thank Boston University and the Smith Richardson Foundation for providing support for the research that went into this article.

1. Michael Mandelbaum, ed., *Post-Communism: Four Perspectives* (New York: Council on Foreign Relations, 1996).

2. Larry Diamond, "Introduction: In Search of Consolidation," in Larry Diamond, Marc Plattner, Yun-han Chu, and Hung-mao Tien, eds., *Consolidating the Third Wave Democracies: Themes and Perspectives* (Baltimore: Johns Hopkins University Press, 1997), p. xlii.

3. Ding Xueliang, *Gongchanzhuyihou yu Zhongguo* (Post-Communism and China) (Hong Kong: Oxford University Press, 1994), p. xxii.

4. William H. Overholt, *The Rise of China* (New York: W.W. Norton, 1993).

5. James Miles, *The Legacy of Tiananmen: China in Disarray* (Ann Arbor, MI: University of Michigan Press, 1996); and Edward Friedman, *National Identity and Democratic Prospects in Socialist China* (Armonk, NY: M.E. Sharpe, 1995). For an overview of prospects and possibilities, see Richard Baum, "China After Deng: Ten Scenarios in Search of Reality," in *The China Quarterly*, no. 145 (March 1996): 153–175.

6. Juan J. Linz and Alfred Stepan, *Problems of Democratic Transition and Consolidation: Southern Europe, South America, and Post-Communist Europe* (Baltimore: Johns Hopkins University Press, 1996); and Juan J. Linz and Alfred Stepan,

"Toward Consolidated Democracies," in Diamond et al., eds., *Consolidating the Third Wave Democracies*, pp. 14–33.

7. Bernard Silberman, *Cages of Reason: The Rise of the Rational State in France, Japan, the United States, and Great Britain* (Chicago: University of Chicago Press, 1993).

8. Shiping Zheng, *Party vs. State in Post-1949 China* (Cambridge: Cambridge University Press, 1997).

9. Barry Naughton, *Growing Out of the Plan: Chinese Economic Reform, 1978–1993* (Cambridge: Cambridge University Press, 1995), pp. 69–74.

10. Hu Qiaomu, "Act in Accordance with Economic Laws: Step up the Four Modernizations," Xinhua, October 5, 1978, trans. Foreign Broadcast Information Service (FBIS), *Daily Report: China*, October 11, 1978, p. E11.

11. Chen Yun, "Jianchi an bili yuanze tiaozheng guomin jingji" (Readjust the national economy in accordance with the principle of proportionality), in Chen Yun, *Chen Yun wenxuan (1956–1985)* (Selected works of Chen Yun, 1956–1985) (Beijing: Renmin chubanshe, 1995), pp. 226–231.

12. Joseph Fewsmith, *Dilemmas of Reform in China: Political Conflict and Economic Debate* (Armonk, NY: M.E. Sharpe, 1994), pp. 87–122; and Naughton, *Growing Out of the Plan*, pp. 119–127.

13. Shang Xiuyun, "Spurring Economic Growth and Making Life Easier; China Scores Marked Achievements in Reform of Circulation Structure," in *Renmin ribao*, overseas edition, October 4, 1995, p. 2, trans. FBIS-Chi-95–229.

14. Hu, "Act in Accordance with Economic Laws," p. E19.

15. Anson Rabinbach, "Social Knowledge, Social Risk, and the Politics of Industrial Accidents in Germany and France," in Dietrich Rueschemeyer and Theda Skocpol, eds., *States, Social Knowledge, and the Origins of Modern Social Policies* (Princeton: Princeton University Press, 1996), pp. 48–89; and Bjorn Wittrock and Peter Wagner, "Social Science and the Building of the Early Welfare State: Toward a Comparison of Statist and Non-Statist Western Societies," in Rueschemeyer and Skocpol, eds., *States, Social Knowledge, and the Origins of Modern Social Policies*, pp. 90–109.

16. Melanie Manion, *Retirement of Revolutionaries in China: Public Policies, Social Norms, Private Interests* (Princeton: Princeton University Press, 1993).

17. Hong Yung Lee, *From Revolutionary Cadres to Party Technocrats in Socialist China* (Berkeley: University of California Press, 1991).

18. Tang Hua, "New Trends in Personnel and Institutional Reforms,' in *Liaowang*, no. 11 (March 13, 1995): 12–13, trans. FBIS-Chi-95–62; and Huang Haixia, "Two Adjustments Shall Be Implemented in Personnel-Related Work," in *Liaowang*, no. 7 (February 12, 1996): 10–11, trans. FBIS-Chi-96–059.

19. Stanley Rosen and Gary Zou, eds., "The Chinese Debate on New Authoritarianism," *Chinese Sociology and Anthropology*, Winter 1990 (22, no. 2), Spring 1991 (23, no. 3), Summer 1991 (23, no. 4), and Fall 1991 (24, no. 1).

20. Tang Tsou, "The Tiananmen Tragedy: The State-Society Relationship, Choices, and Mechanisms in Historical Perspective," in Brantley Womack, ed., *Contemporary Chinese Politics in Historical Perspective* (Cambridge: Cambridge University Press, 1991), pp. 265–327.

21. Adam Pzreworski, *Democracy and the Market: Political and Economic Reforms in Eastern Europe and Latin America* (Cambridge: Cambridge University Press, 1991).

22. Deng Xiaoping, "Zucheng yige shixing gaige de you xiwang de lingdao jiti" (Organize a reformist, hopeful leadership collective), in *Deng Xiaoping wenxuan* (Selected works of Deng Xiaoping), vol. 3 (Beijing: Renmin chubanshe, 1993), pp. 296–301.

23. Joseph Fewsmith, "Reaction, Resurgence, and Succession: Chinese Politics since Tiananmen," in Roderick MacFarquhar, ed., *Chinese Politics: The Eras of Mao and Deng* (Cambridge: Cambridge University Press, 1997), pp. 472–531.

24. Deng Xiaoping, "Zai Wuchang, Shenzhen, Zhuhai dengdi de tanhua yaodian" (Essential points from talks in Wuchang, Shenzhen, and Zhuhai), in *Deng Xiaoping wenxuan*, vol. 3, pp. 370–383.

25. See chapter 4, "The Impact of Reforms on Elite Politics."

26. Fewsmith, "Reaction, Resurgence, and Succession."

27. Paul H. B. Godwin, "Economic Reform and Party-Military Relations in China: The Evolution of a Political Dilemma," in Merle Goldman and Roderick MacFarquhar, eds., *The Paradoxes of China's Post-Mao Reforms* (Cambridge: Harvard University Press, 1999) pp. 76–99.

28. Yang Zhongmei, *Jiang Zemin zhuan* (Biography of Jiang Zemin) (Taipei: Shibao wenhua, 1996), pp. 307–316.

29. Melanie Manion, "Corruption and Corruption Control: More of the Same in 1996," in Maurice Brosseau, Kuan Hsin-chi, and Y.Y. Kueh, eds., *China Review, 1997* (Hong Kong: Chinese University Press, 1997), pp. 33–56.

30. Joseph Fewsmith, "Jockeying for Position in the Post-Deng Era," *Current History*, 94, no. 593 (September 1995): 252–258.

31. Xi Wensi, "Qiao Shi xiatai neimu" (The inside story of Qiao Shi stepping down), *Kaifang*, no. 10 (October): 14–17.

32. In the fall of 1999, many rumors circulated about Jiang's apparent desire to remain as general secretary past the Sixteenth Party Congress, which is expected to be held in 2002. We simply have to wait to see how the political dynamic plays out.

33. Cheng Li and Lynn White, "The 15th Central Committee of the Chinese Communist Party: Full-Fledged Technocratic Leadership with Partial Control by Jiang Zemin," *Asian Survey*, 38, no. 3 (April 1988): 231–264; and Cheng Li, *China's Leaders: The New Generation* (Lanham, MD: Rowman and Littlefield, forthcoming).

34. Yang Qixian, "Guanyu guoyou qiye gaige de lixing sikao" (Thinking rationally about reform of state-owned enterprises), *Jingji yanjiu cankao*, no. 13 (February 13, 1997): 3.

35. Wu Bangguo, "Guanyu guoyou qiye gaige yu fazhan de jige wenti" (Some issues concerning the reform and development of state-owned enterprises), *Zhongyang dangxiao baogaoxuan*, no. 18 (1996): 3.

36. Yang Qixian, "Guanyu guoyou qiye gaige de lixing sikao," p. 4.

37. Nicholas Lardy, "Testimony: Statement Before the Committee on Banking and Financial Services, U.S. House of Representatives," March 20, 1996.

38. Zhiyuan Cui, "Whither China? The Discourse on Property Rights in the Chinese Context," in *Social Text*, no. 55 (Summer 1978): 67–82.

39. Naughton, *Growing Out of the Plan*, pp. 26–33.

40. Jean Oi, *Rural China Takes Off: Institutional Foundations of Economic Reform* (Berkeley: University of California Press, 1999).

41. Hu Angang and Wang Shaoguang, *Jiaqiang zhongyang zhengfu zai shichang jingji zhuanxing zhong de zhudao zuoyong* (Strengthening the central government's leading role in the transition to a market economy) (Shenyang: Liaoning renmin chubanshe, 1993).

42. Joseph Fewsmith, "Jiang Zemin Takes Command," *Current History*, 97, no. 620 (September 1998): 250–256.

43. Linz and Stepan, *Problems of Democratic Transition and Consolidation*, pp. 16–33.

44. Jean Oi, "Fiscal Reforms and the Economic Foundations of Local State Corporatism in China," *World Politics*, 45, no. 1 (1992): 99–126; and Oi, *Rural China Takes Off*.

45. He Qinglian, "Dangdai Zhongguo de ziben yuanshi jilei" (Primitive capital accumulation in contemporary China), *Ershiyi shiji* (April 1996): 150–157.

46. Ibid.; and He Qinglian, *Xiandaihua de xianjing* (The pitfalls of modernization) (Beijing: Jinri chubanshe, 1998), pp. 106–116.

47. Chen Jian, *Liushi de Zhongguo* (Draining away China) (Beijing: Zhongguo chengshi chubanshe, 1998), p. 1.

48. Yan Wen, "Chengzhen jumin shouru chaju zheng kuoda" (The increasing gap in income of urban residents), *Gaige neican*, no. 10 (May 20, 1997): 14–16.

49. Fei Yuanxiu, "Dangqian woguo de geren shouru fenpei wenti" (The question of individual income distribution in contemporary China), *Dangdai sichao*, no. 3 (June 20, 1996): 42–47.

50. He, "Dangdai Zhongguo de ziben yuanshi jilei," p. 153. See also Li Qiang, "Zhongguo jumin shouru chaju wenti baogao" (Report on income differences among Chinese citizens), in Li Peilin, ed., *Zhongguo xin shiqi jieceng baogao* (Report on strata in China's new period) (Shenyang: Liaoning renmin chubanshe, 1995), pp. 334–349.

51. Wu, "Guanyu guoyou qiye gaige yu fazhan de jige wenti."

52. Ibid.

53. Manion, "Corruption and Corruption Control."

54. Jiang Zemin, "Political Report," Beijing Central Television, September 12, 1997, trans. FBIS, *Daily Report*, no. FBIS-Chi-97–255.

55. Jonathan Unger and Anita Chan, "Corporatism in China: A Developmental State in an East Asian Context," in Barrett L. McCormick and Jonathan Unger, eds., *China After Socialism: In the Footsteps of Eastern Europe or East Asia*? (Armonk, NY: M.E. Sharpe, 1996), pp. 95–129; Christopher Earle Nevitt, "Private Business Associations in China: Evidence of Civil Society or Local State Power?" *The China Journal*, 36 (July 1996): 26–45; and David Wank, "Bureaucratic Patronage and Private Business: Changing Networks of Power in Urban China," in Andrew G. Walder, *The Waning of the Communist State: Economic Origins of Political Decline in China and Hungary* (Berkeley: University of California Press, 1995), pp. 153–183.

56. *The China Quarterly*, no. 141 (March 1995), special issue on China's Legal Reforms.

57. See, for instance, Roger V. Des Forges, Luo Ning, and Wu Yen-bo, eds., *Chinese Democracy and the Crisis of 1989: Chinese and American Reflections* (Albany: State University of New York Press, 1993).

58. Yossi Shain and Juan Linz, *Between States: Interim Governments and Democratic Transitions* (New York: Cambridge University Press, 1995).

59. Tang Tsou, "Political Change and Reform: The Middle Course," in *The Cultural Revolution and Post-Mao Reforms* (Chicago: University of Chicago Press, 1986), p. 241.

60. Wang Shaoguang, "Gonggong caizheng yu minzhu zhengzhi" (Public finance and democratic politics), *Zhanlue yu guanli*, no. 2 (April 1996): 32–36.

4

The Impact of Reform on Elite Politics

The changes that have swept Chinese society over the past two decades have stirred hopes for the future just as continued repression has conjured visions of renewed despotism and fears of a more aggressive China. There is no question about the breadth or profundity of the social change that has occurred in China, but there is a great deal of uncertainty and debate about its meaning for the present and future of China. Specialists who follow China closely remain deeply divided over whether China, as it begins the post-Deng era, is emerging as the latest instance of the East Asian developmental state, imploding like other socialist states, on the verge of democratic transition, or rising as a threat to East Asia and the United States.[1] People differ in their assessments of China, at least in part, because they make different assumptions about the impact of broad economic, social, and intellectual changes on the political system. That impact will indeed be critical, for politics, particularly elite politics, will be central to China's transition.[2] As Andrew Walder recently put it, the "ultimate question" about the sustainability of China's economic growth is whether China can maintain social stability and the coherence of its political institutions, "or whether they will become so weakened that growth will stall amidst corruption and political strife."[3] One simply cannot assume either that the political system will remain stagnant in the face of the vast social changes that have taken place or that benevolent political changes will follow as a matter of course.

In thinking about the relationship between social and political change, it is useful to juxtapose two different approaches to state-society relations. One approach emphasizes the relative autonomy of the state.[4] In terms of the "rules of the game" by which elite politics are played, there is every reason to believe that elite politics (at least in China) are relatively autonomous from society, and hence resistant to change. The rules of the game of the political system are not the written constitution or even the formal institutional arrangements at the top of the system but, rather, the assumptions that elite political actors bring with them about the nature of the game that they are playing. Such assumptions are deeply influenced by history ("history matters," as Douglass North reminds us), both in general and in personal terms. If political systems are "path dependent," they are so largely because political actors tend to internalize and replicate the patterns of behavior they have learned in the course of their own careers.[5]

The second approach emphasizes the mutual penetration and interaction between state and society.[6] This approach looks at the expansion of the realm of elite politics in the broad sense, at the various linkages that have developed between state and society, and indeed at the very duality ("amphibiousnes" in the terms of one observer[7]) of various organs of the state. In this perspective, the distinction between state and society is not so sharp or clear cut. Changes in society do have an affect on politics because the various organs of the state are not hermetically sealed off from society and, sooner or later, absorb some of the perspectives and attitudes being adopted by nonstate actors.

As different as these perspectives are, both are useful to our consideration of contemporary People's Republic of China (PRC) politics. The first approach is useful because of the particular *leitmotif* of modern Chinese politics, namely the quest for total dominance, that has characterized elite politics throughout the twentieth century.[8] Over the course of recent decades, political actors, often of quite different ideological persuasions, have nevertheless shared the perception that political power is "monistic, unified, and indivisible." The result of this conception has been that the game of politics has been played as a game to win all.[9] As the Chinese frequently and if rather inelegantly put it, "You die, I live" (*Nisi wohuo*). The influential philosopher Li Zehou and prominent literary critic Liu Zaifu have recently reflected on this tradition, arguing that China "lacks a spirit of compromise" and that "in every political game everyone wants the result of 'I get 100 points and you get zero.'"[10]

This conception of politics, no doubt rooted in the emperor system of traditional China, was greatly strengthened by the end of the dynastic system in 1911, the humiliation suffered at the hands of foreigners, the ravages of internal conflict, the revolutionary ideologies (with their privileged claims to truth) of the Guomindang (GMD) and the Chinese Communist Party (CCP), and the struggle for power between those two political parties.[11] The quest for "national salvation" and revolution (to "solve problems at their root" as CCP cofounder Li Dazhao put it) led to an emphasis on ideological purity and political struggle. As political scientist Tang Tsou has argued, "the basic assumption of CCP politics has been that a group or a coalition of groups can and does decisively defeat a major rival group or coalition, and eliminate it."[12] Assuming that this winner-take-all conception of politics has been a hallmark of CCP politics, the critical question is whether the social, economic, and intellectual changes generated by some two decades of economic reforms are leading to the construction of institutions that can temper, constrain, and perhaps change this conception of politics.

The second approach to state-society relations referred to above (that is, the state in society approach) is thus useful because, even though elite political actors may share certain assumptions about the rules of the game, they must still act within the context of the broader society. It appears that the societal, economic, and intellectual pressures generated by nearly two decades of reforms have begun to challenge the conduct of elite politics, but whether such pressures can result in the growth of new institutions, both formal and informal, that can transform the rules by which politics are conducted or whether those same pressures will touch off a new round of "total conflict," thus reproducing and reinforcing the old rules of the game, is the critical question. As Li Zehou and Liu Zaifu put it, "If this train of thought ['You die, I live'] is not changed, China in the twenty-first century could still replay the extremely violent and painful political game of the twentieth century."[13]

In the short run, it appears that elite political actors have reacted to the rapid economic and social changes affecting Chinese society primarily in accordance with the old rules of the game, thus generating debilitating leadership conflict. This process was apparent in the conflict between "reformers" and "conservatives" that developed as the reforms deepened in the 1980s. These tensions were partly responsible for the political meltdown the CCP experienced in the spring of 1989, suggesting the persistence of dysfunctional patterns of elite politics. Nevertheless, over the longer term, there is reason to believe that these social and economic pressures may yet temper or change the rules of the game. Although it is still too early to say with confidence which way Chinese politics will evolve, it is possible to outline the areas in which the past understanding of politics (as a struggle to win all) has influenced the progress of reform, to recognize where the changes produced by reform have influenced the conduct of politics, and to show how the interaction between these two factors is shaping China's political transition.

Impact of Elite Politics on Reform

Two aspects of elite politics appear to have had a particularly important impact on the development of reform in the late 1970s and early 1980s. The first was the "winner-take-all" assumption. Not only was this assumption apparent in the decision to eliminate the so-called Gang of Four (Jiang Qing, Zhang Chunqiao, Yao Wenyuan, and Wang Hongwen) by arresting them and putting them on trial, but it was also important in the struggle for power between Hua Guofeng and Deng Xiaoping. This struggle, which unfolded in stages between 1977 and 1981, ended with the complete elimination of Hua Guofeng and his supporters from the political scene. These struggles, it should be noted, were not simply over power, but also over policy. Thus, the Gang of Four, Hua Guofeng, and Deng Xiaoping all articulated different ideological rationales that justified their quest for power and the policy goals that they pursued. These were struggles between competing political "lines."[14]

In this power cum policy conflict between Hua Guofeng and Deng Xiaoping, Deng and his supporters articulated a different political line *prior* to Hua's ouster. Hua was Mao's designated successor, and his removal and the inauguration of reform had to be legitimated both in ideological and policy terms. Thus, Deng Xiaoping and his followers explored significantly different approaches to ideology, agricultural and industrial policy, and opening to the outside world. Of these, the most important was ideology, for without putting his own reform efforts on a substantially different ideological basis, Deng and his reforms would have been vulnerable to political challenge.[15] The discussion on "practice as the sole criterion of truth" that began in the spring of 1978 and Deng's emphasis on "seeking truth from facts" were critical in Deng's defeat of Hua at the watershed Third Plenum in December 1978.[16] Ironically, although the reforms themselves aimed at a diminution of the role of ideology in Chinese society, that change itself had to be justified through ideology.

Deng did not win his struggle with Hua simply because he offered a more persuasive political vision. On the contrary, Deng's seniority in the Party, his high-level administrative experience, the high opinion in which he was held by Mao Zedong (despite Mao's purging him twice), Zhou Enlai, and other Party veterans, and, most important of all, his standing in the military, were critical factors in Deng emerging as the supreme leader (the political "core").[17] It is, however, precisely the existence of these elements of substantive power that underscores the importance of articulating a different "line" in this political struggle. Deng did not replace Hua as a result of back room political maneuvers; he championed a different ideological vision publicly before defeating Hua and his followers at the Third Plenum.

If Chinese politics had operated with different assumptions about the rules of the game—if, for instance, Chinese politics had been more institutionalized at the time, and if there had been more of a tradition of political compromise—Deng might have been brought into a coalition leadership with Hua. The result of that type of politics might have been a much more incremental process of change; Deng's reform ideas might have been significantly diluted or compromised. In other words, there is every reason to believe that the implicit rules of the game of elite politics in China played a substantial role in pushing the reforms forward by forcing Deng Xiaoping and his followers (as outsiders and challengers) to articulate a substantially different vision of ideology and policy than that of Hua and his followers (the incumbents).

This is not to suggest that Deng and his supporters did not have significantly different ideas about the direction the country should take in wake of Mao's death. Deng represented a major constituency of veteran cadres within the Party who were victims of the Cultural Revolution. Many of them had long harbored doubts about Mao Zedong's subordination of practical policy to ideological purity. Deng himself had raised his pragmatic slogan "Yellow cat, black cat, whichever catches mice is a good cat" in 1962, as peasants in local areas began adopting forms of individual household contracting following the disaster of the Great Leap Forward.[18] In rejecting such practical approaches to governance in pursuit of revolutionary romanticism, Mao had ultimately undermined his own ideological vision and reconfirmed the pragmatic convictions of Deng and other veteran cadres. Nevertheless, the implicit rules of political conflict placed a premium on Deng's, and his followers,' defining their differences with Hua Guofeng more sharply so as to legitimate the ouster of Hua and the refutation of the policy line he represented. This political process gave the early reforms a momentum they might not otherwise have had.

A second implicit understanding of politics that clearly had an important impact on the inauguration, and the subsequent evolution of reform, was the role of informal, personal relations.[19] Personal relations have always existed uneasily alongside formal institutions and Party norms in CCP politics. Whereas Party discipline demands that personal relationships be based on Party discipline and that personal feelings not deviate from abstract Party principles, informal relations and personal networks have always been an important part of political practice. Moreover, because reform was proceeding in a political atmosphere that was uncertain, uninstitutionalized, and highly contested, it was necessary to rely on the use of personal networks to solidify the new leadership and to oversee the implementation of reform.

Thus, as Deng fought to return to power and then to secure support for his reforms, he turned naturally to those he trusted. These associates included Hu Yaobang as head of the Organization Department and deputy head of the Central Party School, Wan Li in Anhui province, and Zhao Ziyang in Sichuan province. This role of informal politics has continued to be important throughout the reform period.[20] When Hu Yaobang, then general secretary of the Party, was trying to consolidate his power following the Twelfth Party Congress of 1982 and to prepare the country for another round of reform, he, too, placed many of his trusted protégés in important central and provincial leadership positions. Many of these people were drawn from the Communist Youth League (CYL), which Hu had headed for many years. Whereas Deng was able to get away with building such personal networks, Hu was later tagged with engaging in "factionalism," one of the charges that led to his downfall. In the current period, Party head Jiang Zemin seems to be following the same pattern, promoting people whom he has known from his tenure as CCP secretary of Shanghai and elsewhere.

This use of informal politics sometimes involved the creation of "factions" (the clearest case may be Deng Xiaoping's use of people from the Second Field Army, which he had co-led during the Civil War, to secure his control of the military) or the use of trusted followers (as in Deng Xiaoping's use of such people as Wan Li and Zhao Ziyang), but sometimes it meant putting together people who seem to have little relationship either with the leader or with each other but whom the leader thought could do the job and be trusted (Hu Yaobang's use of Wu Jiang and Ruan Ming, two of Hu's followers at the Central Party School, appears to fit in this category). Thus, although one of the objects of reform has been to promote the regularization of personnel administration (discussed below), the inauguration and development of reform have also involved, perhaps necessarily, the politics of personalism.

Reform as a Challenge to the Rules of the Game

If implicit understandings of the conduct of elite politics had an important impact on the unfolding of reform, it is also true that the inauguration of reform challenged the conduct of politics in a variety of ways, both direct and indirect. The essence of the Leninist approach to politics, as Kenneth Jowitt has argued, lies in the fusion of charismatic authority and impersonal organization.[21] The result is an organization, the Party, that is organized around impersonal norms ("comradeship" rather than "friendship," in the terms of Ezra Vogel's well-known article)[22] but which exercises a type of charismatic authority vis-à-vis society. Rather than regularizing its relations with society and conducting itself in accordance with law (as in legal-rational authority), the Party governs society through campaigns and considers itself to be above law. Many Chinese observers, looking at the development of the CCP, have expressed this same thought by saying that the Party has not made the transition from a revolutionary party to a ruling party.[23] This transition is a major focus of reform, and a major reason why reform encounters problems in Leninist systems is precisely because the requisites of being a "ruling" party (adhering to legal-rational norms and regularizing relations with society) clash with the charismatic impersonalism of Leninist systems.

The Third Plenum of the Eleventh Central Committee, which inaugurated reform in December 1978, opened a major breach with the preceding history of the CCP by announcing that "the period of large-scale class struggle" had come to a close.[24] Despite the important qualification that class struggle continued to exist and could, under certain circumstances, expand in scale (a sentence that has provided a basis for various efforts to hamper the development of the reforms), it was nevertheless clear that the Party was renouncing the ideological justification for its repeated campaigns and seeking to regularize its relationship with society. However elusive a regularized relationship with society would prove to be, it was nevertheless clear that a major turning point had been passed and the Maoist order was over. There could be no turning back.

A second benchmark in this turn away from Leninist charismatic impersonalism was the discussion on practice as the sole criterion of truth that took place from May to December 1978. Whereas Mao's invocation of the criterion of practice during the revolution had marked his well-known effort to define an ideology that would work in China (what is often referred to as the Sinification of Marxism), Deng's evocation of the same principle in 1978 marked a retreat from ideology. Deng was saying, in effect, that the Party did not have the answers and that it would have to allow a variety of experiments and see which ones worked. The CCP, like most other revolutionary movements, had based its claim to power on solipsistic knowledge. Deng's invocation of the criterion of practice marked the end of the Party's privileged claim to truth.

The end of the Party's privileged claim to truth was apparent in Hu Qiaomu's July 1978 report to the State Council. Hu, Mao Zedong's former secretary and the Party's leading ideological authority, stated that economic laws are "objective" and that violating them, as the Party had in the Great Leap Forward and the Cultural Revolution, could lead to a "national crisis."[25] The Party obviously needed to discover those objective economic laws and learn to obey them. Such an admission clearly suggested that the Party had no privileged claim on truth and that professional economists might be better equipped than Party ideologues to discover objective economic laws. It soon became apparent that Hu's observations about objective economic laws was being extended to every other field of endeavor as practitioners inevitably claimed that objective laws governed their fields as well. Such efforts were, and are, the subject of intense conflict as the Party has resisted giving up control over various fields. Nevertheless, practitioners from the hard sciences through the social sciences and humanities have persisted in stressing the objective laws in their fields, trying to squeeze Party bureaucrats out.[26]

A third benchmark was the 1982 Party Constitution, which declared that "all political parties" must "take the Constitution as the basic norm of conduct."[27] Although this commitment to operate within the framework of the law has been upheld inconsistently at best, it nevertheless marked a conscious break with Mao's declaration that he was "a monk holding an umbrella," unrestrained by law or heaven.[28] The recognition, even in principle, that there were laws and principles that even the Party had to obey implied the end of solipsistic knowledge as a legitimating principle. It also laid the basis for later efforts to separate the Party from the government, an effort that has gone forward only with great conflict and tension precisely because the principle inherent in bureaucratic rationality conflicts with the privileged claim on truth on which the Party originally based its legitimacy.

Such changes suggest the degree to which the inauguration of reform undermined the Party's claim to authority, diminished the role of ideology, and altered the Party's relationship to society. In giving up its privileged claim to truth, the Party turned naturally to economic performance to bolster its claim to rule. Performance legitimacy—the ability to deliver the goods—replaced the utopian ideological vision that Mao had used to control and mobilize society. Ideology could no longer be the fulcrum for political action. The "Four Cardinal Principles" (the socialist road, Marxism-Leninism-Mao Zedong Thought, the People's democratic dictatorship, and the leadership of the CCP) could only mark a boundary (albeit an ambiguous and shifting one) beyond which speech and action were not to go. Boundaries do not elicit belief and mobilize actions.

The changing nature of the Party's authority and of the role of ideology had ramifications both for the organization of the Party and for the relations between the Party and state on the one hand and society on the other. Ideology was abandoned as a mobilizing device, reducing the center's ability to ensure ideological compliance within the Party, before administrative rationality could provide an alternative mechanism of control. Existing in an uncertain realm between an ideological system that no longer provided guidance or commanded respect and a bureaucratic order that remained undeveloped, individual units (*danwei*) began to assert themselves. Those with a stake in the old system pressed for its preservation, while other units explored the limits of reform. Over time, counterelites—those who held privileged Party and bureaucratic positions but whose views were different from those of the Party leadership—were able to use the very structure that had been established to control society, the *danwei* system, to resist ideological conformity and to propose far-reaching changes in orthodox understandings of Marxism-Leninism, thus further undermining the state's ideological legitimacy.[29]

The same turn from mobilization to administration that undermined compliance within the Party was reflected in the state's pulling back from society (without, it should be noted, giving up its residual right to reintroduce its power whenever and wherever it chose). The "zone of indifference" that emerged around individual activity had the salutary effect of restoring normal family life to China's citizens, allowing them unprecedented (in PRC history) control over their leisure time (which was increased dramatically by the reduction of political demands).[30] Inevitably, some citizens turned their attention to political activities, making demands on the political system and pressing for greater participation in the political process.

These tendencies were strongly reinforced by a reform strategy that effectively circumvented the state apparatus to devolve greater decision-making authority to local levels. In part because of uncertainty or opposition to reforms and in part because the central state itself was quite weak in the aftermath of the Cultural Revolution, reformers adopted a strategy known as *fangquan rangli* (devolving authority and granting benefits), in which the center provided incentives for local areas to undertake reforms. These were enabling reforms that allowed localities the latitude to pursue policies that had been prohibited in the previous history of the PRC. Supported by a revised tax system that allowed localities to garner benefits by developing their economies, the reforms, particularly in the rural areas, took off.[31] This approach to reform allowed China to avoid the titanic institutional struggles that paralyzed reform in the Soviet Union, but it did bring into being a sector of the economy, that of the township and village enterprises, that eventually eroded the profits of state-owned enterprises, constrained the financial position of the central state itself, and gave new vigor to local society.[32]

Reform also challenged the conduct of politics in more direct ways. The common demand of veteran cadres returning to power was that Party norms be "restored." Party norms, it should be noted, stand in an ambivalent relationship with the "rules of the game" of the political system, particularly the assumption that political conflict ultimately results in either total victory or total defeat. After all, Mao had clearly established his dominance at least by the mid-1940s, but concentration of power in Mao's hands did not, at least immediately, mean that there were no norms in the Party. On the contrary, the CCP was at its most effective when Mao's dominance was complemented (*not* balanced) by the coexistence of such norms as democratic centralism and "curing the illness to save the patient" (that is, the practice of limiting the cost of deviance by allowing the offending person to be restored to good political standing after self-criticism and a period of contrition). As Mao's tolerance for the expression of differing views declined—Mao's denunciation of Peng Dehuai at the Lushan Plenum of 1959 for the latter's criticisms of the Great Leap Forward marked the critical turning point— inner-Party norms were destroyed and the vetting of different views within the Party was effectively curtailed for the next twenty years. The destruction of inner-Party norms was widely believed by veteran Party cadres to have been one of the root causes of the Cultural Revolution, so they were determined to restore important Party norms in the aftermath of the Cultural Revolution.

The effort to restore Party norms was reflected in the establishment of the Central Discipline Inspection Commission in January 1979, in the adoption of the "Guiding Principles for Political Life Within the Party" at the Fifth Plenary Session of the Eleventh Central Committee in February1980, and the adoption of new Party and state constitutions (which emphasized that the Party must operate within the scope of the law).[33] This effort to reassert the prerogatives of the Party as an institution was an understandable organizational response to the destruction the Party suffered at Mao's hands during the Cultural Revolution, and it resembles similar efforts in the Soviet Union following Stalin's death.

In important ways, however, this effort to restore Party norms went beyond a restoration of the status quo ante. Indeed, the Party's 1982 decision to abolish the post of Party chairman reflected a sensitivity to widespread feelings that too much power had been concentrated in the hands of one person, and Deng's diminution of the personality cult was his acknowledgment of such feelings. But "collective leadership," as the restored norms demanded, conflicted with traditions of personal dominance, and one finds Chen Yun frequently voicing concerns about the need for collective leadership as Deng consolidated his own authority.

Of greater import than the tension inherent in such efforts to "restore" Party norms was the effort to implement new norms. One such norm concerned retirement. Over the decade from 1978 to 1988, the Party gradually ended (with a few notable exceptions) the system of lifelong tenure and implemented an effective retirement system. By the end of the decade, it appears that most cadres had come to accept the system and agreed to step down from power on time.[34] The institution of the retirement system was an important step in turning the Party from a revolutionary party based on "charismatic impersonalism" into a bureaucratic party, now more authoritarian than revolutionary.

The implementation of the retirement system coincided with efforts to promote younger and better-educated cadres. Hong Yung Lee, who has exhaustively studied the transformation of China's cadre structure, states that by the time of the Thirteenth Party Congress in 1987 the "process of elite transformation was nearly completed" and that "almost all leading positions, from the highest level to the basic level, were filled by the bureaucratic technocrats."[35] This transformation has profound implications for China's political future. As Hong Yung Lee notes, in Western Europe the creation of an efficient state bureaucracy was "the first step toward reducing the patrimonial power of the monarchy."[36]

Further evidence that China's cadre system is becoming more bureaucratic (in the Weberian sense) comes from Yasheng Huang. Contrary to the conventional wisdom, Huang argues that institutional changes made in the 1980s have improved the Party center's ability to manage personnel and monitor their behavior. He argues that "Chinese central authorities have retained a firm grip over the vital aspects of personnel allocations: selection, promotion, and removal."[37] In other words, China's bureaucracy is behaving more like a bureaucracy.[38]

Finally, one should note the simple but, given CCP history, extraordinary fact that Party meetings throughout the post-Mao period have been convened regularly. Given the Party's poor record of holding Party meetings in accordance with constitutional provisions in the years before reform, it is impressive that Party congresses have been held every five years since the Eleventh Congress in 1977, and that plenums have been held at least yearly—and frequently more often—despite the evident conflicts within the Party over the years, including the trauma of Tiananmen. It seems that no matter how serious the disputes may be within the Party, there is now an expectation that issues will be dealt with through some combination of compromise, avoidance (that is, delaying the more controversial issues), and authoritative decision. Purging of leaders is still apparently an acceptable tactic in inner-Party struggle, but delaying a Party conclave is not. The regular convening of Party meetings suggests that there is a process of institutionalization at work that constrains Party conflict, at least to a certain extent.

The first decade of reform reflected the contradictory tendencies of the period. The traditions of personal dominance and the struggle to win all coexisted with restored norms and new norms, while at the same time the role of the political system vis-à-vis society was changing dramatically. A brief overview of reform in the 1980s reveals these contradictions, as well as the continuing importance of the game to win all.

Politics in the Era of Reform

The period of reform, as one would expect, has witnessed an intermingling and interaction between, on the one hand, the continuing legacies of previous understandings of the conduct of politics—understandings derived from China's traditional political culture, its revolutionary history, and the practice of politics at the highest levels of the Party—and, on the other hand, the reassertion of old norms with new content, the emergence of new norms, and the rapidly changing environment in which politics take place. Indeed, it is this interaction that shaped the conflict between "conservatives" and "reformers" within the Party on the one hand and between state and society on the other.

Broadly speaking, political conflict in the 1980s revolved around different understandings of the meaning of "reform." There were those, generally identified as "conservatives," who saw no *fundamental* problem with the CPC's traditional political structure and practice. Headed by such leaders as economic specialist Chen Yun and ideologues Hu Qiaomu and Deng Liqun, conservatives generally attributed the problems of the past to the various political movements launched by Mao Zedong. Once the extreme "leftism" identified with Mao's latter years and with his campaign-style politics was eliminated, they believed, *scientific* socialism could finally come into being. This understanding of reform was strongly supportive of the "restoration" of such Party norms as democratic centralism and collective leadership and of the emergence of some new norms such as retirement. After all, it was Chen Yun who first expressed concern about the problem of an aging cadre force and the need to rejuvenate the ranks.[39] Nevertheless, conservatives thought that reforms should not challenge the central tenets of the Party-state system: the planned economy should be primary, Marxist-Leninist ideology should be actively propagated, and Party building should stress the promotion of "loyal" Marxist-Leninists.[40]

In contrast, reformers, led by Deng Xiaoping, Hu Yaobang, and Zhao Ziyang, believed (or came to believe) that there were fundamental problems with the Party-state system. Generally speaking, they saw "leftist" interferences not as exogenous to the system, as conservatives did, but as responses to the inherent contradictions of the system. Thus, for reformers, it was not sufficient to eliminate "leftism"; it was necessary to eliminate the causes of leftism. In the opinion of many reformers, the excesses of the Mao years were rooted in the ideological system. It was not enough, in their opinion, to curtail political movements; "leftism" would be a recurrent danger if Marxism-Leninism were not fundamentally reinterpreted in ways that were compatible with economic reform, political democratization (however understood), and intellectual freedom. Such views were pressed strongly at the Theory Conference of early 1979, provoking the first of several reactions against "deviating" from the tenets of Marxism-Leninism.[41]

The difference between conservative and reformist approaches was reflected in an early debate over the question of whether the cycles of centralization and decentralization that had been experienced repeatedly in PRC history were caused by "leftism" or were inherent in the planning system itself. Conservatives argued that there was nothing fundamentally wrong with the planned economy as it had been conceived in the early history of the PRC. The problem, in their opinion, was that the various political movements launched by Mao had interfered with the proper functioning of the planning system. Consequently, they argued that it was necessary to restore and revitalize such state organs as the State Planning Commission and to make their operation more scientific. Markets should be allowed, but they should exist around the fringes of the planned economy and not interfere in its operation. In contrast, reformers saw the planning system itself generating such cycles, forcing policy makers to either loosen up the centralized vertical controls (*tiao*) that stifled the economy or to overcome the chaos produced by decentralized horizontal coordination (*kuai*). Reformers argued that the planning system needed to be reformed by incorporating the market mechanism *within* it, and thus they called for "integrating the planned and market *economies*," not just "integrating the planned economy with market *regulation*," which was what conservatives called for.[42]

The question that must be addressed is why such differences of understanding and approach hardened over time, leading to a polarization of opinion within the Party, to increasingly harsh campaigns, to the purge of Hu Yaobang in 1987, and finally to the inner-Party crisis of spring 1989. My contention is that despite the development of norms and the increasing institutionalization (bureaucratization) of the Party organization, political conflict was still conditioned by the perception that the rules of the game revolved around the struggle to win all or lose all. This is not to say that there was not compromise throughout the first decade of reform, but that such compromise was tactical in nature, premised on the belief that sooner or later there would be a final "game" in which one side would win and the other would lose. In other words, compromises were made to gain temporary advantage (or, conversely, to minimize political damage); they were efforts to position oneself for the final game that would have to be played sooner or later. This understanding of the political game allows us to understand many aspects of the development of reform in the 1980s that are otherwise not comprehensible.

First, it allows us to understand the political importance of such debates as that between "integrating the planned and market *economies*" and "integrating the planned economy with market *regulation*," referred to above. Such expressions were not, contrary to appearances, arcane exercises in Marxist-Leninist jargon without real consequences. On the contrary, such phrases were metaphors that encapsulated very different perceptions of the goals of reform. Political battles were fought over such terminology, harsh criticisms launched, self-criticisms made, and victories and losses recorded in the changing vocabulary of official Party documents. One cannot understand the political importance of the 1984 "Decision on the Reform of the Economic Structure," which reflected the growing differences between Chen Yun and Deng Xiaoping, without reference to such debates.[43]

Second, reference to the political game being played allows us to better understand the importance of the structural conflict that underlay the evolution of reform. Generally speaking, conservatives in the 1980s controlled the bureaucracies most closely identified with CCP rule, particularly the State Planning Commission (which was central to the management of the planned economy) and the Propaganda Department (which had as its mission the defending of Marxism-Leninism). Because conservatives dominated such bureaucracies (something to which Deng Xiaoping clearly acquiesced), reformers had to depend largely on extra-bureaucratic networks. Thus, Hu Yaobang had his "intellectual network" (as well as his Communist Youth League network), and Zhao cultivated his economic "think tanks."[44] These networks tended to rely less on formal structures than on informal politics. They tended to be composed of a relatively small number of individuals, often concentrated in research organs. In general, their bureaucratic heft did not match their intellectual firepower. This pattern of authority helps explain why reform followed the course of enabling reforms that allowed latitude to pursue policies heretofore prohibited.

This structural dimension helps us to understand the pattern of conflict that emerged in the 1980s. It is hardly surprising that conservatives in such orthodox bureaucracies as the Propaganda Department would fight ferociously against independent-minded intellectuals, supported directly or indirectly by the general secretary, who developed ideological approaches that undermined the authority of the Propaganda Department. It is also not surprising that bureaucrats in the State Planning Commission and other conservative ministries objected to reform measures that made their jobs more difficult (by creating enterprises that competed with state-owned enterprises, eroding the profits of the latter and creating financial difficulties for the state) but diminished their relevance.

As reform proceeded, the problems associated with partial reform inevitably occurred. On the one hand, such economic problems as excessive investment, redundant industrial construction, local blockades, and inflation developed; on the other hand, reformers blamed the failure to open up the ideological atmosphere and reform the political system for creating obstacles for deepening reform. As such conflicts developed, there was a natural tendency for reformers to push for more reform, even as conservatives sought solutions in reinforcing the old system, both by tightening administrative controls over the economy and by tightening the Party's control over ideology. In some instances, reformers would push ahead even when doing so was not advisable, because slowing down or turning back implied an admission of error, opening them to political attack. A classic instance of this logic occurred in early 1987 when Zhao Ziyang, facing conservative demands to tighten the money supply and strengthen central controls, decided to push ahead and urged a loosening of the money supply, thus fueling inflationary pressures.[45] It seems that Zhao feared that yielding to conservative criticisms on monetary policy would force him to cede greater influence over policy-making to his conservative critics. It was a calculus that appeared to be directly rooted in an intuitive understanding of the rules of the game, and Zhao, it seems, had a better understanding of the politics of the time than of the economics.

In this and similar instances, the dispute was not simply over policy but over power. The political game being played was not one of compromise but one of gradually forcing one's opponent into an indefensible position where he could be destroyed politically. Zhao Ziyang often used the metaphor of a boat being rowed upstream to describe reform—if it is not going forward then it will be pushed backward. This was at least as true politically as it was economically. Had Chinese politics been one of compromise, Zhao might have been more willing to yield on such policy issues without fear of losing power. The logic of "struggle politics" (*douzheng zhengzhi*) was quite apparent in such instances, and as such conflicts accumulated, compromise became even less possible. Zhao's ouster, like that of Hu Yaobang, was the result of the implicit understanding of the game of politics.

This overview of elite conflict in the reform period suggests a basic continuity in the conduct of elite politics as the view of politics as a struggle to win all or lose all colored the actions of both conservatives and reformers. Conservatives articulated a systematic critique of reform, faulting it on economic, organizational, and ideological grounds. As reform deepened, inevitably encountering the problems of partial reforms, conservatives tended to blame the reform project itself, not just the methods by which it was conducted. For their part, reformers pushed ahead, paying scant heed to the concerns of conservatives. The tensions between the two wings of the Party exploded into full view as social pressures built up in the late 1980s. Following the purge of Zhao Ziyang in June 1989, the conservative critique of reform became quite explicit and was clearly directed at Zhao's patron, Deng Xiaoping.[46] Soon Deng was being treated, as Mao once claimed he had been, as a dead ancestor at his own funeral. At one point, Deng is reported to have fumed, "*People's Daily [Renmin ribao]* wants to comprehensively criticize Deng Xiaoping."[47] Indeed, it was not until the Fourteenth Party Congress in September 1992—following Deng's dramatic trip to Shenzhen in January that year and a series of sharp political maneuvers that spring—that one could say that Deng had regained the inner-Party influence that he had enjoyed in the years prior to Tiananmen.[48]

Nevertheless, despite the evident continuity in the rules of the game of elite politics, it is possible to discern an impact of reform on the conduct of elite politics. Although the struggle to win all was evident in the tensions between conservatives and reformers and was particularly conspicuous in the battle between Zhao Ziyang and Premier Li Peng, it did not, in the final analysis, extend to the highest level of the regime. Whatever the tensions between Deng Xiaoping and Chen Yun, and there is no doubt that they were great, even the political crisis of June 1989 did not trigger a decisive showdown between them. This was in part because Chen (as he had in the Maoist period) respected Party norms regarding inner-Party policy differences (in particular, by not challenging Deng openly once Deng had made a decision) and in part because Chen had no ambition to be the number one leader. However, it also appears that the turn away from mobilizing ideology, the reaffirmation of inner-Party norms, and the focus on economic modernization that defined the reform period all contributed to a sense of limitation on elite struggle. As serious as the political crisis of the spring of 1989 was, the scope of conflict was constrained. At the highest level, Deng and Chen continued to coexist with each other (even as they continued to disagree on policy), while at lower levels the anticipated purge was not as wide or deep as anticipated.

The eighteen years since the inauguration of reform have entailed both the destruction (or at least redefinition) of institutions as well as the construction of new institutions. Thus, on the one hand, the span of control of the State Planning Commission and the Propaganda Department were curtailed, while, on the other hand, new or reinstated norms, such as those governing retirement and the regular convening of Party meetings, have developed. Although institutions such as the Organization Department of the Party appear to have been strengthened by attention to bureaucratic rules, many other institutions have become deeply involved in the economy, leading to corruption and the societalization of the state bureaucracy, that is, an intermingling of state and society in ways that seriously corrode the autonomy of the state.

The coexistence of these conflicting trends along with traditional assumptions about the rules of the game of politics have given the reform process an uneven, "jerky" quality. The critical question is whether the changed environment in which elite politics are being played out, the growth of institutionalization, and the elevation of a younger, better-educated, and more technocratic leadership, might finally be affecting the conduct of politics within the highest echelons of the Party. The answer is not yet clear, but perhaps we can gain some insight from the literature on democratic transitions.

Chinese Politics in Transition?

The era of reform, as the above suggests, has been one of intense contradiction, in which the emergence of new norms and institutions stand in tension with longstanding norms and traditions, in which indications of state building coexist with signs of disintegration. The CCP is attempting to carry out the dual task of transforming itself from a Leninist party to an authoritarian party while presiding over the transition from a planned economy to a market economy. This is an enormously difficult economic-cum-political task—as the fates of other communist states suggest.[49] Yet the costs of not making it, given the implicit rules of the political game and the revolutionary *leitmotif* of twentieth century Chinese politics, would be very high indeed.[50] Ding Xueliang, a very knowledgeable observer of contemporary China, has gone so far as to say that "if an anarchic situation appears in China, the violence that Chinese will inflict on each other will far exceed the barbarism inflicted by the Japanese army when it invaded in the 1930s."[51]

Devining the future of China is risky indeed, but some guidance can be garnered from the literature on political transitions. One conclusion of this literature is that the window of opportunity for successful democratic transitions is relatively small and the likelihood of a hardline crackdown, reversal, or unconsolidated democracy is correspondingly great.[52] In general, the combination of a strong state and strong civil society appears to provide the best backdrop for successful transition.[53] Another important factor is the development of a legal framework and the creation of a "usable bureaucracy," both of which might be said to be components of a strong state.[54] Thus, in thinking about China's development, we should direct our attention to such issues as state capacity and social organization.

Viewed from this perspective, China's transition appears delicate at best. As indicated above, there are indeed indications that China's state capacity is increasing. The institution of a retirement system, the recruitment of younger and better-educated cadres, and the procedures that China's central state has put in place to monitor local cadres all point to a rationalization of China's bureaucratic structure. Moreover, as Hong Yung Lee points out, the increasing complexity of tasks undertaken by the bureaucracy and the recruitment of cadres with diverse backgrounds are likely to increase the importance of bureaucratic technocrats and diminish the role of personalistic ties.[55]

At the same time, however, there are trends that suggest that China's state remains far from the Weberian ideal and may in fact be weakening. In his study of the ideological realm, X.L. Ding chronicled the emergence of counterelites as the center's control over ideology declined.[56]

Similarly, Minxin Pei has argued that "reform in the communist systems tends to generate and accelerate the decay of the key institutions it seeks to preserve and revitalize."[57] Andrew G. Walder has argued that this decay occurs because economic reform, in and of itself, changes the structure of incentives and makes lower-level agents of the state less willing to comply with the demands of administrative superiors. Indeed, he argues that reform sets off "a chain of consequences" that often leads "to the point where Communist party rule can no longer be sustained."[58]

The economic decentralization carried out in the course of reform clearly diminished the economic capacity of the central government. The share of total state revenues as a percentage of GDP fell from 35 percent in 1978 to 11.3 percent in 1995, before increasing slightly to 11.4 percent in 1996.[59] Despite the sharp increase in central revenues as a percentage of all government revenues (from 22 percent in 1993 to 55.7 percent in 1994), the central government's bargaining power vis-à-vis the localities appears not to have increased for the simple reason that central tax collection efforts appear to remain in the hands of local tax collectors. As Barry Naughton concludes, "Local governments are much more effective at getting their taxes actually collected than is the central government."[60] While such figures may well exaggerate the degree of decentralization, as Yasheng Huang has argued, they nonetheless indicate the difficulty China has in constructing a "usable bureaucracy."[61]

The biggest change, however, is not the shift of fiscal and financial resources from the central state to local governments but rather from the state as a whole (both central and local) to individuals and, to a lesser extent, enterprises. As Cheng Xiaonong, former head of the Comprehensive Section of the Economic Reform Institute, points out, the percentage of financial resources in the hands of the state, enterprises, and individuals, respectively, changed from 31.6, 18.9, and 49.5 in 1978 to 14.5, 23.8, and 61.7 in 1990. In other words, at the same time financial resources controlled by the state (both central and local) declined by 17.1 percentage points, that held by individuals increased by 12.2 percentage points. This trend, Cheng argues, reflects the state's continual effort to "buy" political compliance by increasing the incomes of individuals. This need to secure political obedience reflects a "softening" of the state that may undermine effective governance in the future.[62]

Potentially the most important weakness in China's central state capacity comes from the entrepreneurial activities of the central government itself. Thus, government bureaucracies facing budgetary shortfalls have gone into business on their own, sometimes spinning off profitable subsidiaries. Even the State Planning Commission, the bulwark of the old planned economy, set up six major investment corporations that have the dual functions of guiding investment in their respective sectors and making profits for themselves. This bureaucratic entrepreneurship has extended to state organs not normally associated with economic activities, such as the Ministry of State Security and the People's Liberation Army (PLA). At least in the case of the military, such entrepreneurship has aroused deep concerns about professionalism and the ability of the PLA to conduct itself as a modern military.[63] What such bureaucratic involvement in the economy suggests is an institutionalization of corruption, making even the organs of the central state itself less responsive to central direction. It also suggests the emergence of a combination of "soft state" and entrenched interests feeding off each other to the detriment of both effective bureaucracy and civil society.[64] It should be noted that Jiang Zemin ordered the PLA out of business in 1998, but whether that will actually happen, and whether it is a harbinger of professionalization of the state bureaucracy as a whole, remains to be seen.[65]

Societies that make successful transitions also tend to have well developed, if not necessarily consistently implemented, legal structures. The existence of legal frameworks can provide a limited but important form of leverage as dissidents try to hold regimes to the standards that they themselves have articulated. Legal frameworks can also provide guidance through the uncertain passage that frequently exists between the fall of the existing order and the establishment of a new order.[66] Although China has made much progress in the articulation of a legal structure since 1978, its starting point was obviously low and it has a very long way to go. Traditional China, with its understanding of law as a means to control society rather than to regulate public-private relations, provided little basis for the growth of modern legal norms and an autonomous legal profession.[67] In the PRC, prior to the Cultural Revolution, Soviet-based views of law as bureaucratic regularity vied with Maoist antibureaucratic and antilegal prescriptions. The overwhelming victory of the latter in the Cultural Revolution meant there was little legal framework as China emerged from that national nightmare. After nearly two decades during which officials have tried to create a legal system almost *de novo*, Chinese law is still largely conceived of as "a tool of state administration."[68] Efforts to elevate law and the legal profession have run aground on deeply embedded concepts of state-society relations (which are generally hostile to the emergence of autonomous entities that might voice the interests of particular groups)[69] as well as such factors as local protectionism and the view that courts are simply one, coequal part of China's bureaucratic apparatus.[70] Even Minxin Pei, who takes an optimistic view of legal progress in China, admits that the enforcement record for the more than six hundred laws passed by the National People's Congress (NPC) remains "abysmal."[71]

Turning to the society side of the equation, it is apparent that Chinese society today remains very much dominated by the state, so much so that many specialists are reluctant to apply the term "civil society" to China at all. Although the state has retreated from society over the course of reform, creating a "zone of indifference" around individuals, the social space created by the retreat of the state appears to have been filled primarily by organic organizations of one sort or another—such as clan organizations or corporatist interest associations—rather than by independent associations of private individuals. Indeed, the process of economic decentralization that has taken place over the course of reform has had the effect of strengthening the role of local government to the detriment of autonomous society.[72] The most important finding of several studies of state-society relations from different perspectives is the degree to which state and society are intermingled and the degree to which nominally autonomous groups are in fact dominated by the state.[73] The *danwei* (unit) system remains the central organizing feature of Chinese life, and the *danwei* continue to conflate state and society as those concepts are generally understood in the West.[74] Although it can be argued that there has been substantial progress from the period of the Cultural Revolution in which there was no civil society, however defined, to the present, the overwhelming fact is that in today's China social groups pursue their interests through the state rather than against the state.

In short, the corrosion of the state bureaucracy (even as there is bureaucratization) has been mirrored by a very weak civil society. What has *not* happened is the emergence of a strong, bureaucratic (in the Weberian sense) state dealing with autonomous social organizations along the lines of what Peter Evans has called "embedded autonomy."[75] States may not have to maintain the hands-off approach to society favored by neoliberal interpretations, but blurring the lines between state and society to the degree China has done it is not conducive either to the formation of a strong state or a strong society, and hence, is very likely not conducive to democratic transition, at least in the short run.

Another factor that must be taken into account in thinking about the state-society relationship in contemporary China is the obvious decline of Marxism-Leninism as a legitimating device. As ideology was transformed from the central fulcrum of the system to a mere border that was not to be transgressed (the "four cardinal principles"), there was an inevitable tendency for reform to diverge increasingly from the previously accepted understanding of "socialism." The cynicism and raw use of power that filled the vacuum left by the collapse of the Maoist ideological system not only left the liberal intelligentsia alienated from the regime but also caused conservative thinkers to rebel against the lack of a moral vision. As the popular neoconservative writer Wang Shan wrote in his 1994 best-selling *Looking at China Through a Third Eye*:[76]

> As soon as the traditional ideology of Mao Zedong's idealism begins to be broken, then the government's defense line must retreat step by step. Local governments continuously extend their hands asking for new "policies" and the central government has no choice but to compromise in the face of [the need to] solve new problems. China's economic structural reform was really created this way. Now, when we look back, what is left of Mao's inheritance? How much is left? Deng Xiaoping has repeatedly said that the four cardinal principles must be upheld, but how much has really been upheld?

On the one hand, the decline of ideology and legitimacy deprive the Leninist party of a powerful tool for eliciting compliance, while, on the other hand, the resulting failure of social norms makes it difficult to create new, impersonal norms around which bureaucratic structures could be built.[77]

One reaction to the decline in Marxism-Leninism and the resulting ideological confusion has been the rise of nationalism.[78] Nationalism has always been a concomitant part of the Communist revolution (and the Nationalist revolution before that); indeed it helped fuel those revolutions and bolstered their ideological claims. What is different about the current wave of nationalistic feeling is that it is occurring outside of, indeed as a replacement for, the formal ideological structure of Marxism–Leninism–Mao Zedong Thought. National power is being touted as a value, in and of itself.

It should be noted that rising nationalism in China is occurring not just because the influence of Marxism–Leninism–Mao Zedong Thought is declining, but also because of China's growing confidence in its own economic strength and development, and because of the widespread perception that the twenty-first century will indeed be a Pacific century.[79]

To the extent that the growth of nationalism reflects a decline in ideology and secularization of politics, it should be welcomed as a normal and even a healthy part of state building (what Michel Oksenberg calls "confident nationalism"),[80] one that can give the state a raison d'être and bolster central government authority vis-à-vis lower levels. If, however, nationalism becomes a significant component of elite political competition, it will work against emerging pressures to "normalize" politics. Moreover, nationalism easily turns toward organic metaphors, which are deeply embedded in Chinese culture in any case, and, as Adam Przeworski notes, "organicist views of the nation are incompatible with the toleration of partial interests" necessary for democratic transitions.[81]

What is perhaps most troubling about the current rise of nationalist feeling is the resonance this has with the recent past. As Li Zehou has argued, one of the preeminent themes of twentieth-century China has been the struggle between "enlightenment" and "salvation." The New Culture and May Fourth movements were efforts to reconceive and, in some ways, to remake Chinese culture in order to better respond to the pressures (and opportunities) represented by "Mr. Science" and "Mr. Democracy." This effort to remake Chinese culture "drop by drop," as Hu Shi put it, was interrupted then, and has been interrupted many times since, by the demand to save the nation.[82] The demand for salvation, fueled by the rise of modern nationalism, repeatedly overwhelmed the enlightenment project and became an integral part of China's revolutionary history and "struggle" politics. If nationalism again becomes central to elite politics, it will indeed be difficult for Chinese politics to say "farewell to revolution."

Conclusion

The reform process has witnessed conflicting political impulses, as the concept of politics as a struggle to win all has coexisted with the reassertion of old Party norms and the generation of new, more legal and rational norms. With the death of Deng, there will be an opportunity to assess which of these conflicting principles will dominate.

Although both state implosion and hardline authoritarian rule are possible, there is reason to be cautiously optimistic about the future.

The winner-take-all tradition of Chinese politics suggests that sooner or later one person will emerge as the preeminent leader. Jiang Zemin seems to have taken a significant step in this direction at the Fifteenth Party Congress in September 1997. But whether Jiang or someone else ultimately emerges triumphant from this process, that person will not have the personal authority of Deng Xiaoping, much less of Mao Zedong. Thus, once the post-Deng power struggle is settled, the leader is likely to have to rely more heavily on formal authority and institution building, both to secure his authority vis-à-vis his Politburo colleagues and to increase the state's authority vis-à-vis society. Thus, these processes will entail a process of legitimization, institutionalization, and legalization.

Indeed, the very effort to secure authority in the post-Deng era seems to require a greater reliance on the invocation of norms and the building of institutions. For instance, Jiang Zemin's successful ouster of Beijing mayor Chen Xitong in 1995, which certainly involved a struggle for power, was nevertheless conducted in terms of a campaign against corruption. In other words, even if the purpose of such campaigns as that against corruption is not primarily to strengthen Party norms, they could in fact have that effect. Similarly, the retirement of NPC head Qiao Shi at the Fifteenth Party Congress, which similarly contained elements of power struggle, was accomplished by invoking Party rules governing retirement, a norm that Jiang himself may have to adhere to at the next Party congress.

Furthermore, the decentralization of the economy, which many see as undermining the authority of the central state and leading to institutional decay, could lead to the institutionalization of more stable authority relations. The readjustment of the incentive structure associated with the devolution of authority and development of the local economy has been absolutely vital to economic reform, marketization of the economy, and the development of the economy. However, even strong advocates of decentralization and democracy admit that the process has gone too far and threatens the stability of the state.[83] Two measures appear essential to stabilizing central-local relations, and both would contribute to institutionalization and state-building. The first is to turn the blueprint of a national tax system, adopted in the 1994 tax reform, into a reality. This would build a level playing field both in terms of types of ownership and geographical location and thereby regularize central-local relations. Second, the center should grant the localities greater participation in decision making in exchange for their yielding greater fiscal control to Beijing.[84]

Some years ago, Tang Tsou wrote, "The Chinese have never succeeded in finding a set of arrangements in which the formal institutions are firmly established and in which informal relationships are supplements to the formal institutions, enabling the latter to function effectively and efficiently instead of overwhelming them and turning them into empty symbols."[85] They have not done so largely because of the nature of elite politics as a game to win all. Today, generational succession, the promotion of younger and better-educated cadres, the institution of a more professional bureaucracy, the decentralization of the economy, and other factors make it conceivable that China will finally address this historical problem. Whether or not China can do so depends largely on whether the political conflict can be contained in ways that do not trigger the logic of the game to win all. If so, the processes of institutionalization outlined above will have a better chance to take hold, eventually facilitating a transition toward a more benevolent understanding of politics. The present, however, is a moment of great fluidity. As Li Zehou and Liu Zaifu put it in their recent work, "China is again in the midst of a new social transformation. China at the present time is full of hope and also full of danger: It could really rise up from here, but it could also decline (*chen lun*)."[86]

Notes

1. For contrasting views of China's future, see William H. Overholt, *The Rise of China* (New York: W.W. Norton, 1993); James Miles, *The Legacy of Tiananmen: China in Disarray* (Ann Arbor: University of Michigan Press, 1996); Chalmers Johnson, "Nationalism and the Market: China as a Superpower," Japan Research Institute, Working Paper No. 22 (July 1996); Edward Friedman, *National Identity and Democratic Prospects in Socialist China* (Armonk, NY: M.E. Sharpe, 1995); and Richard Baum, "China After Deng: Ten Scenarios in Search of Reality," *The China Quarterly*, no. 145 (March 1996): 153–175.

2. The literature on democratic transition takes the role of political elites in negotiating or resisting political change as one of the central variables. See Guillermo O'Donnell and Philippe C. Schmitter, *Transitions from Authoritarian Rule: Tentative Conclusions About Uncertain Democracies* (Baltimore: Johns Hopkins University Press, 1986).

3. Andrew Walder, "China's Transitional Economy: Interpreting Its Significance," *The China Quarterly*, no. 144 (December 1995): 976.

4. See Peter B. Evans, Dietrich Rueschemeyer, and Theda Skocpol, eds., *Bringing the State Back In* (New York: Cambridge University Press, 1985).

5. Douglass C. North, *Institutions, Institutional Change and Economic Performance* (New York: Cambridge University Press, 1990).

6. Joel S. Migdal, Atul Kohli, and Vivienne Shue, eds., *State Power and Social Forces: Domination and Transformation in the Third World* (New York: Cambridge University Press, 1994).

7. X.L. Ding, *The Decline of Communism in China: The Legitimacy Crisis, 1977–1989* (New York: Cambridge University Press, 1994).

8. This proposition is controversial within the China field, but this is not the place to defend or develop it. Suffice it to say, this approach does not conflict with a bureaucratic politics approach, which deals with a different level of the political system. For an elegant restatement and elaboration of the winner-take-all approach, see Tang Tsou, "Chinese Politics at the Top: Factionalism or Informal Politics? Balance-of-Power Politics or a Game to Win All?" *The China Journal*, no. 34 (July 1995): 95–156.

9. Zou Dang [Tsou Tang], *Ershi shiji Zhongguo zhengzhi: cong hongguan lishi yu weiguan xingdong jiaodu kan* (Twentieth-century Chinese politics: Viewed from the perspective of macro history and micro actions) (Hong Kong: Oxford University Press, 1994).

10. Li Zehou and Liu Zaifu, *Gaobie geming: Huiwang ershi shiji Zhongguo* (Farewell to revolution: Looking back on twentieth-century China) (Hong Kong: Cosmos Books, 1995), p. 85.

11. Zhengyuan Fu, *Autocratic Tradition and Chinese Politics* (New York: Cambridge University Press, 1993).

12. Tang Tsou, "Prolegomenon to the Study of Informal Groups in CCP Politics," in Tang Tsou, *The Cultural Revolution and Post-Mao Reforms: A Historical Perspective* (Chicago: University of Chicago Press, 1986), p. 99.

13. Li and Liu, *Gaobie geming*, p. 23.

14. It has often been noted that much of Hua Guofeng's economic program was formulated by Deng Xiaoping before Deng was purged again in 1976. Politics might have taken a different course if the oil wells that were being madly dug in 1978–1979 in support of Hua's economic program had struck oil, but they did not. In the event, Deng adopted a different approach to economic development. On China's efforts to strike oil, see Barry Naughton, *Growing Out of the Plan: Chinese Economic Reform, 1978–1993* (New York: Cambridge University Press, 1995), pp. 70–74.

15. The obvious comparison is to the early 1960s, when efforts to sum up the lessons of the Great Leap Forward could not be articulated in ideological terms for the obvious reason that Mao was still alive.

16. Much has been written, in both Chinese and English, about the discussion on "practice as the sole criterion of truth." See Michael Schoenhals, "The 1978 Truth Criterion Controversy," *The China Quarterly*, no. 126 (June 1991): 243–268; Merle Goldman, *Sowing the Seeds of Democracy: Political Reform in the Deng Xiaoping Era* (Cambridge: Harvard University Press, 1994), pp. 35–41; Wu Jiang, *Shinian zhi lu* (The course of ten years) (Hong Kong: Mirror Post Cultural Enterprises, 1995); Ruan Ming, *Deng Xiaoping diguo* (The Deng Xiaoping empire) (Taipei: Shibao chuban gongsi, 1991); and Su Shaozhi, *Shinian fengyu: Wengehou de dalu lilunjie* (Ten years of storms: The mainland's theoretical circles after the Cultural Revolution) (Taipei: Shibao wenhua, 1996), pp. 38–78.

17. Frederick C. Teiwes, "The Paradoxical Post-Mao Transition: From Obeying the Leader to 'Normal Politics,'" *The China Journal*, no. 34 (July 1995): 55–94.

18. Deng Xiaoping, "Zenyang huifu nongye shengchan" (How can agricultural production be restored?), in *Deng Xiaoping wenxuan (1938–1965)* (The selected works of Deng Xiaoping, 1938–1965) (Beijing: Renmin chuban she, 1983), p. 305. Over the years, the colors of the cats changed to black and white as Deng's aphorism was repeated, but, as Deng might say, the color of the cats does not matter!

19. Lowell Dittmer, "Chinese Informal Politics," *The China Journal*, no. 34 (July 1995). It should be noted that the "game to win all" and informal politics do not exist on the same level. After all, the term "game to win all" suggests the nature of the game being played, whereas informal politics are merely one of the ways of playing the game. Other means of playing the game could be elaborated.

20. Joseph Fewsmith, "Formal Structures, Informal Politics, and Political Change in China," chapter 2 in this volume.

21. Kenneth Jowitt, *The Leninist Response to National Dependency* (Berkeley: Institute of International Studies, University of California, 1978).

22. Ezra Vogel, "From Friendship to Comradeship: The Change in Personal Relations in Communist China," *The China Quarterly*, no. 21 (January–March 1965): 46–60.

23. See, for instance, Pang Song and Han Gang, "Dang he guojia lingdao tizhi de lishi kaocha yu gaige zhanwang" (A historical investigation of the Party and the state's leadership structure and the outlook for reform), *Zhongguo shehui kexue* (Chinese social science), no. 6 (November 10, 1987).

24. Communiqué of the Third Plenary Session of the Eleventh Central Committee. There were a number of important decisions that followed from this change. Intellectuals, who had been denounced as the "stinking ninth category" during the Cultural Revolution, were now regarded as "part of the working class." In addition, the Party made formal decisions to remove the label from landlords and to reaffirm the role of the "national bourgeoisie."

25. Hu Qiaomu, "Act in Accordance with Economic Laws, Step Up the Four Modernizations," Xinhua, October 5, 1978, trans. in Foreign Broadcast Information Service, *Daily Report–China* (FBIS-Chi), October 11, 1978, pp. E1–E22.

26. On such conflict in the sciences, see H. Lyman Miller, *Science and Dissent in Post-Mao China: The Politics of Knowledge* (Seattle: University of Washington Press, 1996).

27. "Xuyan" (Preamble) to *Zhonghua renmin gongheguo xianfa* (Constitution of the People's Republic of China), in Zhonggong zhongyang wenxian yanjiushi, ed., *Shi'erda yilai zhongyao wenxian xuanbian* (Important documents since the Twelfth Party Congress), 3 vols. (Beijing: Renmin chubanshe, 1986), vol. 1, p. 219.

28. Tang Tsou, "Reflections on the Formation and Foundations of the Communist Party-State," in Tsou, *The Cultural Revolution and Post-Mao Reforms*, pp. 313–315.

29. See especially Ding, *The Decline of Communism in China*.

30. Shaoguang Wang, "The Politics of Private Time: Changing Leisure Patterns in Urban China," in Deborah Davis et al., eds., *Urban Spaces in Contemporary China*, (New York: Cambridge University Press, 1995), pp. 149–172.

31. Jean Oi, *Rural China Takes Off: Institutional Foundations of Economic Reform* (Berkeley: University of California Press, 1999).

32. Barry Naughton, "Implications of the State Monopoly over Industry and Its Relaxation," *Modern China*, 18, no. 1 (1992): 14–41.

33. "Guanyu dangnei zhengzhi shenghuo de ruogan zhunze" (Guiding Principles for Political Life Within the Party), in Zhonggong zhongyang wenxian yanjiushi, ed., *Shiyijie sanzhong quanhui yilai zhongyao wenxian xuandu* (Selected readings in important documents since the Third Plenary Session of the Eleventh Central Committee), 2 vols. (Beijing: Renmin chubanshe, 1987), vol. 1, pp. 163–184.

34. Melanie Manion, *Retirement of Revolutionaries in China: Public Policies, Social Norms, Private Interests* (Princeton: Princeton University Press, 1993).

35. Hong Yung Lee, "China's New Bureaucracy?" in Arthur Lewis Rosenbaum, ed., *State and Society in China: The Consequences of Reform* (Boulder, CO: Westview, 1992), p. 56. See also Hong Yung Lee, *From Revolutionary Cadres to Party Technocrats in Socialist China* (Berkeley and Los Angeles: University of California Press, 1991).

36. Lee, "China's New Bureaucracy?" p. 67.

37. Yasheng Huang, *Inflation and Investment Controls in China: The Political Economy of Central-Local Relations During the Reform Era* (New York: Cambridge University Press, 1996), p. 119.

38. This is so in its control functions, but there is an important difference between the Chinese bureaucracy and Weber's model of the legal-rational authority. As Huang notes, the central authorities are able to keep such tight control over the bureaucracy because of the stress on "ideological conformity." See ibid.

39. Chen Yun, "Tiba peiyang zhongqingnian ganbu shi dangwu zhi ji" (Promoting and cultivating young and middle-aged cadres is an urgent task at present), in *Chen Yun wenxuan (1956–1985)* (Selected works of Chen Yun, 1956–1985), (Beijing: Renmin chubanshe, 1995), pp. 262–266.

40. For a classic statement of the conservative position on Party building, see Chen Yeping, "Have Both Political Integrity and Ability, Stress Political Ability: On Criteria for Selecting Cadres," *Renmin ribao*, September 1, 1991, trans. FBIS-Chi, September 6, 1991, pp. 26–31.

41. On the Theory Conference of January–April 1979, see Goldman, *Sowing the Seeds of Democracy*, pp. 47–61. See also Su, *Shinian fengyu*, pp. 80–117.

42. Joseph Fewsmith, *Dilemmas of Reform in China: Political Conflict and Economic Debate* (Armonk, NY: M.E. Sharpe, 1994), esp. chapter 3.

43. "Decision of the Central Committee of the Communist Party of China on Reform of the Economic Structure," Xinhua, October 20, 1984, trans. FBIS-Chi, October 22, 1984, pp. K1–K19. This decision endorsed the creation of a "socialist planned *commodity* economy." The term "commodity economy" had implications that had long been resisted by conservatives within the Party. Obviously, the decision of the Fourteenth Party Congress in 1992 to endorse the creation of a "socialist *market* economy" went an important step further. See Jiang Zemin, "Political Work Report," Beijing Central Television, trans. FBIS-Chi (Supplement), October 13, 1992, pp. 23–43.

44. Joseph Fewsmith, "Institutions, Informal Politics, and Political Transition in China," *Asian Survey*, 36, no. 3 (March 1996): 230–245.

45. Fewsmith, *Dilemmas of Reform in China*, pp. 219–220.

46. Joseph Fewsmith, "Reaction, Resurgence, and Succession: Chinese Politics since Tiananmen," in Roderick MacFarquhar, ed., *The Politics of China*, 2d ed. (New York: Cambridge University Press, 1997), chapter 6.

THE IMPACT OF REFORM ON ELITE POLITICS 115

47. Gao Xin and He Pin, *Zhu Rongji zhuan* (Biography of Zhu Rongji) (Taipei: Xinxin wen wenhua shiye gufen youxian gongsi, 1993), pp. 231–232.

48. Fewsmith, "Reaction, Resurgence, and Succession," pp. 505–508.

49. Minxin Pei has stressed the difficulty of this dual transition. See his *From Reform to Revolution: The Demise of Communism in China and the Soviet Union* (Cambridge, MA: Harvard University Press, 1994).

50. This is the major thesis of Li and Liu, *Gaobie geming*.

51. Ding Xueliang, *Gongchanzhuyihou yu Zhongguo* (Post-communism and China) (Hong Kong: Oxford University Press, 1994), p. xxii.

52. Adam Przeworski, *Democracy and the Market: Political and Economic Reforms in Eastern Europe and Latin America* (New York: Cambridge University Press, 1991), p. 37; and Axel Hadenius, ed., *Democracy's Victory and Crisis* (Cambridge: Cambridge University Press, 1997).

53. Adam Przeworski et al., *Sustainable Democracy* (Cambridge: Cambridge University Press, 1995).

54. Yossi Shain and Juan J. Linz, eds., *Between States: Interim Governments and Democratic Transitions* (Cambridge: Cambridge University Press, 1995), pp. 10–14; and Juan J. Linz and Alfred Stepan, *Problems of Democratic Transition and Consolidation: Southern Europe, South America, and Post-Communist Europe* (Baltimore: Johns Hopkins University Press, 1996), pp. 16–37.

55. Lee, *From Revolutionary Cadres to Party Technocrats in Socialist China*, pp. 402–408.

56. Ding, *The Decline of Communism in China*.

57. Pei, *From Reform to Revolution*, p. 49.

58. Andrew G. Walder, "The Quiet Revolution from Within: Economic Reform as a Source of Political Decline," in Andrew G. Walder, ed., *The Waning of the Communist State: Economic Origins of Political Decline in China and Hungary* (Berkeley: University of California Press, 1995), p. 3.

59. Barry Naughton, "Fiscal and Banking Reform: The 1994 Fiscal Reform Revisited," in Maurice Brosseau, Kuan Hsin-chi, and Y.Y. Kueh, eds., *China Review, 1997* (Hong Kong: Chinese University Press, 1997), p. 255.

60. Ibid., p. 262.

61. Yasheng Huang, *Inflation and Investment Controls in China*. For a contrary interpretation, see Jia Hao and Lin Zhimin, eds., *Changing Central-Local Relations in China: Reform and State Capacity* (Boulder, CO: Westview, 1994).

62. Cheng Xiaonong, "Weichi wending yu shenhua gaige: Zhongguo mianlin de jueze" (Maintaining stability and deepening reform: A choice confronting China), *Dangdai Zhongguo yanjiu*, nos. 1 and 2 (1995), trans. in "Wang Shaoguang Proposal (II)," *Chinese Economic Studies*, 28, no. 4 (July–August 1995): 88–125.

63. On the military, see Richard H. Yang and Gerald Segal, eds., *Chinese Economic Reform: The Impact on Security* (London: Routledge, 1996).

64. Xiao Gongqin, "Dongya quanwei zhengzhi yu xiandaihua" (Asian authoritarian politics and modernization), in *Zhanlue yu guanli*, no. 2 (1994).

65. On Jiang ordering the PLA out of business, see Xinhua, July 13, 1998, in FBIS, *Daily Report*-Chi-98–195 (July 14, 1998); and Zhu Rongji, "Unify Thinking, Strengthen Leadership, and Swifty and Sternly Crack Down on the Criminal Activities of Smuggling," *Qiushi* (Seeking truth), no. 17 (September 1, 1998), trans. FBIS, *Daily Report*-Chi-98–245 (September 2, 1998).

66. Shain and Linz, *Between States*.

67. William P. Alford, *To Steal a Book Is an Elegant Offense: Intellectual Property Law in Chinese Civilization* (Stanford: Stanford University Press, 1995), pp. 9–29.

68. William P. Alford, "Seek Truth from Facts—Especially When They Are Unpleasant: America's Understanding of China's Efforts at Law Reform," *Pacific Basin Law Journal*, 8 (1990): 182. Quoted in Stanley Lubman, "Introduction: The Future of Chinese Law," *The China Quarterly*, no. 141 (March 1995): 2.

69. William P. Alford, "Tasseled Loafers for Barefoot Lawyers: Transformation and Tension in the World of Chinese Legal Workers," *The China Quarterly*, no. 141 (March 1995): 35.

70. Donald C. Clarke, "The Execution of Civil Judgments in China," *The China Quarterly*, no. 141 (March 1995): 65–81.

71. Minxin Pei, "'Creeping Democratization in China," in Larry Diamond, Marc F. Plattner, Yun-Han Chu, and Hung-mao Tien, eds., *Consolidating the Third Wave Democracies: Regional Challenges* (Baltimore: Johns Hopkins University Press, 1997), p. 216.

72. Jean Oi, "Fiscal Reform and the Economic Foundations of Local State Corporatism in China," *World Politics*, 45, no. 1 (1992): 99–126.

73. Jonathan Unger and Anita Chan, "Corporatism in China: A Developmental State in an East Asian Context," in Barrett L. McCormick and Jonathan Unger, eds., *China After Socialism: In the Footsteps of Eastern Europe or East Asia?* (Armonk, NY: M.E. Sharpe, 1996); David Wank, "Private Business, Bureaucracy, and Political Alliances in a Chinese City," *The Australian Journal of Chinese Affairs*, no. 33 (January 1995); and Christopher Earle Nevitt, "Private Business Associations in China: Evidence of Civil Society or Local State Power?" *The China Journal*, no. 36 (July 1996): 26–45.

74. Ding, *The Decline of Communism in China*.

75. Peter Evans, *Embedded Autonomy: States and Industrial Transformation* (Princeton: Princeton University Press, 1995).

76. Luo yi ning ge er [Wang Shan], *Disanzhi yanjing kan Zhongguo* (Looking at China through a third eye) (Taiyuan: Shanxi renmin chubanshe, 1994), p. 61.

77. Lowell Dittmer and Lu Xiaobo have found an *increase* in personal politics even as *danwei* become more formal in their structure. See their "Personal Politics in the Chinese *Danwei* Under Reform," *Asian Survey*, 36, no. 3 (March 1996): 246–267.

78. Nationalist sentiment was given expression in the much-talked-about book *Zhongguo keyi shuo bu* (China can say no) (Beijing: Zhonghua gongshang lianhe chubanshe, 1996), which spawned a cottage industry of similar books. It should be noted that the Chinese government subsequently banned such books, and offered criticism of nationalism in Xiao Pang, ed., *Zhongguo ruhe miandui xifang* (How China should face the West) (Hong Kong: Mingjing chubanshe, 1997), among other works. For a more historical treatment of nationalism, see Jonathan Unger, ed., *Chinese Nationalism* (Armonk, NY: M.E. Sharpe, 1996).

79. See, for instance, Song Taiqing, *Zhongguo shidai: Ershiyi shiji da yuyan* (The age of China: A great prediction for the twenty-first century) (Guiyang: Guizhou renmin chubanshe, 1993).

80. Michel Oksenberg, "China's Confident Nationalism," *Foreign Affairs*, 65, no. 3 (1987): 501–523.

81. Pzreworski et al., *Sustainable Democracy*, p. 61.

82. Li Zehou, *Zhongguo jindai sixiangshi lun* (History of modern Chinese thought) (Beijing: Renmin chubanshe, 1979); and Li Zehou, *Zhongguo xiandai sixiangshi lun* (History of contemporary Chinese thought) (Beijing: Dongfang chubanshe, 1987). See also Vera Schwarcz, *The Chinese Enlightenment: Intellectuals and the Legacy of the May Fourth Movement of 1919* (Berkeley: University of California Press, 1986).

83. Wu Guoguang and Zheng Yongnian, *Lun zhongyang—difang guanxi* (On central-local relations) (Hong Kong: Oxford University Press, 1995).

84. This proposition follows the lines of the suggestions for readjusting central-local relations contained in Wang Shaoguang and Hu Angang, *Jiaqiang zhongyang zhengfu zai shichang jingji zhuanxing zhong de zhudao zuoyong* (Strengthen the guiding functions of the central government during the transition to a market economy) (manuscript, 1993), trans. as "Wang Shaoguang Proposal," *Chinese Economic Studies*, 28, nos. 3 and 4 (May–June and July–August 1995).

85. Tang Tsou, "Political Change and Reform: The Middle Course," in Tsou, *The Cultural Revolution and Post-Mao Reforms*, p. 241.

86. Li and Liu, *Gaobie geming*, p. 4.

5

Historical Echoes and Chinese Politics: Can China Leave the Twentieth Century Behind?

As the twentieth century wound to a close in China, it was impossible not to be struck by two somewhat contradictory thoughts. One was that the echoes of the major political anniversaries of the past century still ring with unnerving clarity, suggesting just how relevant the issues of the late nineteenth and early twentieth centuries remain at the turn of another century. The other was that the social and political changes that are underfoot are so dramatic and fundamental that China really is moving into a new era in which those echoes will finally grow fainter. Which of these impressions becomes the more accurate depends much on the course of the next ten years or so.

There seem to be nothing but anniversaries these days in China. The hundredth anniversary of the "Hundred Day" reform—the radical reform movement championed by Kang Youwei and Liang Qichao in the closing days of the Qing dynasty—fell in 1998, and Beijing University, which was founded in the course of that movement and became the symbol of political liberalism in modern China, marked its centenary in a grand but contested ceremony. At the same time, 1998 marked the twentieth anniversary of the Third Plenary Session of the Eleventh Central Committee, at which Deng Xiaoping decisively launched China on the course of reform, thus leading everyone to discuss even more fervently the successes and failures of the past two decades.

The following year, 1999, was perhaps even more portentous. It marked the eightieth anniversary of the May Fourth Movement, the iconoclastic cultural and nationalistic movement that gave birth simultaneously to liberalism and communism. The fiftieth anniversary of the founding of the People's Republic of China was celebrated with elaborate ceremonies and a well-orchestrated military parade on October 1, 1999. Most sensitive of all, 1999 also marked the tenth anniversary of the Tiananmen demonstrations and their suppression, an event that cuts the reform period neatly in half and has generated continuing controversies about the meaning of reform and the course China should follow in the future.

Finally, the year 2000 marks the hundredth anniversary of the Boxer Rebellion, the xenophobic peasant movement whose magic was believed to protect its adherents from bullets. This anniversary has taken on new saliency as demonstrations and armed outbursts pock the countryside, and as the Falun Gong (Buddhist Law Society) movement, which combines traditional *qigong* exercises with a potent spiritual message, has attracted millions of adherents and most famously mobilized ten thousand people to sit in sudden and silent protest outside Zhongnanhai on April 25, 1999, before the government tried to suppress it (not completely successfully) in a virulent and widespread crackdown that started in July.

These anniversaries resonate with the present because they raise issues of continuing importance: China's relationship with the West (politically, economically, and culturally); the simultaneous desire for wealth and power and social fairness; popular political expression and participation; and the relationship of the present to the past, which is to say the value of the revolution. Moreover, the meanings of these anniversaries remain contested; indeed, it is precisely because they are contested that they continue to have such salience. In fact, one way to try to comprehend the state of Chinese society at the turn of the century is to contrast the way these anniversaries echo today with the way they did just a decade ago. Doing so underscores how very different the China of the 1990s is from the China of the 1980s.

A decade ago, prior to Tiananmen, intellectuals almost universally keyed on the upcoming seventieth anniversary of the May Fourth Movement to push the themes of intellectual freedom and democratization further. The West, particularly the United States, was viewed as a model, or at least as a useful embodiment of ideals that could be evoked to propel reform forward. The fortieth anniversary of the founding of the PRC, in contrast, was something few intellectuals were in a mood to celebrate; the phrase from the Confucian *Analects* saying that "at forty one should not have doubts" (*sishi er buhuo*) could not but be cited with irony. Cosmologist Fang Lizhi wrote off the history of the PRC as "forty years of failure";[1] others may have demurred from such an extreme judgment, but not by much.

These concerns and doubts reflected the experience of intellectuals and were broadly shared by other sectors of society. Coming out of the Cultural Revolution, intellectuals were obsessed by a desire to understand where the revolution had gone wrong and by a profound wish to prevent anything resembling the Cultural Revolution from ever happening again. Intellectuals placed the blame squarely on "leftism." The enormous excesses of the Chinese revolution—from the "socialist transformation" of the mid-1950s to the anti-rightist movement of 1957, the Great Leap Forward of 1958–60, and finally the Cultural Revolution of 1966–76—were attributed to a "leftism" that accepted uncritically a (contradictory) mix of Stalinist economic planning and Maoist mobilization, that rejected the importance of rationality and hence of intellectuals, that emphasized the "class nature" of human beings to the detriment of their humanity, and that turned the nation inward, rejecting the importance of learning from the West. These trends were also encompassed by the term "feudalism," a word of opprobrium that had nothing to do with its meaning for the economic and political history of the West or even its traditional meaning of local self-rule in China, but instead connoted everything negative that had been attributed to Chinese traditional society through the long course of China's revolution, including patriarchalism, authoritarianism, bureaucratism, anti-intellectualism, and fanaticism. As China's revolution had increasingly criticized capitalism, trying desperately in the course of the Cultural Revolution to "cut off the tail of capitalism" and to criticize the "bourgeois right," feudalism had flourished. "Leftism" was thus rooted in "feudalism," and the task of intellectuals and reform-minded Party people was to expunge these evils and thus set China on a course toward "modernity."

Given this basic, if somewhat oversimplified, diagnosis of what was wrong with China, it was natural that intellectuals turned to the May Fourth tradition for inspiration and moral sustenance. The May Fourth tradition had always contained contradictory elements: a radical critique of traditional Chinese culture and the demand to learn from the West and to introduce science and democracy were combined with a nationalism that rejected cosmopolitanism in favor of nativism. Chinese Academy of Social Sciences (CASS) Philosophy Institute scholar Li Zehou articulated for his generation of 1980s scholars the need to disentangle the "liberal" elements of the May Fourth tradition, those that emphasized "enlightenment," from those that were caught up in nationalistic efforts to "save the nation." Every time the cultural critique seemed to offer hope of introducing new enlightenment values into Chinese culture, Li argued, it was overwhelmed by nationalism ("national salvation") as China faced one crisis after another.[2] Now, in the 1980s, it was finally time to take up the task of enlightenment and carry it through to fruition.

This enlightenment project dominated intellectual discourse in the 1980s. Whether it was discussions of "alienation" in socialism,[3] efforts to bring an end to lifelong tenure and create a rational civil service,[4] policy proposals to marketize the Chinese economy,[5] translations of Western thinkers,[6] nascent writings about human rights and democracy,[7] or "reconceptualizations" of capitalism and socialism to emphasize their similarities, the task was to expunge "leftism" from Chinese social, economic, and political life. This focus on the dangers of leftism and feudalism assigned a lofty position to the West, particularly the United States. The United States took on an aura of modernity that provided a mirror opposite of the leftism that intellectuals sought to root out. Western culture provided fuel for ongoing critiques of Chinese culture, thus continuing the May Fourth rejection of traditional values, while Western economic and political systems served as foils against which to criticize the planned economy and authoritarian political system of China. If discussions of the United States and other Western countries in the 1980s were superficial, it was because the point was not to understand how those systems actually worked but to provide a fulcrum from which faults in the Chinese system could be criticized. However superficial these discussions may have been, their participants clearly saw themselves as lying within the May Fourth enlightenment tradition and providing a cosmopolitanism that helped support the political relationship being forged with the West as well as with reformers within the Party.

A decade later, the May Fourth legacy appears badly tattered. The liberal tradition of the May Fourth period has been ignored and suppressed many times since 1919, as Li Zehou points out, because revolution or foreign war seemed more pressing. But never in the seven decades since then had intellectuals themselves come to see the May Fourth tradition as outdated or irrelevant to their concerns. That changed in the 1990s, and the turn away from the enlightenment project of the May Fourth Movement marks a major, one is tempted to say fundamental, change in the way many intellectuals view China and its place in the world.

The change in the intellectual atmosphere in China can be dated fairly precisely to the 1992–93 period. It was in 1992 that Deng Xiaoping made his famous journey to the south of China to reinvigorate his reform program.[8] Deng was highly successful not only in changing the political atmosphere but also in setting off a major upsurge in economic activity (bolstered by a loose monetary policy) and, more important, a critical structural shift in the economy as the private sector finally emerged as a major factor in its own right and as foreign investment expanded greatly.[9] These changes, which have generally received high praise in the Western press, have been greeted by greater skepticism in China because they have challenged vested interests, have created new vested interests, and have been accompanied by a host of social problems: rapidly rising intra- and interregional income inequalities, corruption on a scale that would have been unimaginable in 1989 (when students took to the streets to protest corruption), a massive stripping of state-owned assets as officials have taken advantage of their positions to preside over a large-scale de facto privatization, a large increase in the number of migrant workers looking for employment outside their native areas, increases in crime and other social-order problems, and a growing unemployment problem as hard-pressed state-owned factories finally began to move to reduce the size of their labor forces.

In short, in the eyes of many intellectuals, the problematique of China had shifted dramatically from the need to push reform forward by criticizing leftism and feudalism to the need to deal with the effects of reform. For these intellectuals, the left was no longer a problem; it was a spent force that had little, if any, practical effect on China. Marketization was likewise no longer a problem; it had succeeded, perhaps too well. And opening to the outside world, that counterpart to Dengist domestic reforms, had also succeeded. Not only was China opened to the outside world, but it found itself inextricably linked to a new global order that was not necessarily benevolent—as the Asian financial crisis demonstrated forcefully and brutally. Such concerns led many intellectuals to become quite critical of the effects of reform in China and of the global order China was trying to join. This was a wholly different set of concerns from that which had dominated the intellectual agenda in the 1980s.[10]

Ironically, these intellectuals were far more familiar with the West and with the intellectual trends of the West than were those who had dominated intellectual discourse in the 1980s. Many of them had studied extensively in the West before either returning to take up prestigious positions within China or staying in the West in university teaching positions. Indeed, this internationalization of intellectual discourse distinguished the 1990s from the 1980s. In the first decade of reform, Chinese intellectuals generally resided in China and discussed issues with other intellectuals in China; by the 1990s, particularly with the spread of the Internet, the conversation had become truly global, encompassing not only intellectuals in China and those who were studying or working in the West but also non-PRC Chinese intellectuals from Taiwan, Hong Kong, and elsewhere.

What this new, sophisticated, and international group of intellectuals latched onto as they focused on a new set of social problems was a variety of perspectives that are generally referred to as "critical methodologies" in the West: postmodernism, postcolonialism, deconstructionism, critical legal studies, analytic Marxism, world systems theory, and so forth.[11] Such methodologies are highly critical of capitalism and globalization and are determined to "unmask" the various power relations that were said to be hidden behind "hegemonic" rhetoric. Although such critiques are widespread within U.S. and European academe, they have remarkably little impact on public policy, standing as academic critiques of a very dominant capitalist order.[12]

In China, however, their position is quite different and hence highly controversial. First, instead of representing minority critiques of a dominant trend, critical methodologies have arguably become the mainstream of intellectual discourse in China. Second, although advocates of critical methodologies in China argue that they want to transcend such dualities (usually said to be a legacy of Cold War thinking) as East/West, tradition/modernity, and capitalist/socialist, their very focus on these dualities tends to accentuate their importance. For instance, Chinese scholars following in Edward Said's footsteps to unmask the relationship between "Orientalist" rhetoric and the power interests of the United States invariably end up not transcending the East/West duality but emphasizing the need for a nativist response to a Western "hegemonic" discourse.[13]

Third, it is difficult for followers of critical methodologies to escape from nationalist modes of discourse, and indeed many seek to adopt such rhetoric either because they are concerned with the way they see China being absorbed into an international capitalist order in which it has little say or because they share a sense of frustration with (largely) U.S. rhetoric and policies in the post–Cold War era. In this sense, those who promote critical methodologies ironically adopt a nationalistic attitude that is far from the orientation of those using parallel methodologies in the West. Those opposed to critical methodologies criticize, sometimes in extremely harsh terms, those who adopt them for becoming, in their view, spokespersons for the government, while those who adopt critical methodologies state with equal validity that they are highly critical of the government and its policies.[14]

To point to such harsh polemics is to suggest another feature of the 1990s landscape that is different from that of the 1980s or arguably even earlier. Although there have been some notably harsh polemics throughout the twentieth century, intellectuals in China have generally shared a sense that they were one group. This sense was particularly strong in the 1980s, as intellectuals had endured a common fate during the Cultural Revolution and generally shared a desire to move China as far away from that period as possible. By the 1990s, however, the traditional world of Chinese intellectuals had largely vanished. Some had moved into the government and its think tanks as specialists and technocrats, others had retreated into academia to pursue specialized research, and still others had responded to the rapidly growing commercialization of culture by writing popular literature and the like. Indeed, one of the most interesting intellectual debates of the 1990s, and arguably the only one that was truly indigenous, was about the loss of the "humanistic spirit" (renwen jingshen) among intellectuals.[15] It was a debate that reflected the growing marginalization of intellectuals in the face of commercialization. In short, by the end of the 1990s, it was difficult to speak of China's intellectuals as a coherent social stratum or as the "conscience" of Chinese society, their traditional role.

Critical methodologies, as just mentioned, have an affinity with nationalism, even if they are inherently critical of the government and the course of reform as well. Nationalism is hardly new in China; it has in fact been the leitmotif of twentieth-century China. Chinese intellectuals were just as nationalistic in the 1980s as they were in the 1990s, but in the earlier decade their nationalism took a more cosmopolitan approach, seeking a path to wealth and power through learning from the West.[16] As noted above, this learning from the West simultaneously served the purposes of criticizing "leftism" and "feudalism" and promoting reform. As intellectuals have become more critical of reform, they have simultaneously become more critical of the neoclassical economics and political liberalism that have been offered up as models for China's reform. There has been a new desire in the 1990s to forge a uniquely Chinese path to reform, and this desire to explore a "native" approach to reform that conforms with Chinese culture and tradition necessarily entails an emphasis on asserting Chinese identity.

This assertion of Chinese identity, however, has mingled with other feelings of suspicion directed primarily against the United States that are an outcome of the specific atmosphere that has prevailed in U.S.-China relations since Tiananmen. The sea change in public opinion came in the 1992–93 period when President Clinton, trying to bridge the gap between his campaign rhetoric and the realities of international relations, extended China's most-favored-nation status conditionally. This flawed decision, later reversed, was followed by other gaffes that reflected a sensitivity to certain opinion groups in the United States and an insensitivity to opinion in China. Such decisions included the opposition to China's bid to host the summer Olympics in the year 2000 and the forceful inspection of a Chinese ship, the *Yin He*, believed to be transporting chemicals that could be used in the manufacture of chemical weapons to Iran.

One of the most interesting aspects of Chinese intellectuals' response to these and similar incidents is the widespread and deep-seated assumption that the United States was taking such measures in a well-calculated effort to "contain" China. Whereas few officials or scholars in the United States could identify a clear-cut "China policy" in the early Clinton administration, much less one that was implemented consistently, Chinese intellectuals could explain in detail how various measures were all clear expressions of a U.S. "national interest" in keeping China down. This new intellectual focus on "interests" speaks volumes about the intellectual atmosphere in contemporary China. Intellectuals have been twice disillusioned regarding idealism, first by the Cultural Revolution, which turned into a nightmare, and second by the liberalism of the 1980s, which ended in political disaster. Particularly in the atmosphere of commercialism that has prevailed in recent years, any talk of idealism seems out of place. In some ways, the blunt discussions of "national interest" are a refreshing change from the ideological stridency of the past, but they reflect not so much realism as it is conceived by Western students of international relations as out-and-out cynicism. Since ideological pretensions have been unmasked in China, so the logic seems to go, it is inconceivable that a nation such as the United States would not be a careful calculator of its national interests.

This "cynical realism" was deeply reflected in Chinese reactions to the war in Kosovo and especially to the tragic bombing of the Chinese embassy in Belgrade. Even before the bombing, there were elaborate scenarios set out to explain how the NATO action in Kosovo reflected U.S. national interests. These generally focused on the shift in NATO's mission statement to reflect an expanded, "out-of-area" role and explained the conflict in Kosovo as simply a first step in the U.S. plan to dominate the world. Following the bombing incident, the explanations became even more fanciful and far-fetched.[17] Chinese critics were deaf to explanations that suggested that the United States and other nations were in fact concerned with human rights and that the military action with respect to Kosovo largely reflected idealism (whether misguided or not).

Not only has the nature of nationalism changed in China in the course of the 1990s, but its base has also widened substantially. The broadening of nationalist appeals is part and parcel of the decline of "elite" culture and the consequent "flattening out" of public discourse. The widening of intellectual discourse started in the 1980s, but it is the commercialization of culture in the1990s that has reshaped the public arena. The market for Wang Shuo's anti-establishment "hooligan" literature reflected a new populist culture and a new social mood. Wang, who is not college educated, flouted the conventions of Chinese literature and showed no deference to his better-educated colleagues. Another turning point was the popularity of "Yearnings" (Kewang),[18] a soap opera featuring stock characters but written in part by respected writers Zheng Wanlong and Wang Shuo (who were quickly accused of selling out). The show attracted a huge audience and marked a turning point in the commercialization of culture. As Li Xiaoming, the chief scriptwriter, put it, "If you're a television writer, and you know that the majority of your Chinese audience had to save up for years to buy a TV set, then you'd better come to terms with them."[19]

Popular nationalism then emerged on the scene in 1994 with the publication of Wang Shan's book, Looking at China through a Third Eye.[20] This was a highly critical look at the state of Chinese society and the impact of the reforms as well as a bold statement of nationalism. Two years later, the better-known China Can Say No was published and became an instant best-seller.[21] A whole series of similar books soon appeared, cashing in on the market that China Can Say No had pioneered.[22] Indeed, one of the hallmarks of the new era of the 1990s was the way in which official books had to compete more with nonofficial books to influence public opinion. Thus, books such as Heart-to-Heart Talks with the

General Secretary and *China Should Not Be 'Mr. No'* (discussed below) appeared on the market to oppose the upsurge of nationalism.[23] These books were soon followed by others touting the U.S.-China "constructive strategic partnership" as Jiang Zemin and Clinton exchanged summits.

This expansion of the public realm, which was due both to secular changes in Chinese society and to the government's recognition that the sort of heavy-handed ideological campaign it had pursued following Tiananmen was counterproductive, begins to make more explicable the public reaction to the bombing of the Chinese embassy in Belgrade. However, one must also factor in the frustrations that are evident in Chinese society.

Political Implications of Socioeconomic Change

The very different intellectual atmosphere in China, as well as the fractionalization of intellectuals and their very different relationship with the state, is one of the profound changes that have taken place in state-society relations over recent years. Although these changes have their roots in the early years of reform, they have accelerated in recent years as the marketization, internationalization, and diversification of the Chinese economy have accelerated. Whereas through much of the 1980s most social groups gained from reform, as the 1990s progressed, there were increasingly obvious differences between "winners" and "losers." And as more people joined the ranks of the losers, or at least the relative losers, there were widely felt implications for politics. Put simply, the very different socioeconomic environment that has emerged in recent years not only fuels the tensions that erupt in worker and farmer protests but also generates the critical attitude many intellectuals have adopted and undermines Party discipline as well as the confidence that many Party members and social elites have in the future of the Party, which in turn stimulates the corruption, illegal transfer of wealth abroad, and cynicism that are themselves so much a part of the problem that China's political elite faces. Management of this complex and rapidly changing sociopolitical environment presents a formidable political challenge, arguably one greater than that faced by Mao or Deng, and inevitably leads to sharply differing political views within the elite.

The single most important change in Chinese society has been the emergence of a class of nouveaux riches. In the mid-1980s, there was fevered talk in the Chinese press, which turned out to be exaggerated, of the emergence of "ten-thousand-yuan households" (*wanyuanhu*)—almost unimaginable in a period when the average rural resident earned only about 350 yuan per year. A decade or so later, the reality was that there were at least one million households with annual incomes exceeding one million yuan. This was an enormous change with profound social, psychological, and political implications. In many ways, of course, this was a long overdue and healthy change seemingly marking the appearance of a middle class, albeit one that was still quite small in terms of China's population, even if one considered only its urban population. Nevertheless, the new middle class, including the much more prosperous nouveaux riches, drove the new consumerism of the 1990s, changing the nature and role of culture in Chinese society by commercializing it and diversifying it.

In part, this new middle class marked the internationalization of the Chinese economy; by the mid-1990s, there were some hundred thousand joint-venture enterprises employing perhaps eighteen million people, and most of them paid salaries that far exceeded those of state-owned enterprises (SOEs). Enterprise managers who formed joint ventures or jumped into the international economy sometimes made very large incomes indeed. The new middle class also marked an important structural change in the Chinese economy as the "knowledge economy" boomed; new high-tech firms sprouted up everywhere. As knowledge became a commodity, some intellectuals, whose incomes had lagged behind in the 1980s, found that their skills were valuable and began enjoying a comfortable lifestyle. Whereas previously their only choice had been to join a university or government research organ, now intellectuals could hang out their own shingles as consultants. Such people developed a stake in the system, and as they did so radicalism waned. Other intellectuals, it should be noted, did not do as well, and were profoundly discomforted by the fact that income, not intellectual prowess, had become the measure of success.

The seamy side of this story is that those who did the best in this new economy—and some did very well indeed—almost always seemed to have strong political connections. Sometimes they were bureaucrats who had tired of the office routine and jumped into the sea of business but retained their connections to colleagues who could offer all-important approvals or access to scarce resources. Sometimes they were family members of officials still in office. Sometimes they were enterprise heads who used their positions to siphon off large amounts of state-owned

assets to private firms that they controlled directly or indirectly. Often
they were the offspring of high cadres who used their family connections to amass large sums of money. In other words, corruption—massive corruption—was a major part of the story of income redistribution
in the 1990s.

A recent study calls this nouveau riche group the "never-left-out
class" (*bu luokong jieji*) because every time Chinese society has entered a new round of adjustment in which resources are reallocated,
this group has benefited the most. The same study argues that this
group possesses "comprehensive" (*zongtixing*) capital resources, meaning that it is able to mobilize its multidimensional economic and political contacts to monopolize the best opportunities.[24] This is the same
group of people that economic journalist He Qinglian described in
her 1998 best-seller when she argues that through the "marketization
of politics," officials or those with close relations with officials have
directed millions of dollars' worth of assets into private hands, bringing about a form of "primitive socialist accumulation" that rivals anything Marx and Engels observed about "primitive capitalist
accumulation." The result, He argues, has been income inequality sur-
passing that in either Japan or the United States (keeping in mind that
China had a much more equal distribution of income than either of
those countries less than a decade ago), the rise of secret societies, and
mass resentment. China, she argues, seems to be heading not toward
liberal democracy and capitalism but toward a "government and mafia
alliance."[25]

The losers in this process are, at least in a relative sense, urban workers, particularly those in smaller cities and towns, who are thrown out of
work, furloughed (*xiagang*), not paid for months at a time, or simply
made anxious about their prospects. According to official figures, 3.1
percent of the urban workforce—some 5.7 million workers—were registered as unemployed at year-end 1998, and an additional 8.9 million
workers were furloughed,[26] giving a total unemployment rate of about 8
percent. Unofficial estimates suggest an unemployment rate that is considerably higher.[27] To be a worker in a state-owned enterprise used to be
an honored and secure position in society, but today it is relatively less
well paid and much less secure, making many workers resentful. There
is also an economic impact as workers, worried about their futures, hoard
their savings, exerting a deflationary pressure on the economy. Ironically, the "tiger" of savings that economists had long worried would

come leaping out of its cage to drive up inflation now cannot even be lured out!

Rural agricultural workers have also lost out, at least in a relative sense. Rural incomes have not increased as quickly in recent years, and local exactions appear not to have abated despite repeated directives from Beijing. Potentially more destabilizing, there remain some 150 million agricultural workers who are grossly underemployed and should shift out of agriculture. But there is no apparent outlet for their services. In the 1980s and 1990s, over 100 million farmers were able to shift out of agriculture by finding jobs in the township and village enterprises (TVEs) that were springing up. By the late 1990s, however, TVEs were undergoing their own readjustment, and many were encountering the same sort of problems that SOEs had previously faced—debts that had been contracted through political relationships and now could not be paid back.[28]

The large numbers of urban and rural people who have been relative losers over the past decade of reform (in contrast to the 1980s when they did relatively well) provide a base of discontent that fuels a constant stream of protest that threatens social order. In a passage worth quoting at length, the authors of the study referred to above write:

> Along with the proliferation of labor disputes, hired workers in many urban and rural enterprises, in an attempt to vent their dissatisfaction with the system, have taken to all sorts of destructive measures, such as burning down factories, sabotaging machinery, and even personal damage to managerial personnel. Such incidents have already become fairly commonplace in the economically developed areas in Southern China. In addition, there are all sorts of focused social movements and actions, such as demonstrations, presentations of petitions and appeals, and labor strikes. Incidences of such petitions and strikes, in which workers in enterprises in large and medium-sized cities raise slogans demanding that their basic livelihood be protected and assured, have become increasingly numerous. Although such information and news is almost never reported in the newspapers—out of consideration for "social stability"—it is already an "open secret."[29]

It is precisely such discontent that provides a potential basis for large-scale social protest and explains why sects—such as the Falun Gong—frighten the leadership so much.

The existence of widespread, if unorganized, discontent explains the leadership's concern with providing jobs. Generating sufficient numbers of jobs in a country in which the workforce grows by more than eight million a year is never easy. Rapid economic growth is critical for creating the necessary jobs: each additional percentage point of growth accounts for about 1.2 million jobs, so growth rates have been at the top of the government agenda. So far, growth has managed to keep the government ahead of the curve—unemployment is up but not unmanageable, and both urban and rural incomes have continued to increase—but the margin for error is not great. Given widespread resentment of corruption and income inequality, the potential for social unrest is real.

The profound socioeconomic changes of recent years offer both hope and concern. On the one hand, the growing wealth of a significant number of mostly urban residents, even if much of that wealth has been acquired in a less than pristine manner, could pave the way for the emergence of a genuine middle class, something that China has never had in its more than two thousand years of history. Such a development would have profound, and profoundly positive, implications for Chinese culture, society, and politics. At the moment, Chinese society falls well short of such a development, but nevertheless, there is emerging a group of people who have a real stake in the stability of Chinese society, who are outside of (if well connected with) the political system and positioned to make demands on that system, and who may well discover (however belatedly) an interest in law and property rights. Moreover, as Shanghai historian and social critic Xiao Gongqin points out, the diversification that has taken place in Chinese society over recent years means that most problems are localized. Workers and farmers raise demands specific to their own circumstances, and the prospects for societywide social movements are correspondingly reduced.[30] Such optimistic scenarios, however, require a period of continued high-speed economic growth. Unfortunately, the prospects for that are uncertain at best. Should there be a major slowdown in economic growth, to say nothing of a crisis similar to those experienced by many other Asian nations in recent years, the potential for social violence is high.

On the other hand, if this nouveau riche group, as the study cited above suggests, squeezes out an emerging middle class and forms the sort of corrupt relationship with the political elite that has long plagued Latin American politics, then the prospects for social and political stability, not to mention democratization, are much less.

There are many indications that China's top leadership is aware of and intensely concerned about these socioeconomic problems and their political implications. The repeated crackdowns on corruption and the efforts to get the military out of business and to stop (or at least significantly slow) smuggling and the illegal remittances of funds abroad reflect this awareness.[31] So too do the ideological campaigns that seem so incomprehensible to Westerners, not to mention many of those forced to take part in them. One of the few tools the Party has to fight social and political disintegration is to force Party members to study official documents and to write self-examinations in an effort to bolster compliance, but the "three stresses" (*sanjiang*) campaign that Beijing has carried out since early 1999 seems to have created as much resentment among those forced to participate as it has compliance. Campaigns may buy the Party some time, but they are not an effective way to build institutions.

Politics in an Era of Domestic Change and Globalization

When one turns to the more specifically political aspects of contemporary China, it is apparent that there are important shifts under way both as generational change forces new adaptations and as the very changed intellectual and socioeconomic environment in which the government operates presents challenges to which the government must learn to respond with greater rapidity and flexibility if it is to survive.

The single greatest change in the political system in recent years has been the passing of the revolutionary generation and the emergence of a new, better-trained, but less authoritative generation. Although there remain veteran revolutionaries who continue to constrain the top leadership in various ways, Deng Xiaoping's death in February 1997—which followed the deaths of other senior leaders such as Chen Yun (April 1995), Li Xiannian (June 1992), and Hu Qiaomu (September 1992)— really brought about the demise of the first generation of Chinese Communist Party (CCP) leadership and of revolutionary legitimacy as well. Deng liked to refer to himself as the "core" of the "second generation" of leadership in order to distinguish himself from the discredited leadership and policies of Mao Zedong. But Deng, born in 1904, was merely a decade younger than Mao and had participated in all the great revolutionary struggles, including most significantly the Long March. It was a generation that felt assured both of its right to rule and of its ability to do so. By and large, these claims were accepted by younger people in the Party and by society at large.

No such natural legitimacy accrues to Jiang Zemin and his colleagues. In part because neither his nor the Party's legitimacy is assured in the way Deng's was, Jiang is intensely conscious of ideology. He understands that both the coherence of the Party and the legitimacy of the government depend significantly on articulating a rationale for their continued rule. Reflecting on the challenge he faced, Jiang reportedly once said that Mao Zedong's generation had the theory of revolutionary socialism and Deng Xiaoping's generation had the theory of building socialism with Chinese characteristics, but the third generation (that is, Jiang Zemin's generation) had not yet put its ideological stamp on politics.[32] The absence of such an ideological stamp reflected both the very different state-society relationship Jiang faced and the more particular problem of establishing Jiang's legitimacy vis-à-vis his colleagues. In terms of the Party-state's relationship to society, Jiang had (and has) the unenviable task of trying to build an institutionalized, regularized relationship. In a sense, Mao and Deng had the easy jobs: Mao centralized, and Deng decentralized. Neither built viable institutions regulating the central government's relationship either with local levels of government or with the broader society. That task falls to Jiang.

In terms of the narrower political question of establishing his authority vis-à-vis his colleagues, Jiang had the task of replacing leaders of his own generation and older who felt, with some legitimacy, that they were as well qualified as Jiang and thus were reluctant to take orders from him with a younger group who would, he hoped, be more compliant. This was a process that Jiang undertook in several steps, first defeating a challenge from military leader Yang Shangkun in 1992, then elevating protégés at the Central Committee's Fourth Plenum in 1994, and then significantly rejuvenating the Central Committee at the Fifteenth Party Congress in 1997. Yet Jiang has never believed that simply replacing people is sufficient either to ensure his own control or to maintain the Party's control over society. The explosion of corruption and smuggling as well as the fusion of Party and business, not only in the Party but also in the military, was testimony to the erosion of Party discipline and the loss of faith not only in any ruling ideology but perhaps in the future of the Party as well.[33] That is why Jiang places so much emphasis on ideology and Party discipline.

If legitimacy has been Jiang's number one problem, coping with the very rapidly changing socioeconomic conditions outlined above has ranked a close second. There were at least two aspects of this problem.

One was that as Chinese society and economy diversified and as the Party lost much of its ability to command allegiance, the role of interests became conspicuously greater. Although there continued to be problems with those who objected to reforms on ideological grounds, the influence of the "Old Left"—the ideologically more orthodox wing of the Party identified with senior ideologue Hu Qiaomu before his death and former propaganda head Deng Liqun—waned after 1992 though it has resurged periodically.[34] Meanwhile, it has been complemented by a variety of interests—regional, local, ministerial, and sectoral—that seemed to defend their turf more vigorously and more directly than before. Moreover, a strong sense of nationalism has taken the place on the ideological spectrum once occupied by the Old Left.

Second, the hard nut of SOE reform, which was inextricably bound up with the increasingly severe problems in the fiscal system, presented an increasing drag on the economy as well as on state resources. Although the size of the state-owned economy shrank from some 75 percent of GNP at the beginning of the reforms to less than 35 percent by 1995, it continues to dominate some sectors of the economy, particularly heavy industry. Because these are important sectors of the economy and because their reform (or lack thereof) has strong implications for the viability of the banking sector, SOE reform is something that simply cannot be avoided. Moreover, half measures have arguably made the situation worse, not better.[35]

Both the "interest group" nature of contemporary Chinese politics and the severity of sectoral problems in the economy are closely related to China's role in the international economy, particularly to its probable entry into the World Trade Organization (WTO). Exports are essential for shoring up the economy, but entry into the WTO would present formidable competitive challenges to many industries.

The conflicting demands on the political system are reflected both in the composition of the top leadership and in the group of people Jiang has gathered around him to advise on policy. Within the top leadership, there are conservative figures, headed by former premier Li Peng (now head of the National People's Congress), who have extensive ties throughout the government bureaucracy and with Party elders. There are also bold reformers, personified by the current premier Zhu Rongji, who understand the need to bring about a rapid and dramatic restructuring of the economy. Within Jiang's own entourage, there is likewise a diversity of people, reflecting Jiang's need to keep in close touch with different

constituencies in the Party. There are, for instance, conservative officials such as Teng Wensheng, Deng Liqun's protégé, who heads the Policy
Research Office of the Central Committee, and Ding Guan'gen, the conservative head of the Propaganda Department, who Jiang continues to
employ despite his being widely disliked within the Party, not to mention among intellectuals. At the same time, there are more "liberal" ad-
visors, such as former Shanghai mayor and all-around political mentor
Wang Daohan, who has played a critical role in helping Jiang navigate
the hidden shoals of elite politics, has shaped much of Jiang's approach
to foreign affairs, and has been invaluable as a liaison with the intellectual community. There is also Liu Ji, Jiang's close friend from Shanghai
who served as vice president of the Chinese Academy of Social Sciences from 1993 to 1997 and has continued to play a very active if much
lower profile role since leaving CASS. In between, there are a number
of people who have worked to further Jiang's interests bureaucratically.
The most important of these is Zeng Qinghong, who served as head of
the Central Committee's General Office from 1993 to 1998 and then
moved over to head the important Organization Department. Zeng was
promoted to alternate member of the Politburo at the Fifteenth Party
Congress in 1997 and may well one day emerge as leader of China in his
own right.[36]

This effort to pull together, or at least accommodate, divergent views
and interests within the Party has been reflected in Jiang's political stewardship over the past several years, particularly since he began to come
into his own following the Fourth Plenum in late 1994. In general, what
Jiang has done has been to steal a page from Deng Xiaoping's book of
political strategy by trying to carve out a "middle course" that encom-
passes a fairly wide spectrum of opinion within the Party but nevertheless isolates both ideological hardliners and "bourgeois liberals."[37]

If one looks back to 1995, one can see the ideologically conservative
side of Jiang on display. Coming out of the Fourth Plenum the previous
fall, and meeting the challenge raised by the Old Left in the first of a
series of "ten-thousand-character manifestos" (*wanyanshu*), Jiang
stressed ideological orthodoxy by calling for "talking politics" (*jiang
zhengzhi*).[38] This was, perhaps, a natural outcome of the Fourth Plenum,
which had taken "Party building" as its theme, and of Jiang's overall
efforts to secure his own authority in the face of obvious challenges
from both the left and the right. By late 1995 and early 1996, one sees
Jiang trying to define his program in somewhat more positive terms by

giving a series of internal speeches distinguishing Marxism from anti-Marxism in seven areas, including socialist democracy versus Western parliamentary democracy, developing a diverse economy with a predominant public sector versus privatization, and studying what is advanced in the West versus fawning on the West. As such distinctions suggest, Jiang was reaching for a formula that would permit him to move pragmatically beyond the ideological strictures of the Old Left without leaving him open to the charges of being "lax" on "bourgeois liberalization" that had toppled his two immediate predecessors, Hu Yaobang and Zhao Ziyang.

The most systematic effort to define a middle course and respond to the criticisms of the left came when Xing Bensi, vice president of the Central Party School, published a long article in the *People's Daily*. Apparently angered by the silence with which the *People's Daily* greeted his speeches—a silence apparently induced by the inability of top leaders to agree on how to respond—Jiang arranged for the publication of Xing's article.

In trying to define what constituted "real" Marxism (and thus refute the Old Left that positioned itself as the defender of the faith), Xing argued that a lot had changed since the birth of Marx 150 years before. Xing argued that there are parts of Marxism that contain universal truth and are still applicable, parts that need to be supplemented, and parts that are "completely unsuitable for use, which should not be continued or upheld in the present day."[39] Thus, Xing stated, "The criterion for determining the border dividing Marxism and anti-Marxism has to rest on developed Marxism; in present day China the 'only correct' criterion for distinguishing Marxism and anti-Marxism is the 'theory of socialism with Chinese characteristics established by Deng Xiaoping'"—most importantly upholding the "one center [economic construction] and two basic points [the four cardinal principles and emancipating the mind]." Xing thus juxtaposed "Deng Xiaoping theory" against leftist thought and referred explicitly to the first ten-thousand-character manifesto when he criticized those who declared that reform had created a "new bourgeoisie."

At the same time, Xing defined a "right" that was just as anti-Marxist as the left. Xing cited several manifestations of rightism, including "privatization" and revisionist interpretations of Chinese history that implied that China had taken the wrong road in pursuing the revolutionary path and that it was now necessary to say "farewell to revolution." This was a reference to a well-known book of the same title by prominent philosopher Li Zehou and leading literary critic Liu Zaifu, both of whom were then living in the United States.[40] The criticism of their book appears to have been a useful bit of political artifice. Although *Farewell to Revolution* does raise uncomfortable legitimacy issues, its primary function in Xing's piece appears to have been to provide a "right" to complement the "left" and thus define a "middle course" for Jiang. It may also have been chosen as a symbol of rightist thinking to warn liberal thinkers to hold their peace as Jiang turned his primary attention to warding off the left.[41]

Another sign of Jiang's effort to distinguish his own political program from those of the left and right was the publication, in late 1996, of *Heart-to-Heart Talks with the General Secretary*. This book brought together fourteen young scholars, mostly based at CASS, to flesh out the contents of the speech Jiang had made on twelve major problems confronting China at the Fifth Plenum the previous year. Part of the intent of the book was to counter the rising tide of nationalism and to point the way to adopting the shareholding system for SOEs, which would be made official the following year at the Fifteenth Party Congress. What was most eye-catching about the volume was the preface and endorsement by Liu Ji, vice president of CASS and close friend of Jiang Zemin. *Heart-to-Heart Talks with the General Secretary* anticipated the publication of a new series of books, called *Contemporary China's Problems* (*Dangdai Zhongguo wenti*), under the sponsorship of Liu Ji, that would eventually include more than twenty titles.

Following Deng's death in February 1997, Jiang began to move with remarkable self-confidence. In his eulogy at Deng's funeral, Jiang quoted Deng as saying when he returned to power in the late 1970s that there are two possible attitudes: "One is to act as a bureaucrat, the other is to work."[42] It seemed a risky quotation for Jiang to cite, given his reputation for caution. In retrospect, however, it seems that Jiang was using Deng to make a personal declaration, namely, that he was determined to "work," too. Indeed, he did, for by the time of Deng's death, Jiang had the Fifteenth Party Congress clearly in mind. Within a month of Deng's death, a draft of Jiang's report to the Fifteenth Party Congress, which would make important revisions to the Party's understanding of "socialist ownership," was circulated for comment.

Although economic liberals welcomed Jiang's report, ideological conservatives hated it. Rather than again tacking to the left, as he had many times in the past, Jiang went to the Central Party School in late

May to give the most important political speech of his career. In a thinly veiled jab at the left, Jiang declared that "there is no way out if we study Marxism in isolation and separate and set it against vivid development in real life." In the unpublicized portion of the speech, Jiang went further, explicitly criticizing the left and laying out his rationale for reform of the ownership structure. Deng had raised the slogan "Guard against the right, but guard primarily against the left" in his 1992 trip to the south, but it had been largely dropped from the official media (except for inclusion in formal Party resolutions) following the Fourteenth Party Congress later that year. Now Jiang was reviving it and identifying himself with Deng's reforms. For a leader often criticized as bland, cautious, and technocratic, Jiang was beginning to reveal a boldness previously visible only in his deft maneuvers against political enemies.

The relaxation of the political atmosphere that was associated with the discussions leading up to and following the Fifteenth Party Congress brought about what is sometimes called the "Beijing spring," a period of limited opening up of public discussion that actually started the previous fall. This limited opening can perhaps be traced to the letter that Beijing University economics professor Shang Dewen sent to the Central Committee in August 1997, the first of three such missives. Shang argued that economic reform could not go further without an opening of the political system. In October, a month after the Party congress, Fang Jue, a reform-minded official in the southeastern province of Fujian, distributed a statement calling for political reform.[43] In December, Hu Jiwei, the crusading former editor-in-chief of the *People's Daily*, published a series of articles calling for political reform in a major Hong Kong daily.[44] In January, the economics journal *Reform* carried an article advocating political reform written by Li Shenzhi, the highly respected former head of the Institute of American Studies at the CASS, who had been removed in the wake of Tiananmen.[45] In March, the little-known journal *Methods*, carried several articles calling for political reform.[46] And in May, a rapidly edited book called *Beijing University's Tradition and Modern China* took advantage of the approaching centennial anniversary of Beijing University to emphasize the liberal tradition in China. A preface by Li Shenzhi noted that liberalism is not native to China but that since its introduction into China through Beijing University, liberalism has struck roots and become a part of China's tradition.[47]

The most controversial book of the spring was *Crossed Swords*

(*Jiaofeng*). Written by two journalists at the *People's Daily*, the book starts by tracing the history of the emergence of the Dengist reforms—particularly the opening up of intellectual freedom—against the opposition of Mao's successor, Hua Guofeng. *Crossed Swords* goes on to link this early period of relaxation to the heated debates surrounding Deng Xiaoping's trip to the south in 1992. Finally, and most controversially, the book details the sharp political debates of 1995–97. These debates pitted those who wanted to advance reform further against those leftist ideologues who continued to oppose the marketization, and especially the privatization, of the Chinese economy, as well as China's continued integration into the world economy and the progressive abandonment of Marxism. Ignoring certain historical realities—particularly that much of Deng's animus in his 1992 trip was directed against Jiang Zemin, who was then seen as lukewarm at best toward reform—the book portrays Jiang as inheriting and pushing forward the "emancipation of the mind" begun in 1978.[48] Picking up on Jiang's report to the Fifteenth Party Congress and Li Peng's remarks at the same time, the book calls the current opening China's "third emancipation of the mind."

Crossed Swords was even more controversial than other works published during the Beijing spring because it was included in Liu Ji's series, *Contemporary China's Problems*, mentioned above. Despite Liu Ji's close relationship with Jiang Zemin, it seems that the publication of *Crossed Swords* was part of the ongoing conduct of the "court politics" surrounding the Party leader, thus reflecting the inevitable conflicts among the diverse group of people Jiang had brought together under his wing. For instance, Wang Renzhi, the former head of the Propaganda Department who was forced to step down following Deng's trip to the south and take up the position of Party secretary of CASS, took a very negative view of the publication of *Heart-to-Heart Talks with the General Secretary* and quarreled on more than one occasion with Liu Ji. This may well have influenced Liu's willingness to allow the publication of *Crossed Swords*. In any event, it was clear that the publication of *Crossed Swords* did set off a political maelstrom. Ding Guan'gen, the conservative head of the Propaganda Department, quickly condemned the book. Wang Renzhi was predictably outraged, as was conservative elder Song Ping. On the liberal side, Party elder Wan Li had an unusual meeting with the authors in which he defended the book. Nevertheless, leftists, who were angered by the wholesale criticism of them in *Crossed Swords*, organized a meeting in April to criticize the book, to which they invited Communist ideologues from Russia (provoking liberals to mock the event as a gathering of the "Communist International"). Eventually, the editors of the conservative journal *Zhongliu*, which had published some of the "ten-thousand-character manifestos," took the authors of *Crossed Swords* to court, charging copyright violation. The court eventually dismissed the charges, but not until after some dramatic political theater.[49]

Jiang's limited movement to the "right" reflected an interesting intersection of domestic and foreign policy. On the domestic front, in view of the very difficult problems facing the economy, Jiang had clearly decided to distance himself from Li Peng's more cautious approach to economic reform and had decided to endorse Zhu Rongji's bold moves to restructure the government, the economy, and the relationship between the two. Major reform measures simply require a more open political atmosphere in China. At the same time, the political relaxation on the domestic front was related to a broad-ranging effort to repair relations with the United States. The nationalist mood that had welled up in the wake of the *Yin He* incident and particularly following Taiwan president Lee Teng-hui's visit to the United States hampered both domestic reform and the stability of China's international environment, which was seen as essential to continued economic reform and development, which in turn depended on both stable export markets and a large amount of investment from abroad.

Indeed, the evidence strongly suggests that as Jiang was coming into power, his strategy was to ease China's international relations so as to create a better environment for domestic reform and to support a major restructuring of the economy (including making the necessary ideological revisions) while nevertheless sounding certain conservative ideological themes both to shore up support among the conservative wing of the Party and to try to reinforce Party discipline. Thus, in early 1995, Jiang tried to ease relations across the Taiwan Strait, only to have the policy blow up in his face as Lee Teng-hui traveled to the United States and made highly provocative comments while visiting his alma mater, Cornell University. The crisis that soon unfolded in the Strait, however, ironically provided a new opportunity to relax international tensions as both the United States and China worked to back away from the abyss.

Part of this effort consisted of quasi-official initiatives to depict the United States in a more favorable light. That there was a need to do so says much about the public resentment that had built up against the United States in the mid-1990s and about the role that public opinion was beginning to play, even in the formulation of foreign policy. Perhaps the most important of these initiatives was the publication of *China Should Not Be 'Mr. No'* by Shen Jiru, a senior researcher with CASS's Institute of World Economics and Politics. Part of Liu Ji's *Contemporary China's Problems* book series, *China Should Not Be 'Mr. No'* joined the longstanding debate about the causes of the collapse of the Soviet Union. Shen argued that it had been the steadfast refusal of the Soviet leaders to cooperate with other countries and open their country up (which earned Soviet foreign minister Andrei Gromyko the nickname of "Mr. No") that had brought about its demise. In opposition to conservatives' argument that it was reform that led to collapse, Shen argued that it was the lack of reform that had brought about the failure of socialism in the Soviet Union and Eastern Europe.[50]

Jiang's strategy reflected at least in part the growing recognition in Beijing, particularly in the wake of the Asian financial crisis, that China's fate was bound up with joining the world, not with resisting global trends. Thus, Jiang stated in March 1998, "We have to gain a complete and correct understanding of the issue of economic 'globalization' and properly deal with it. Economic globalization is an objective trend of world economic development, from which none can escape and in which everyone has to participate."[51] It was this recognition that lay behind the exchange of summits between Jiang and President Clinton in October 1997 and June 1998. It also lay behind the far-ranging reforms announced at the Fifteenth Party Congress in September 1997 and the First Session of the Ninth National People's Congress in March 1998 (when a major restructuring of the government was announced), as well as the sweeping efforts made to join the WTO in 1999. Overall, Jiang was remarkably successful in combining this recognition with domestic politics in the first year following Deng's death; he would not be so lucky in 1999.

A Politically Sensitive Year

By late 1998, it was already apparent that the last year of the century was shaping up to be one of extraordinary political sensitivity—but no one could have predicted the bizarre twists that would occur. The Asian financial crisis, which had seemed at first to have bypassed China, began to bite as exports became more difficult and foreign investment began to fall. The slowed economy, accompanied by a fall in the consumer index, made the ongoing economic restructuring even more politically sensitive as more than the expected number of workers lost their jobs or could not find employment in the first place. Reports of violence in the countryside, suggested the volatile situation there.

It was under these conditions that the Chinese leadership faced the most politically sensitive season in a decade, which would include the fortieth anniversary of the Tibetan revolt (March 10), the eightieth anniversary of the May Fourth Movement, the tenth anniversary of Hu Yaobang's death (April 15), the tenth anniversary of Tiananmen (June 4), and, finally, the fiftieth anniversary of the founding of the PRC (October 1). The leadership was clearly already thinking about this series of anniversaries: one of the construction projects that was to be completed before October 1 was a renovation of Tiananmen Square, which somehow required the square to be surrounded by a solid fence for some seven months between December and July, denying the public space to potential demonstrators. Caution was clearly the order of the day as Jiang and others focused on orchestrating a grand birthday party for the PRC.

As carefully as the leadership planned, events would conspire to make 1999 a less than successful year. Neither foreign relations nor the domestic situation fell into place, raising new questions about the ability of the regime to provide a political "soft landing."

Jiang Zemin's November 1998 summit meeting in Japan provided an intimation of what was to come. This trip was intended as the capstone of a successful year of diplomacy. The exchange of summits with the United States and Jiang's trip to Russia just prior to his Japanese sojourn had seemingly repaired or improved all of China's great power relations. The trip to Japan would display Jiang's diplomatic prowess by showing that he could promote good relations on terms favorable to China. But Jiang overreached. Japan had offered a full apology for its history of aggression in Korea to Kim Dae-Jung, and Jiang thought he could extract a similar statement. He also wanted to push Japan on the Taiwan issue, asking that it repeat the "Three No's" that President Clinton had offered during his trip to China. The trip was new foreign minister Tang Jiaxuan's first big test. A diplomat trained as a Japan specialist, Tang might have been expected to orchestrate a smooth visit, but domestic pressures in China made it difficult to pull off. The results were disappointing. Jiang gave his hosts a long lecture on history,[52] and a prepared joint communiqué was left unsigned. Japanese public opinion was alienated by Jiang's seemingly rude behavior, and Jiang returned home not in triumph but to new doubts about his diplomatic skills.

More unexpected, and more serious, than Jiang's diplomatic dustup in

Japan was the downturn in U.S.-China relations. The exchange of summits had created a significantly better atmosphere, but this goodwill quickly dissipated as old problems returned and new ones came up. The human rights issue, seemingly tempered by the summit meetings, suddenly returned to plague the relationship as China moved to jail a number of dissidents trying to form a new political party. The arrest and sentencing to long jail terms of Xu Wenli, Wang Youcai, and other China Democracy Party activists in December 1998 was merely the prelude to further arrests and sentencings the following year. Critics quickly charged China with blatant hypocrisy: it signed the UN Covenant on Political and Civil Rights in October and then rounded up dissidents in December.

These new outcries came at a time when charges of campaign finance violations involving the United States were once again heating up. Stories of Chinese contributions had first been raised in the winter of 1997–98 but had died down after the Thompson hearings failed to produce any solid evidence. In May 1999, however, the charges acquired new life as Democratic fund-raiser Johnny Chung finally testified before Congress. According to Chung, Ji Shengde, head of China's military intelligence, had given him $300,000 toward support of President Clinton's presidential campaign—only $35,000 of which was actually passed to the Democrats.[53]

The most explosive charges, however, came from the committee headed by Christopher Cox, which alleged that the Chinese government had systematically stolen the United States' most advanced nuclear weapons designs. The release of the declassified version of the report in March created a new upsurge of anti-Chinese sentiment—despite the fact that the report was so hedged with suppositions that most weapons experts distrusted its conclusions, or at least the farthest-reaching of its conclusions, doubting that the Chinese had acquired anywhere near as much as the Cox report intimated or that they had put it into production.[54] Chinese American scientist Wen Ho Lee was removed from his job at Los Alamos laboratory, eventually indicted, but then released after a plea bargain that admitted only the mishandling of classified data.

Against this background, the United States began to bomb Yugoslavia on March 24. Frustrated by its failure to persuade Yugoslav president Slobodan Milosevic to sign a compromise agreement at Rambouillet and by its repeated failure to cow him with threats, NATO embarked on a course of military action intended to force an end to systematic human rights violations in Kosovo. The United States and its NATO allies clearly saw going through the United Nations as fruitless, whereas the Chinese leadership just as clearly saw the failure to do so as a gross violation of international law. There was certainly much hypocrisy in the position of the Chinese leaders—they consistently ignored Serbian violations of human rights and made no effort to bring about a viable solution in the United Nations—but the willingness of NATO to simply ignore the United Nations raised China's worst fears about U.S. intentions.

It was in this poisonous atmosphere that Premier Zhu Rongji arrived in the United States on April 6 to discuss China's accession to the WTO. With his unique ability to combine humor and intelligence, Zhu almost single-handedly turned back the wave of anti-Chinese sentiment that had grown up in the preceding months. Making sweeping concessions, Zhu made clear that China wanted to join the WTO and the world. This was a leadership that understood the importance of trade and the inevitability of globalization.

Then, as if to prove that history really does progress without rhyme or reason, mistakes started happening. The first was made by President Clinton. Presented with an opportunity to top off the years he had devoted to improving U.S.-China relations (after notably contributing to their decline during his first two years in office), the president flinched. Once again the trees blinded him to the forest. Trent Lott, in stating his unalloyed opposition to China's entry into the WTO, left no doubt in the president's mind that China policy would be a divisive domestic issue.[55] At the same time, Secretary of the Treasury Robert Rubin, perhaps not adequately briefed on the total package, voiced doubts over the banking and securities portions of the agreement. So the president, perhaps feeling that a yet better deal could be done, sided with the doubters over the advice of his national security advisor Sandy Berger and Secretary of State Madeleine Albright.

Zhu returned to Beijing on April 21 to accusations that he had given up too much, but before Zhu had a chance to overcome the naysayers, the domestic atmosphere in China was transformed once again. In spite of having prepared for months for the possibility of demonstrations in the spring, the leadership was caught completely unawares on April 25 when ten thousand members of the Falun Gong—many of them elderly—appeared suddenly and without warning outside of Zhongnanhai, the leadership compound. There were no speeches or protests; the crowd simply sat and meditated, directing their *qi* (inner spirit) at the CCP leadership.

Zhu Rongji, the "passionate premier" as some in Beijing call him, sent people to the gate of Zhongnanhai to ask what was going on. In response, five members of the Falun Gong were deputed to talk to Zhu in Zhongnanhai. What must have been more disturbing than anything said was the rank of the representatives. At least three of the five were reportedly very high-ranking, albeit retired, officials, including one retired major general who had worked in the military intelligence section of the People's Liberation Army's General Staff Department.[56]

Jiang Zemin was clearly disturbed by the demonstration. Sometime after midnight, he reportedly took pen in hand and wrote a letter to his colleagues in the Politburo Standing Committee. Saying that he could not sleep because of the day's events, he wondered how such a large demonstration could have occurred without any warning from any central department. His concerns could only have been compounded when he received a long letter from Li Qihua, former head of the 301 hospital (the top military hospital that serves the leadership). Li said that Marxism-Leninism could explain many things about the natural world but that there were many things beyond the natural world that it could not explain. The teachings of the Falun Gong filled this void and should not be seen as incompatible with Marxism-Leninism. Jiang Zemin reportedly wrote him a long letter criticizing his views. Li was then visited by two high-ranking officials and subsequently wrote a two-page self-criticism recanting his views.[57]

The subsequent crackdown on the Falun Gong, including arrests, detentions, study sessions, and a very wide-ranging and harsh propaganda campaign, has evoked new concerns abroad with human rights issues. No doubt the campaign has been, as all such campaigns are, harsher and more ham-handed than necessary, but the government's crackdown draws more on a two-thousand-year tradition of political autocracy than it does on Marxism-Leninism or communist dictatorship—just as the Falun Gong itself draws on a long millenarian tradition of combining martial arts with spiritual mysticism. What obviously disturbed Jiang Zemin and other leaders most was the extent of the Falun Gong's organization, its obvious ability to mobilize people quickly, and its deep penetration into the military and security ranks, which potentially diluted the Party's ability to control those important pillars of rule.[58] Jiang thus reacted just as China's imperial governments had acted before him; the risk was that the crackdown would further politicize the Falun Gong or similar movements, just as imperial crackdowns had provoked rebellion from the White Lotus, Taiping, and other sects.[59]

Domestic politics and international relations came crashing together dramatically and unexpectedly early on the morning of May 8 (Beijing time) when five laser-guided U.S. bombs slammed into the Chinese embassy in Belgrade, killing three and injuring twenty. The Chinese leadership was stunned and confused. It spent three days in an intense round of meetings, reflecting both the weakness of China's crisis-management system and the array of conflicting opinions that existed at high levels. It is clear that domestic considerations were the highest priority. The depth of public anger was real and should not be underestimated. Talk of "mistakes" was quickly dismissed by most of the public; not only had the bombs clearly been targeted to hit the building, but also the people believed that U.S. intelligence could not make a mistake of that magnitude. And the event seemed to fit into a pattern of U.S. efforts to hold China down: everything from human rights concerns to the Cox report to U.S. support for Taiwan seemed to reflect hostility toward China. Understanding the need for a public release of anger, the leadership quickly yielded to students determined to march on the U.S. embassy. The government provided buses to bring the students to the embassy area; directed them to march past the ambassador's residence, the embassy, and the visa section; allowed them to throw stones, bricks, and ink bottles; and then bused them back to their campuses. It was a way of channeling genuine public anger and preventing the alternative, namely, that students would take to the streets outside Zhongnanhai if they perceived the Chinese government as being "weak."

Despite this public show of anger, the Chinese leadership quickly came to two basic conclusions: first, whatever the reason for the bombing, it did not reflect policy at the highest levels of the U.S. government, and second, U.S.-China relations were too important to be sacrificed to the emotions of the moment. Trade and a stable international environment were essential for China's continued economic development, and domestic stability was impossible without economic development.

This basic understanding hardly meant that the Chinese government was unified. Hardliners quickly spun out scenarios that "proved" that the bombing was deliberate and, more important, that the United States was engaged in a long-term strategy to "contain" China.[60] The military quickly demanded more money to counter the perceived strategic threat. Even sophisticated and open-minded intellectuals viewed international trends in ominous terms. The focal point for much of this anger and frustration was Zhu Rongji. Conservatives had cautioned against Zhu's going to the United States in the first place (because of the Kosovo situation) and were particularly angered when it was revealed (by the U.S. Trade Representative office's unilateral posting on the Internet) that he had made sweeping concessions in order to win WTO entry.

Zhu was abused mercilessly by public opinion and criticized within the government. Articles on the Internet as well as student demonstrators labeled him a "traitor" (*maiguozei*). At the same time, some old cadres were known to mutter that the government's readiness to accept globalization was like Wang Jingwei's willingness to serve as head of Japan's puppet government in occupied China during World War II. Others have called Zhu's compromises in Washington the "new twenty-one demands selling out the country"—a reference to Japan's infamous demands of 1915 that sought to reduce China to a near colony.[61]

By the time the Party retreated in late July for its annual conclave at the seaside resort of Beidaihe, Chinese politics had taken on a more conservative tone. Backing away from the limited liberalization of the "Beijing spring," Jiang had directed Party cadres to put their thoughts in order through a rectification campaign known as the "three stresses." Then, in response to Falun Gong activities, Jiang ordered the detention or arrest of numerous leaders as well as special study sessions for Party members who were also members of the Falun Gong. Still adhering to a middle course, Jiang was nevertheless closer in 1999 to the ideological conservative that he had been in the earlier years of his stewardship than to the more open-minded leader he had seemed in 1997–98.

Neither Jiang's efforts to bolster his own and the Party's authority through study campaigns nor his efforts to prevent social unrest by cracking down on democracy activists suggested a retreat to the old days. Jiang and the Party recognize the need to move forward with economic reform, as the Fourth Plenary Session of the Fifteenth Central Committee in September 1999 demonstrated. Nevertheless, the Party seems reluctant to endorse the far-reaching measures needed. Following a series of speeches on the reform of state-owned enterprises over the spring and summer, the Party endorsed a plan to move economic reform forward by further "corporatization" of SOEs. But further introduction of the shareholding system is not likely to revive the state sector unless hard-budget constraints can be enforced. And the intermingling of enterprise Party committees with the managerial boards of enterprises— which Jiang called for—seems designed more to make sure the "never-left-out class" never gets left out than to enforce market-conforming behavior.[62] The unstable social and political environment undoubtedly makes the Party reluctant to take more decisive measures, while the failure to implement more fundamental reforms, including political reforms, breeds further instability.

Conclusion

There is a "presentness" in the historical anniversaries that fell in the last years of the twentieth century not only because China is a country with a deep historical consciousness and not even because it is a country obsessed with its modern history but particularly because the unfolding of its reforms over a twenty-year period, during which both the domestic and international situations have changed dramatically, has allowed for a continual reflection on the meaning of history, on the roads taken and not taken, and on the choices for the future. The major issues that have roiled China's political waters over the past few years—China's relations with the United States, Japan, and Taiwan; the enormous socioeconomic changes brought about by the growth of the nonstate sector and the continuing problems in the state-run sector; and the problem of maintaining political control in the face of generational change, rising interest-group politics, an orgy of corruption, and a loss of political faith—all raise profound issues that are embedded in Chinese history, either the history of the revolution or the history of reform. This is why the intellectual debates outlined at the beginning of this chapter are of such importance and have taken on such a harsh tone.

During the decade of the 1980s, reformers could dismantle much of what Mao had built without fear of going "too far." However, with the student demonstrations of 1989, the poles around which debate had centered in the 1980s—reformers versus conservatives—were joined by a third possibility: political collapse and social disorder. The 1989 crisis provoked not only a political reaction but also, especially in light of the experience of Eastern Europe and the Soviet Union, a profound and sometimes painful intellectual reflection. Widespread concerns over "stability" were soon joined by new frustration over the corruption that accompanied marketization, especially the explosion of profiteering that occurred in the wake of Deng Xiaoping's trip to the south. If reformers in the 1980s, whether in policy-making circles or among the intelligentsia, had wanted to introduce "capitalism" (then more delicately called "market forces") to shake off the heavy hand of a bureaucratized ministerial economy, to create millions of new jobs, and to pursue China's comparative advantage internationally, China seemed to have too much capitalism by the mid-1990s—particularly the raw sort associated with Dickens' novels and Engels' early writings.

Does one continue to introduce more capitalism to right the wrongs of the capitalism that has already been introduced? And if one does, is there anything left to the revolution that cost China millions of lives and untold hardship? Is there anything of value in China's revolutionary legacy or was it all a mistake? These are some of the painful questions that lurk behind the very changed intellectual atmosphere of the 1990s, but they also affect, however indirectly, the political leadership as it tries to secure the loyalty, or at least the compliance, of the citizenry and to shore up its own legitimacy.

The political difficulties of dealing with the diverse problems of China at the turn of the century are formidable. The optimism of the 1980s that reform could easily rectify the problems of the past if only "leftism" and "feudalism" could be eradicated has faded. Economic development, diversification, and decentralization have created interests that erode compliance, while ideology has lost the attraction it once had. Nationalism has emerged as the ridgepole supporting the Party's claim to rule, but it is also a double-edged sword. Nationalism not only distinguishes China from a world its leadership knows China must join but also presents a powerful, populist critique of the leadership. Nationalism is inherently critical of the "never-left-out class" that has gorged itself at public expense for the last decade and more, and it demands that the political system open up to accommodate the "true" representatives of the people. The leadership senses a need to open up (hence the "Beijing spring" of 1998), but it also fears the challenges that come with doing so.

Both the pressures that Beijing faces and the problems of postrevolutionary succession have forced the leadership to look, albeit tentatively and uncertainly, to institutions—including tax reform, local elections, institutionalized retirement, property-rights reform, law, and the National People's Congress—to shore up the center's control, to allow different voices to be heard, and to regularize the relationship between state and society. Such changes, accompanying the far-reaching socioeconomic changes outlined above, could lead to broad, though by no means instantaneous, changes in the conduct of politics. But institution building has come late to China. Not only have socioeconomic changes eroded much of the basis for institutional compliance at local levels, but the CCP itself seems conflicted about the desire for institutions. As institutions start to come into being, there are inevitably challenges to the CCP's control over power, and the Party responds with campaigns designed to shore up Party discipline—which inevitably undermine the institutions that are necessary for fundamental political change.

The answer to the question raised in the title of this chapter—can China leave the twentieth century behind?—depends on whether Jiang Zemin and other leaders of the CCP can deal with the various international and domestic political problems they face in ways that can absorb, channel, and institutionalize the socioeconomic changes that have taken place in recent years rather than yield to the pressures of interests that seek protection in the face of domestic and international competition, back down in the face of corruption that threatens to undermine all notions of law and order, and stifle all voices calling for change. Such changes would not revivify the CCP, at least in the traditional sense (whether or not the Party survives), but rather would change the zero-sum conception of political contestation that has so dominated and distorted twentieth-century politics.[63] The alternatives, as China enters the new century, are to allow the growth of pluralism and institutionalization or to replay much of the tragic history of the past century.

Notes

1. Fang Lizhi, "China's Despair and China's Hope," *New York Review of Books*, February 2, 1989, reprinted in Fang Lizhi, *Bringing Down the Great Wall* (New York: Alfred A. Knopf, 1991), pp. 250–57.

2. Li Zehou, *Zhongguo xiandai sixiangshi lun* (History of contemporary Chinese thought) (Beijing: Dongfang chubanshe, 1987). Vera Schwarcz's masterful study *The Chinese Enlightenment: Intellectuals and the Legacy of the May Fourth Movement of 1919* (Berkeley: University of California Press, 1986) builds on some of Li's insights.

3. Wang Ruoshui's *Wei rendao zhuyi bianhu* (In defense of humanism) (Beijing: Sanlian chubanshe, 1986) is the classic work in this regard.

4. Yan Jiaqi is one of the first and best-known advocates of instituting a civil-service system. See Yan Jiaqi, *Toward a Democratic China: The Intellectual Biography of Yan Jiaqi*, trans. David S. K. Hong and Denis C. Mair (Honolulu: University of Hawaii Press, 1992).

5. Wu Jinglian is probably the best-known of the early advocates, but there are many others. See Joseph Fewsmith, *Dilemmas of Reform in China: Political Conflict and Economic Debates* (Armonk, NY: M.E. Sharpe, 1994).

6. Gan Yang edited a famous series of translations under the general title *Culture: China and the World*. See Chen Fong-ching and Jin Guantao, *From Youthful Manuscripts to River Elegy: The Chinese Popular Cultural Movement and Politi-

cal Transformation, 1979–1989 (Hong Kong: Chinese University Press, 1997), pp. 159–85.

7. Su Shaozhi was an early and consistent advocate of democratization. See Su Shaozhi, et al., *Marxism in China* (Nottingham: Russell Press, 1983). See also Su's memoirs, *Shinianfengyu: Wengehou de dalu lilunjie* (Ten years of storms: The mainland's theoretical circles after the Cultural Revolution) (Taibei: Shibao wenhua, 1996).

8. Suisheng Zhao, "Deng Xiaoping's Southern Tour: Elite Politics in Post-Tiananmen China," *Asian Survey*, vol. 33, no. 8 (August 1993), pp. 739–56.

9. Figures on the size of China's private economy are notoriously hard to pin down, but the official figures give a sense of the explosion of such activity in the wake of Deng's trip to the south. In 1992 there were 139,633 registered private enterprises selling 9.1 billion yuan of goods; the following year there were 237,919 private enterprises with sales of 68.1 billion yuan. See Li Peilin, ed., *Zhongguo xinshiqi jieji jiceng baogao* (Report on classes and strata in China's new period) (Shenyang: Liaoning renmin chubanshe, 1995), p. 225.

10. Perhaps the best summation of the changed intellectual atmosphere and concerns of these intellectuals is Wang Hui, "Dangdai Zhongguo de sixiang zhuangkuang yu xiandaixing wenti" (Contemporary Chinese thought and the problem of modernity), *Tianya* (Frontier/Haikou) (September 1997), pp. 133–50.

11. A large number of books and articles have been published from various critical perspectives. See, for instance, Wang Hui and Yu Guoliang, eds., *90 niandai de 'houxue' lunzheng* (Post-ism in the nineties) (Hong Kong: Chinese University Press, 1998); and Cui Zhiyuan, *Di'erci sixiang jiefang* (The second thought liberation) (Hong Kong: Oxford University Press, 1997).

12. Areas in which such critiques have had a visible impact are those of gender and race.

13. See Zhang Kuan, "Wenhua xinzhimin de keneng" (The possibility of cultural neocolonialism), *Tianya* (April 1996).

14. See, for instance, the critical essays contained in Wang and Yu, eds., *90 niandai de 'houxue' lunzheng*.

15. Wang Xiaoming, ed., *Renwen jingshen xunsi lu* (Reflections on the humanistic spirit) (Shanghai: Wenhui chubanshe, 1996).

16. Joseph Fewsmith and Stanley Rosen, "The Domestic Context of Chinese Foreign Policy: Does 'Public Opinion' Matter?" in David M. Lampton, *The Making of Chinese Foreign and Security Policy in the Era of Reform: 1978–2000* (Stanford: Stanford University Press, forthcoming).

17. For instance, Wang Jian, an economist with the State Planning Commission, posted an article on the *Jianchuan zhishi* web site on June 2 arguing that the United States bombed the Chinese embassy to keep the war going because it wanted to maintain the value of the U.S. dollar vis-à-vis the euro.

18. Jianying Zha, *China Pop* (New York: New Press, 1995).

19. Zha, *China Pop*, p. 38.

20. Luo yi ning ge'er (pseud.), *Disanzhi yanjing kan Zhongguo* (Looking at China through a third eye), trans. Wang Shan (Taiyuan: Shanxi renmin chubanshe, 1994). See also Joseph Fewsmith, "Review of *Disanzhi yanjing kan Zhongguo*," *Journal of Contemporary China*, no. 7 (fall 1994), pp. 100–104.

21. Song Qiang, Zhang Zangzang, and Qiao Bian, *Zhongguo keyi shuobu* (China can say no) (Beijing: Zhonghua gongshang lianhe chubanshe, 1996).

22. The authors of *China Can Say No* were the first to exploit their own success with a quick sequel called *Zhongguo haishi neng shuo bu* (China can still say no) (Beijing: Zhongguo wenlian chuban yongsi, 1996). Imitations quickly followed. See, in particular, Li Xiguang and Liu Kang, *Yaomo Zhongguo de beihou* (Behind the demonization of China) (Beijing: Zhongguo shehui kexue chubanshe, 1996).

23. Weng Jieming et al., eds., *Yu zongshuji tanxin* (Heart-to-heart talks with the general secretary) (Beijing: Zhongguo shehui kexue chubanshe, 1996); and Shen Jiru, *Zhongguo bu dang 'bu xiansheng'* (China should not be 'Mr. No') (Beijing: Jinri Zhongguo chubanshe, 1998).

24. "Zhongguo shehui jiegou zhuanxing de zhongjinqi qushi yu yinhuan" (Trends and hidden shoals in the transformation of China's social structure in the near and mid-term), *Zhanlue yu guanli* (Strategy and Management/Beijing), no. 5 (1998), pp. 1–17.

25. He Qinglian, *Xiandaihua de xianjing* (Pitfalls of modernization) (Beijing: Jinri Zhongguo chubanshe, 1998). See Liu Binyan and Perry Link, "A Great Leap Backward?" *New York Review of Books*, October 8, 1998, pp. 19–23; and Ming Xia, "From Comraderie to the Cash Nexus: Economic Reforms, Social Stratification, and Their Political Consequences in China," *Journal of Contemporary China*, no. 21 (July 1999), pp. 345–58.

26. Ma Hong and Wang Mengkui, eds., *1998–1999 Zhongguo jingji xingshi yu zhanwang* (China's economic situation and outlook, 1998–1999) (Beijing: Zhongguo fazhan chubanshe, 1999), p. 162.

27. "Zhongguo shehui jiegou zhuanxing de zhongjinqi qushi yu yinhuan" (p. 11) cites a study by CASS researcher Feng Lanrui that estimates that unemployment in "cities and towns" will peak at around 21.4 percent during the ninth Five-Year Plan period (1996–2000), meaning that some 153 million people would be jobless. Unfortunately, the citation for Feng's study is not given, so the basis for these calculations cannot be checked.

28. Ma and Wang, eds., *1998–1999 Zhongguo jingji xingshi yu zhanwang*, pp. 25–26.

29. "Zhongguo shehui jiegou zhuanxing de zhongjinqi qushi yu yinhuan," p. 13.

30. Xiao Gongqin, "Zhongguo shehui ge jieji de zhengzhi taishi yu qianjing zhanwang" (The political attitudes of the various strata in China's society, and their prospects for the future), *Zhanlue yu guanli* (Strategy and Management/Beijing), no. 5 (October 1998), pp. 36–43.

31. Joseph Fewsmith, "China in 1998: Tacking to Stay the Course," *Asian Survey*, vol. 39, no. 1 (January/February 1999), pp. 99–113.

32. Joseph Fewsmith, "Jockeying for Position in the Post-Deng Era," *Current History*, vol. 94, no. 593 (September 1995), pp. 252–58.

33. Joseph Fewsmith, "Reaction, Resurgence, and Succession: Chinese Politics since Tiananmen," in *The Politics of China: The Eras of Mao and Deng*, ed. Roderick MacFarquhar, 2nd ed. (New York: Cambridge University Press, 1997), pp. 472–531.

34. The term "Old Left" generally refers to a group of older CCP cadres who remain wedded to more orthodox understandings of Marxism-Leninism and worried about the impact of trends, such as the growth of private business and new interpretations of ideology, that undermine the traditional social and ideological bases of Party rule. In addition to the Old Left, there are many people with nationalistic or

conservative ideas who are not particularly identified with the Old Left but who constitute a Party constituency that is threatened by the changes that are taking place, both domestically and internationally. This pressure must be taken seriously by Jiang Zemin and other top Party leaders.

35. Edward Steinfeld, *Forging Reform in China* (New York: Cambridge University Press, 1998), pp. 13–22; and Nicholas Lardy, *China's Unfinished Economic Reform* (Washington, D.C.: Brookings Institution Press, 1998).

36. This paragraph draws on Gao Xin, *Jiang Zemin de muliao* (Jiang Zemin's counselors) (Hong Kong: Mirror Books, 1996).

37. On Deng's middle course, see Tang Tsou, "Political Change and Reform: The Middle Course," in Tang Tsou, *The Cultural Revolution and Post-Mao Reforms* (Chicago: University of Chicago Press, 1986), pp. 219–58.

38. The "ten-thousand-character manifestos" were a series of conservative ideological statements circulated informally but widely between 1995 and early 1997 that challenged the direction of reform. Although they represented a rear-guard action by the Party's more ideologically orthodox wing, they presented a real problem for Jiang at the time. See Shi Liaozi, ed., *Beijing dixia 'wanyanshu'* (Beijing's underground ten-thousand-character manifestos) (Hong Kong: Mirror Books, 1997).

39. Xing Bensi, "Jianchi Makesi zhuyi bu dongyao" (Uphold Marxism without wavering), *Renmin ribao* (People's Daily), June 6, 1996, p. 9.

40. Li Zehou and Liu Zaifu, *Gaobie geming: Huiwang ershi shiji Zhongguo* (Farewell to revolution: Reviewing twentieth-century China) (Hong Kong: Cosmos Books, 1996).

41. Shen Hongpei, "Ershi shijimo gongchan zhuyi dalunzhan" (The great debate over communism at the end of the twentieth century), *Beijing dixia 'wanyanshu,'* ed., Shi Liaozi, p. 9.

42. Xinhua, February 25, 1997.

43. Fang Jue, "China Needs a New Transformation: Program Proposals of the Democratic Faction," *China Rights Forum* (spring 1998). This discussion draws on my article, "Jiang Zemin Takes Command," *Current History*, vol. 97, no. 620 (September 1998), pp. 250–56.

44. Hu Jiwei, "If the Party Is Correct, Bad Things Can Be Turned into Good Things; If the Party Is Wrong, Good Things Can Be Turned into Bad Things," *Hsin Pao*, December 29, 1997, trans. in FBIS-CHI-97-363 (December 29, 1997); Hu Jiwei, "Despotic Dictatorship Lingers On—Notes on Studying the Political Report of the 15th Party Congress," *Hsin Pao*, December 30, 1997, trans. in FBIS-CHI-97-364 (December 30, 1997); and Hu Jiwei, "Given a Good Central Committee, We Will Have a Good Party; Given a Good Party, We Will Have a Good State—Notes on Studying the Political Report of the 15th Party Congress," *Hsin Pao*, December 31, 1997, trans. in FBIS-CHI-97-365 (December 31, 1997).

45. Li Shenzhi, "Cong genbenshang shenhua gaige de sixiang" (Fundamentally deepening thinking about reform), *Jiefang wenxuan (1978–1998)* (Beijing: Jingji ribao chubanshe, 1998).

46. See *Fangfa* (Methods/Beijing) (March 1998), pp. 4–15.

47. Li Shenzhi, "Hongyang Beida de ziyou zhuyi chuantong" (Extol the liberal tradition of Beijing University), preface to *Beida chuantong yu jindai Zhongguo* (Beijing University's tradition and modern China), ed. Liu Junning (Beijing: Zhongguo renshi chubanshe, 1998), pp. 1–5.

48. Ling Zhijun and Ma Licheng, *Jiaofeng: Dangdai Zhongguo disanci sixiang jiefang shilu* (Crossed Swords: The third thought liberation campaign in contemporary China) (Beijing: Jinri Zhongguo chubanshe, 1998).
49. Vivien Pik-Kwan Chan, "Reformers Hail Leftist Defeat in Lawsuit Ruling," *South China Morning Post*, August 27, 1999.
50. Shen, *Zhongguo bu dang 'bu xiansheng.'*
51. *Renmin ribao*, March 9, 1998, p. 1.
52. Jiang Zemin, "Take a Warning from History and Usher in the Future," *Xinhua*, November 28, 1998, trans. in FBIS-CHI-98-333.
53. David Johnson, "Committee Told of Beijing Cash for Democrats," *New York Times*, May 12, 1999, p. A1; and Ann Scott Tyson, "Tale of Deep Pockets and Diplomacy," *Christian Science Monitor*, May 17, 1999, p. 1. Ji was later reassigned. See Henry Chu and Jim Mann, "Chinese Reassign Intelligence Chief Implicated in Fund Raising Scandal," *Los Angeles Times*, July 3, 1999, p. A4.
54. Patrick E. Tyler, "Who's Afraid of China," *New York Times Magazine*, August 1, 1999, pp. 46–49.
55. Paul Blustein and Steven Mufson, "Clinton Urges China Foes Not to Stoke a New Cold War," *Washington Post*, April 8, 1999, p. A2.
56. Author's interviews; John Pomfret, "China Sect Penetrated Military and Police; Security Infiltration Spurred Crackdown," *Washington Post*, August 7, 1999, p. A15.
57. Author's interviews; "Resolutely Support the Party Central Committee's Policy Decision, and Forever Listen to and Follow the Party, *Jiefangjun Bao*, July 30, 1999, trans. in FBIS-CHI-1999-0823 (August 24,1999); and Seth Faison, "Ex-General, Member of Banned Sect, Confesses 'Mistakes,' China Says," *New York Times*, July 31, 1999, p. A5.
58. Pomfret, "China Sect Penetrated Military and Police."
59. Daniel L. Overmyer, *Folk Buddhist Religion: Dissenting Sects in Late Traditional China* (Cambridge, MA: Harvard University Press, 1976).
60. Zhang Wenmu, "Kesuowo zhanzheng yu Zhongguo xinshiji anquan zhanlue" (The Kosovo war and China's security strategy in the new century), *Zhanlue yu guanli* (June 1999), pp. 1–10.
61. Joseph Fewsmith, "The Impact of the Kosovo Conflict on China's Political Leaders and Prospects for WTO Accession," *NBR Briefing*, no. 6 (July 1999).
62. See "Zhongguo gongchandang di shiwujie zhongyang weiyuanhui di sici quanti huiyi gongbao" (Communiqué of the fourth plenary session of the Fifteenth Central Committee of the CCP), Xinhua, September 22, 1999. According to the communiqué, the plenum adopted the "Decision on Issues Related to State-Owned Enterprise Reforms and Development," the text of which was not available at the time this chapter was written. A pretty good idea of the content can be gathered from Jiang Zemin's long speech, "Strengthen Confidence, Deepen Reform, Create a New Situation in Development of State-Owned Enterprises," Xinhua, August 12, 1999, trans. in FBIS-CHI-1999-0817 (August 18, 1999).
63. See Tang Tsou's observation that Chinese politics have been dominated by a conception that political power is "monistic and indivisible." Zou Dang [Tsou Tang], *Ershi shiji Zhongguo zhengzhi: cong hongguan lishi yu weiguan xingdong jiaodu kan* (Twentieth century Chinese politics: Viewed from the perspective of macro history and micro actions) (Hong Kong: Oxford University Press, 1994), p. 244.

Index

Agriculture. *See* Rural reform
America's Failure in China (Tsou), viii
Anhui Party, 40-41, 45

Beijing spring discussions, 138

Campaign contributions, 143
Capitalism
  cultural tradition and, 23-24
  modernization and, 23-24
  openness policy, 18-19, 22
Central Advisory Commission, 66-67
Chen Xitong, 72-73, 110
Chen Yizi, 41, 42
Chen Yun
  democratization, 64
  political prospects, 132
  political systems
    1980s, 46-52
    1990s, 53, 54, 55, 56-57
    rural reform and, 41
  reform impact, 98, 100, 102-3
Cheng Li, vii-viii
Chiang Kai-shek, xi-xii
Chinese Academy of Social Sciences
  (CASS), 41, 42, 120, 135, 137,
  141

Chinese Communist Party
  democratization and
    ideology, 64-65
    institution building, 63-64, 67
    leadership succession, 70-75
    partial reform, 78, 79-80
    recruitment, 67
    reform, 64-65, 67
  political prospects and
    Beijing spring discussions, 138
    conservatism, 134-40, 147-48,
      153n.38
    Falun Gong, 144-45, 147
    generational politics, 132-33
    ideology, 133-40, 147-48
    liberalism, 135-40
    nationalism, 134
    Old Left, 134, 135-37, 152n.34
    socioeconomic change, 127
  political study and, viii-x
  political systems and
    enterprise reform, 42-43
    ideology, 39-40, 44-46
    1980s, 46-47, 48, 49
    1990s, 52, 53, 54-55
    rural reform, 40-42
    spiritual pollution campaign, 36-37

Dengist reforms, historically *(continued)*
societal depoliticization, 4-5
Special Economic Zones, 15, 21
state authority and
limitation of, 4-5
private/public sphere, 9-13
summary, 28-30
technological revolution (1983),
18-19, 33n.35
Tiananmen Square, xiv-xv, 3, 4, 6, 7
Western influence
cultural tradition, 22, 23-24, 26, 28
modernization, 22, 23-24, 26, 28
nationalism, 19-22, 33n.39
Dengist reforms, political impact
Chinese Communist Party and
authority diminishment, 93, 94, 95
cadre structure, 97
class system, 92-93, 113n.24
conservatives, 98, 99, 100-101, 102
factionalism, 91-92
ideology, 92-94, 98-99, 101
impersonal norms, 92-93
informal politics, 91-92
Leninism, 92-93, 104
local government, 95
Marxism-Leninism, 94, 98-99, 100
1980s conflict, 98-103
Party meetings, 97
Party norms, 95-96
reformers, 98-99, 100-101, 102
retirement system, 96-97
ruling transition, 92
societal relations, 92-93, 94-95
truth criterion, 93, 94
win/lose politics, 88
Cultural Revolution and, 90, 93, 95,
96, 106
formal structures, 100-101, 111
Guomindang and, 88
ideology and
Chinese Communist Party, 92-94,
98-99, 101
leadership, 89-91, 92-94, 98-99

Dengist reforms, political impact
(continued)
informal politics, 91-92, 111, 113n.19
leadership and
Chen Yun, 98, 100, 102-3
Deng Liqun, 98
Deng Xiaoping, 89-91, 93, 98-99,
100, 102-3
Gang of Four, 89
Hu Qiaomu, 98
Hu Yaobang, 91, 98-99, 100
Hua Guofeng, 89
ideology, 89-91, 92-94, 98-99
informal politics, 91-92, 113n.19
Jiang Qing, 89
Jiang Zemin, 91
Mao Zedong, 89, 90, 93-94,
95-96, 98, 99
policy, 89
Wan Li, 91
Wang Hongwen, 89
win/lose politics, 89
Yao Wenyuan, 89
Zhang Chunqiao, 89
Zhao Ziyang, 91, 98-99, 100,
101-2
Leninism and, 92-93, 94, 98-99, 100,
104, 108
local government, 95, 105, 110
Marxism and, 94, 98-99, 100, 108
1980s conflict
conservatives, 98, 99, 100-101, 102
formal structures, 100-101
ideology, 101
partial reform, 101
planned/market economies, 99,
100, 114n.43
power struggle, 101-2
Propaganda Department, 100, 101,
103
reformers, 98-99, 100-101, 102
State Planning Commission, 99,
100, 101, 103
win/lose politics, 99-100, 102-3

Openness policy *(continued)*
 reform history and
  capitalism, 18-19, 22
  Chinese Communist Party, 6-7,
   17-19
  ideology, 18-19
  Leninism, 17-22
  nationalism, 19-22
  planned/market economies, 17-18
  technological revolution (1983),
   18-19, 33n.35

People's Bank of China, 66
Planned/market economies
 democratization and, 65-66
 1980s, 47-48
 1990s, 53
 reform history and
  Chinese Communist Party, 14-17
  openness policy, 17-18
  reform limitation, 14-17
 reform impact, 99, 100, 104, 114n.43
Policy politics, viii, 35
Political culture, viii, 36
Political prospects
 Chinese Communist Party and
  Beijing spring discussions, 138
  conservatism, 134-40, 147-48,
   153n.38
  Falun Gong, 144-45, 147
  generational politics, 132-33
  ideology, 133-40, 147-48
  liberalism, 135-40
  nationalism, 134
  Old Left, 134, 135-37, 152n.34
  socioeconomic change, 127
 intellectual critique
  Chinese containment, 125
  critical methodology, 123-25
  Cultural Revolution, 120, 124, 125
  economic reform, 122, 124-25,
   151n.9
  event anniversaries, 118-20
  feudalism, 120-21, 122, 124

Political prospects, intellectual critique
 (continued)
  leftism, 120-21, 122, 124
  May Fourth Movement, 118-19,
   120-21
  modernization, 120-21
  nationalism, 118-19, 120-21,
   124-27
  openness policy, 122-24
  socioeconomic change, 127
  Western model, 119-21, 122-27
 leadership and
  Beijing spring discussions, 138
  Chen Yun, 132
  conservatism, 134-40, 147-48,
   153n.38
  Deng Xiaoping, 132, 133, 135, 137
  Ding Guan'gen, 135, 139
  generational politics, 132-33
  Hu Qiaomu, 132
  ideology, 133-40, 147-48
  Jiang Zemin, 133-41
  leftism, 134-40, 152n.34
  liberalism, 135-40
  Li Peng, 134, 140
  Li Xiannian, 132
  Liu Ji, 135, 139
  Mao Zedong, 132, 133
  Marxism, 135-36, 138, 145
  middle course politics, 135, 136,
   137
  nationalism, 134
  openness policy, 134, 138-39,
   140-41
  socioeconomic change, 127,
   128-29, 131-32, 133-34
  state-owned enterprises, 134
  Teng Wensheng, 135
  Wang Daohan, 135
  Western model, 135-36
  Yang Shangkun, 133
  Zeng Qinghong, 135
  Zhu Rongji, 134, 140, 144-45,
   146-47

democratization, 76-77
reform impact, 105
Technological revolution (1983),
18-19, 33n.35
Teng Wensheng, 135
Third wave, 61
Third Wave, The (Toffler), 18-19, 22
Tiananmen Square period
democratization and, 69-77
economic realm, 75-76
fiscal realm, 76-77
ideology, 70
institution building, 70-71, 75-77
leadership, 69-75
state-owned enterprises, 75-76
tax system, 76-77
township/village enterprises, 75,
76
political study, xiv-xv
reform history, xiv-xv, 3, 4, 6, 7
Toffler, Alvin, 18-19, 22
Totalitarianism, viii, xiii, xv-xvi
Township/village enterprises
democratization, 65, 75, 76
political prospects, 130
Trade relations, 134, 144, 147
Tsou, Tang, viii-xv

Unemployment, 129-31, 152n.27
United States, 143-44, 146-47
See also Western influence

Wan Li
reform history, 13-14
reform impact, 91
rural reform, 40-41, 42, 45, 59n.17
Wang Daohan, 135
Wang Dongxing, 44
Wang Hongwen, 89
Wang Qishan, 41-42
Wang Renzhong, 53

Wealth distribution, 79
Wen Ho Lee, 143
Western influence
political prospects and, 119-21,
122-27, 135-36
United States, 143-44, 146-47
political study, x-xi
reform history and
cultural tradition, 22, 23-24, 26,
28
modernization, 22, 23-24, 26, 28
nationalism, 19-22, 33n.39
Win/lose politics
political study, x, xii-xiv, xvii-xviii,
xxii(n32)(n33)
reform impact, 87-88, 89, 99-100,
102-3
World Trade Organization (WTO),
134, 144, 147
Wu Lengxi, 44

Yang Shangkun, 71-72, 133
Yao Wenyuan, 89
Yao Yilin, 41-42, 69
Yu Guangyuan, 43
Yugoslavia, 143-44

Zeng Qinghong, 135
Zeng Xisheng, 40
Zhang Chunqiao, 89
Zhao Ziyang
democratization, 68, 69
political systems, 48-52
reform impact, 91, 98-99, 100, 101-2
technological revolution (1983),
18-19, 33n.35
Zhou Yueli, 40
Zhu Rongji
democratization, 80
political prospects, 134, 140, 144-45,
146-47

Joseph Fewsmith is Professor of International Relations and Director of the East Asia Interdisciplinary Studies Program at Boston University as well as associate-in-research at the John King Fairbank Center for East Asian Research at Harvard University. He has written numerous articles on the politics and economics of contemporary China and is editor of *The Chinese Economy,* a journal of translations published by M.E. Sharpe. His previous books are *Party, State, and Local Elites in Republican China* (1985), and *Dilemmas of Reform in China* (M.E. Sharpe, 1994).